*Refiguring* **ENGLISH STUDIES**

Refiguring English Studies provides a forum for scholarship on English studies as a discipline, a profession, and a vocation. To that end, the series publishes historical work that considers the ways in which English studies has constructed itself and its objects of study; investigations of the relationships among its constituent parts as conceived in both disciplinary and institutional terms; and examinations of the role the discipline has played or should play in the larger society and public policy. In addition, the series seeks to feature studies that, by their form or focus, challenge our notions about how the written "work" of English can or should be done and to feature writings that represent the professional lives of the discipline's members in both traditional and nontraditional settings. The series also includes scholarship that considers the discipline's possible futures or that draws upon work in other disciplines to shed light on developments in English studies.

**Volumes in the Series**

David B. Downing, editor, *Changing Classroom Practices: Resources for Literary and Cultural Studies* (1994)

Jed Rasula, *The American Poetry Wax Museum: Reality Effects, 1940–1990* (1995)

James A. Berlin, *Rhetorics, Poetics, and Cultures: Refiguring College English Studies* (1996)

Robin Varnum, *Fencing with Words: A History of Writing Instruction at Amherst College during the Era of Theodore Baird, 1938–1966* (1996)

Jane Maher, *Mina P. Shaughnessy: Her Life and Work* (1997)

Michael Blitz and C. Mark Hurlbert, *Letters for the Living: Teaching Writing in a Violent Age* (1998)

Bruce Horner and Min-Zhan Lu, *Representing the "Other": Basic Writers and the Teaching of Basic Writing* (1999)

Stephen M. North, with Barbara A. Chepaitis, David Coogan, Lâle Davidson, Ron MacLean, Cindy L. Parrish, Jonathan Post, and Beth Weatherby, *Refiguring the Ph.D. in English Studies: Writing, Doctoral Education, and the Fusion-Based Curriculum* (2000)

Stephen Parks, *Class Politics: The Movement for the Students' Right to Their Own Language* (2000)

Charles M. Anderson and Marian M. MacCurdy, editors, *Writing and Healing: Toward an Informed Practice* (2000)

Anne J. Herrington and Marcia Curtis, *Persons in Process: Four Stories of Writing and Personal Development in College* (2000)

Amy Lee, *Composing Critical Pedagogies: Teaching Writing as Revision* (2000)

Derek Owens, *Composition and Sustainability: Teaching for a Threatened Generation* (2001)

Chris W. Gallagher, *Radical Departures: Composition and Progressive Pedagogy* (2002)

Robert P. Yagelski and Scott A. Leonard, editors, *The Relevance of English* (2002)

Shari J. Stenberg, *Professing and Pedagogy: Learning the Teaching of English* (2005)

# Composition and/or Literature
## The End(s) of Education

Edited by

LINDA S. BERGMANN
*Purdue University*

EDITH M. BAKER
*Bradley University*

National Council of Teachers of English
1111 W. Kenyon Road, Urbana, Illinois 61801-1096

NCTE Editorial Board: Arnetha F. Ball, Evelyn B. Freeman, Jeffrey N. Golub, Carol Jago, Tonya B. Perry, Carol A. Pope, Mark Reynolds, Sharon Taberski, Morris Young, Zarina M. Hock, Chair, ex officio, Kent Williamson, ex officio, Kurt Austin, ex officio

Manuscript Editor: Jane M. Curran
Production Editor: Bonny Graham
Interior Design: Jenny Jensen Greenleaf
Cover Design: Barbara Yale-Read

NCTE Stock Number: 08075

ISSN 1073-9637

©2006 by the National Council of Teachers of English.

All rights reserved. No part of this publication may be reproduced or transmitted in any form or by any means, electronic or mechanical, including photocopy, or any information storage and retrieval system, without permission from the copyright holder. Printed in the United States of America.

It is the policy of NCTE in its journals and other publications to provide a forum for the open discussion of ideas concerning the content and the teaching of English and the language arts. Publicity accorded to any particular point of view does not imply endorsement by the Executive Committee, the Board of Directors, or the membership at large, except in announcements of policy, where such endorsement is clearly specified.

Every effort has been made to provide current URLs and e-mail addresses, but because of the rapidly changing nature of the Web, some sites and addresses may no longer be accessible.

**Library of Congress Cataloging-in-Publication Data**

Composition and / or literature : the end(s) of education / edited by Linda
    S. Bergmann, Edith M. Baker; foreword by Winifred Bryan Horner.
        p. cm. — (Refiguring English studies)
    Includes bibliographical references and index.
    ISBN 0-8141-0807-5 (pbk)
    1. English language—Composition and exercises—Study and
teaching. 2. English language—Rhetoric—Study and teaching (Higher)
3. Literature—Study and teaching (Higher) I. Bergmann, Linda S.,
1950–    . II. Baker, Edith M., 1944–    . III. Series.
PE1404.C622 2006
808'.0420711—dc22

2005034170

*For the Bernies*
*Linda Bergmann*


*For Bruce and Sara*
*Edith Baker*

# Contents

FOREWORD: A REFLECTION ON LITERATURE AND COMPOSITION, TWENTY YEARS LATER
 Winifred Bryan Horner ................................. ix
PREFACE ............................................. xiii
ACKNOWLEDGMENTS ..................................... xv

1 Introduction: "What Do You Folks Teach over There, Anyway?"
 Linda S. Bergmann ........................................ 1

## I Institutional Contexts

2 Composition, Literary Studies, and the End(s) of Civic Education
 Dominic DelliCarpini ..................................... 17

3 Restructuring in Higher Education and the Relationship between Literature and Composition
 Timothy J. Doherty ...................................... 36

4 Causes and Cures for Our Professional Schizophrenia
 Edward A. Kearns ....................................... 54

5 Rhetoric, Literature, and the Ruined University
 Eve Wiederhold ........................................ 73

## II Departmental Cultures

6 In this Corner . . .
 Barry M. Maid .......................................... 93

7 Along the DMZ between Composition and Literature
 John Heyda ........................................... 109

8 Whole English, Whole Teachers: Maintaining the
Balance between Rhetorical and Literary Expertise
Dennis Ciesielski . . . . . . . . . . . . . . . . . . . . . . . . . . . . . . . . . . 124

III Applications in the Classroom

9 Computer-Mediated Communication and the
Confluence of Composition and Literature
Katherine Fischer, Donna Reiss, and Art Young . . . . . . . . . . . . 143

10 Composing English 102: Reframing Students'
Lives through Literature
Edith M. Baker . . . . . . . . . . . . . . . . . . . . . . . . . . . . . . . . . . . 171

11 The Missing Voice in the Debate: What Students
Say about Literature in Composition
Mary T. Segall . . . . . . . . . . . . . . . . . . . . . . . . . . . . . . . . . . . 191

AFTERWORD: A COMPLEX AFFIRMATION OF READING AND WRITING
Patricia Harkin . . . . . . . . . . . . . . . . . . . . . . . . . . . . . . . . . . . 205

WORKS FOR FURTHER CONSULTATION
Linda S. Bergmann . . . . . . . . . . . . . . . . . . . . . . . . . . . . . . . . 221

INDEX . . . . . . . . . . . . . . . . . . . . . . . . . . . . . . . . . . . . . . . . . . . . 231

EDITORS . . . . . . . . . . . . . . . . . . . . . . . . . . . . . . . . . . . . . . . . . . 243

CONTRIBUTORS . . . . . . . . . . . . . . . . . . . . . . . . . . . . . . . . . . . . . 245

# Foreword: A Reflection on Literature and Composition, Twenty Years Later

Winifred Bryan Horner
*University of Missouri*
*Texas Christian University*

When I first conceived the idea for the book *Composition and Literature: Bridging the Gap*, I was organizing a program for the Teaching of Writing division at the Modern Language Association conference. I was very aware of the deep division between literature and composition and the isolation of composition studies in English departments around the country. Teaching and research in literature was considered the primary business of the department, and salaries, promotion, and tenure were awarded for success in that field. Composition, on the other hand, was considered peripheral, and the teaching was assigned to graduate students, adjuncts, and anyone else who might be handy. Research in composition was pursued by a hardy few who did so at their own professional peril.

It was that separation that I wanted to address in the MLA program. I also wanted to gain respectability for research in composition and rhetoric, and for that end I had to enlist the top scholars. I picked up the phone and called Wayne Booth, who, I knew, shared my concerns. He could not participate in the program because he was already committed, but he readily agreed to join in the idea for a book. In fact, he replied, he was at the moment reading papers from his own composition class. He had also recently returned from a meeting with the editorial board of the University of Chicago Press, and they had agreed that they

*Foreword*

needed to publish more books in the field of rhetoric and composition. Within an hour the editor of the press telephoned, and the book was launched. With Wayne Booth's name in the table of contents and an upcoming contract with the University of Chicago Press, I had little trouble recruiting other participants. Call it luck or the right moment. I knew I had an opportunity, and I wanted to do it right.

My target audience was literary scholars whom I wanted to convince of the importance of the teaching of composition and the ways in which research in literature could enrich research in writing. In order to get the attention of my proposed audience I aimed for the best scholars and researchers in both literature and rhetoric/composition. That turned out to be quite easy with Wayne Booth's name on the roster and the prospect of a contract with a prestigious press.

Since that time, some twenty years ago, much has changed. There are new developments, new questions, and possibly new answers as proposed in this anthology, *Composition and/or Literature: The End(s) of Education*, edited by Linda S. Bergmann and Edith M. Baker. I am interested that their title with the "and/or" suggests a combination or a dichotomy. In 1983 I only hoped to "bridge the gap." I have been proved wrong since then as the teaching of writing has in some instances moved out of the English department altogether into campus writing programs. In other institutions it has been incorporated in disciplines across the university in the important Writing Across the Curriculum programs.

The historical reasons that I outlined in the 1983 book have not really changed or been drastically altered by the addition of another twenty years to that history. The full study of rhetoric has for three centuries tended to reduce itself to a minimalist approach in the form of stylistic tricks, elocution, or composition. Today at larger universities with graduate programs, the budget of the composition program still supports graduate students who in turn enroll in the professors' seminars. The low wages paid to these temporary, part-time instructors in the composition programs is a money-saving device for budget-conscious administrators. It is a win-win situation firmly entrenched in many institutions even after twenty years.

Institutions, departments, and classrooms, on the other hand, have changed dramatically over the last twenty years, and Bergmann and Baker divide their book into these three categories: Institutional Contexts, Departmental Cultures, and Applications in the Classroom. Each author in this volume speaks from his or her own perspective in a particular department and a particular institution. The authors write from their experience in large public universities and small private ones—some with graduate programs and others that are four-year liberal arts colleges and community colleges. They write from widely differing institutional contexts.

Of the three categories, probably the classroom applications have changed the most, brought on by the technology of word processing and the ready communication of e-mail. Students feel more familiarity with writing on the computer, and e-mail allows for an exchange of information between the students and their teachers, among the students themselves, and even among students and teachers from different institutions across the country. Professors Fischer, Reiss, and Young write of their experience with "computer-mediated composition" at three institutions. At the same time, the teaching of writing gained new importance as departments responded to students' demands. They also responded to the demands of the larger academic and business communities for better writing from their students and employees. As a result, rhetoric programs expanded, and jobs in rhetoric and composition increased while positions in literature shrank. English departments responded by enlarging their rhetoric and composition faculty and establishing graduate programs. In addition, the Writing Across the Curriculum program first suggested by Elaine Maimon's article in the 1983 book moved the teaching of writing outside the composition classroom and beyond the English department to the university community as a whole, thus placing writing at the center of the educational endeavor.

These articles attest to the continuing discussion of whether literature should be included in the composition classroom. Edward P. J. Corbett argued against it in 1983, maintaining that the "siren song of literature" would detract from the main thrust of the composition course, while Frederick Crews advocated its inclusion. Literature was still confined to belles lettres, a body of work separated from "theme" writing by an immeasurable gulf.

In this new volume, Eve Wiederhold argues for a return to the literary texts that produce the beliefs and values that comprise the commonplaces upon which communication within a culture depends. But other authors in this collection add a new dimension to the discussion by questioning the insistence on literature as only belles lettres. Edith M. Baker, while arguing for the inclusion of literature in the teaching of writing, also recommends a broader view of literature to include "multiple forms and a variety of texts." Mary T. Segall presents evidence of students' preferences for reading "imaginative literature" rather than nonfiction in their writing classes, but I suspect that here again we face the "siren song of literature" for students as well as instructors. The question remains an open one.

Finally, Dominic DelliCarpini's essay, the leading article in this collection, issues a challenge to all teachers of composition, calling them to abandon the triviality of many of their disagreements. Rather than going over the well-worn questions about the use of literature in the composition classroom or the use of stylistic models or the location of writing programs in the academy, he reaches out and advocates civic education as "our central purpose in the teaching of writing." Although English departments have eschewed getting involved in politics and such forays have often been disastrous, he advocates a return to rhetoric, since politics is the realm of language in action, and rhetoric is the language of politics. He argues not only that literature should not be included in the composition course but also that such inclusion has come at a great cost to rhetoric's natural relationship to civic education. It is far safer, he maintains, to function in the sanitized world of literary language and avoid the world of actual politics. Such a program of citizenship across the curriculum would look to current political issues . . . and to the history of rhetoric as its foundational documents.

In the past, writing programs have failed to embrace a full rhetoric within a civic education that must include how we use language and a study of how language can be used against us. That is the business of teachers that becomes clear as the authors in this volume explore the role of a full rhetoric and the place of the teaching of writing and reading in the university and in the culture as a whole.

# Preface

The idea for this book grew out of a panel presentation for the 1999 Midwest Modern Language Association Conference. Linda chaired a panel on the relationship between literature and composition; Edith presented a paper, which Linda had selected. At the end of the session, Edith said to Linda, "We should write a book on this topic." Linda said, "Well, someone should. I have no time right now, but we need to complete this project." And thus began a collaboration between two people who had only met over e-mail. We sent out a call for papers for the book and, by the summer of 2000, we had received twice as many papers and proposals as we could include. Over the years, we continued to hone the chapters to those found in this book. We still find the subject engaging—perhaps even more so because we have worked with authors who come at it from substantially different directions.

We chose this topic because we both were trained in literature and composition at the graduate school level. With over forty-five years of full-time teaching experience between us (and many sections as part-timers), as well as administrative experience as chairs and WPAs, we have seen issues related to literature and composition surface in at least eight different departments where we have been employed. We wanted this book to be timely, theoretical, and practical. We intended to create a book that speaks to genuine concerns of instructors in classrooms so that faculty will no longer have to wrestle with these issues in furtive conversations and isolated departments.

We hope this book will extend faculty discussions about literature and composition, as well as challenge departments that have not reconsidered the relationship between literature and composition in recent years. And so, as Anne Bradstreet says in "The Author to Her Book," we send this collection out to see where

*Preface*

"may'st . . . [it] roam." May it roam freely and widely, sparking and provoking discussion between our colleagues. Our greatest hope is that teachers and scholars will write many sequels to it.

# Acknowledgments

During the five years of production of this book, many individuals have helped in its creation. Our deep thanks go to Kurt Austin, Bonny Graham, and Jane Curran at the National Council of Teachers of English. Duane Roen of Arizona State University suggested that we contact Kurt Austin, whose astute guidance has been generous, unflappable, and trenchant. The anonymous reviewers of the manuscript at two different stages also made suggestions that helped us sharpen the focus. We appreciate their thoughtful critiques.

Thanks to Chair Peter Dusenbery of the Department of English at Bradley University; Claire Etaugh, dean of LAS at Bradley and acting provost; and the Faculty Writing Group of the Writing Across the Curriculum Program at Bradley University, who have offered suggestions and encouragement. Carolyn Rosser has provided clerical support. Colleagues at BU commented on an early draft of Edith's chapter. During this book's creation, Edith received a one-semester sabbatical and also a research grant from Bradley's Office of Teaching Excellence.

The Dr. Beverly Bowen Moeller Writing Center at the University of Missouri–Rolla hosted several of our working sessions, and the clerical support of Margaret Peterson and Lorraine Woolsey kept us organized in the process. The Department of English at Purdue University provided a research leave for Linda, and Charlotte Hartlep of the Writing Lab provided crucial clerical support in final manuscript preparation. Shirley Rose, professor of English at Purdue University, also offered generous advice throughout the process.

Finally, we have to thank the writers of these chapters and colleagues with whom we have discussed these issues at conferences, on chat lists and listservs, and in e-mails. All the initial authors have stayed with our proposal and provided support and revisions over the years, helping us produce a scholarly book that is timely and theoretical, yet located in praxis by instructors with many years of experience in the classroom.

Our deep gratitude also goes to Winifred Bryan Horner, whose collection about bridging literature and composition in the early 1980s started many of the discussions continued in this book. She generously agreed to set a context for revisiting the relationship between literary studies and the increasingly professionalized field of composition. Horner's historical perspective has helped us to complicate the metaphor of the bridge, to apply it to the idea of the "ruined"—or at least changing—university that Bill Readings describes, and to develop new ways of seeing and relating to our English department colleagues.

Throughout the inception and creation of this text, Patricia Harkin of the University of Illinois at Chicago has been a gentle guide. She critiqued many of the chapters in early versions and not only made thoughtful suggestions for revision, but also reminded us of the importance of linking all the language arts: reading, writing, speaking, and listening.

In the process of collecting, judging, editing, writing, and working together for five years, we have developed a distinctive method of collaboration, which surprised both of us. We each have gained deep respect for the other's abilities, and we have come to believe that if one perseveres, the whole can be greater than the sum of the parts.

CHAPTER ONE

# Introduction: "What Do You Folks Teach over There, Anyway?"

LINDA S. BERGMANN
*Purdue University*

The title of this introduction reiterates a question I've spent nearly an entire career trying to answer, a question asked (not unkindly) by colleagues across the disciplines as I worked with various Writing Across the Curriculum projects and programs. It has not been an easy question to answer. Most English departments have lists of goals or outcomes that state what is taught in composition, many of the more recent of them derived from the Council of Writing Program Administrators Outcomes Statement developed in the mid-1990s (Harrington et al.). But what WPAs profess to do and what actually happens in composition classrooms often vary widely, depending on who is actually teaching the classes. In part, this difference occurs because so many composition programs are located in English departments dominated by literary studies, and because so many composition courses are taught by instructors rooted in literature. The theoretical differences and intra-departmental strife between compositionists and literary scholars have resulted in the establishment of separate departments of writing or of rhetoric and composition at a number of institutions, several of which are considered in this collection. This collection is not, however, given solely to arguing for separating writing programs from English departments—although Barry Maid makes a compelling case for that institutional structure in his chapter. Instead, it examines the pressures the relationship between literary studies and composition put on the teaching of writing. Moreover, it undertakes a broader examination of whether and how the study of literature can be compatible with and integrated into composition studies. Because rhetoric and composition has by this time clearly differentiated itself as a discipline, it seems an appropriate point at which to reconsider the question of how compositionists—as members (most of us) of English departments and as teachers and scholars of rhetoric and composition—interface with instructors who teach writing from the substantially different intellectual background of literary studies.

The purposes of this collection of essays—over twenty years after Winifred Horner's *Composition and Literature: Bridging the Gap*—are to reconsider the teaching of literature in composition classes, to examine the extent to which the division between literature and composition affects teaching practices in colleges and universities of various kinds, and to document cases of success and failure in attempted collaborations between literature and composition. In some venues, these issues may no longer seem to be questions, since the problems of the relations between literature and composition have been widely discussed for at least two decades. The debate between Erika Lindemann and Gary Tate, begun at the Conference on College Composition and Communication annual convention and published in *College English* in 1993, generated substantial discussions throughout the profession. Also in the 1990s, James Berlin looked back at the history of rhetoric as a profession, to describe how the separation between poetics and rhetoric is tied into at least a century of academic politics. Thomas Miller (*Formation*) and Sharon Crowley (*Composition*) have continued to historicize the connections, differences, and collisions between the fields. In the context of this history, the present situation of composition and literature can be seen as a precarious balance of claims for utility, critique, and personal growth.

Although most English departments consider teaching literature their primary focus, the common sense and practice of most composition programs (particularly at large research universities) is to avoid teaching literature in writing courses, maintaining the distinction between the two fields. The practice is very different, however, in smaller institutions, where composition is an undergraduate course or two, not a graduate program, and where all or most of the literature faculty teach composition—

Introduction: *"What Do You Folks Teach over There, Anyway?"*

often as they think best and as they have always done it. These institutions can be splendid places in which to learn and to teach, but they offer a different configuration of relationships between composition and literature, and thus complicate the issue of how to separate the two fields—or to keep them productively intertwining and interacting. So, in spite of the established and growing body of disciplinary knowledge in the field of composition, the issue of its relation with literature is still faced department by department and course by course. Because institutional practices and situations vary so greatly in the many kinds of institutions that teach (and usually require) first-year composition, questions about the place of literature in composition courses continue to be raised.

One implication of this collection is that if composition programs are situated in English departments (as compared to independent writing programs), those departments need to initiate and sustain ongoing, productive discussions and collaborations between the fields of literature and composition, rather than merely serving as sites for exerting disciplinary power. The editors and authors of this book have intended to provide models for such ongoing conversations about the institutional and theoretical relations between composition and literary studies. Moreover, these chapters not only show mutual accommodation between composition and literature but also demonstrate how departmental and institutional politics can undermine rational discussions about the purposes and practices of composition courses and thereby render accommodation impossible. Chapters such as those by Timothy Doherty, Barry Maid, and John Heyda document what happens when—for any number of reasons—such conversations break down. And Dominic DelliCarpini makes a clear case for a mission of writing as public discourse that cannot be fulfilled by the teaching of literature as usually defined, that is, as imaginative writing valued primarily by aesthetic criteria.

*Composition and/or Literature: The End(s) of Education* tries to offer teachers from both sides of the literature/composition divide an opportunity to reflect upon pedagogical theory, classroom practices, and the institutional situation of composition instruction, as well as to consider whether and how they can work together. Thus, we offer a series of accounts of, responses to, and compromises with the tensions between literature and composition, between reading and writing, that have beleaguered English departments for decades. While this description might sound like we are proposing a clear move toward reconciliation between literature and composition—as fields and as faculties—both the editors and authors have seen this collection less as offering a prescription for relaxing these tensions, and more as suggesting ways to approach and even use them. The collection is divided into three sections, emphasizing different (although interconnected) aspects of how literature and composition do, do not, and might work with each other: Institutional Contexts, Departmental Cultures, and Applications in the Classroom. The first section reviews some of the theoretical underpinnings of the rift between composition and literature; the next section considers how these differences are set in institutional contexts and departmental cultures; and the final section recounts classroom applications that argue for or exemplify an informed integration of materials and practices drawn from both literature and composition. In selecting the essays for this collection, the editors paid particular attention to pieces that bring to the book the kind of feisty political savvy that often emerges on the Council of Writing Program Administrators e-mail list. The WPA list often voices an acute sensitivity to the potential applications of an idea and to the unanticipated consequences of good intentions. This kind of awareness tends to be blunted in formal publications, but for this collection we sought chapters that keep that practical vision strong.

Many of these chapters began as e-mail or face-to-face conversations among the authors, lamenting the uncomfortable discrepancy between composition theory and the practices that take place in specific programs or classrooms. Many WPAs have seen literature returned to composition courses through the back door, by faculty and graduate students primarily trained in and identifying with literary studies. It seems apparent that over time tacit changes by individual faculty members can substantially alter the focus of a program. For example, despite considerable research arguing that writing is embedded in larger systems of activity and purpose (Russell; Petraglia), "general writing skills instruc-

Introduction: *"What Do You Folks Teach over There, Anyway?"*

tion" continues to remain the rationale that sustains most required writing courses.[1] Literature instructors who have some awareness of composition theory (often expressivist) nonetheless tend to teach what they always have taught. Discipline-specific writing instruction, other than training students to write literature papers, can simply fade away—without discussion. Even such a cornerstone of composition theory as the process approach can be subverted by student resistance, by a lack of commitment or understanding by the faculty who teach it, and by institutional demands for accountability that require drill in "the basics." Under these circumstances, a genuine process approach to writing can easily revert to producing note cards and outlines, revision can become grammar drill, and group work can be subordinated to solitary authorship.

This book, then, provides an opportunity to reconsider the relations between composition and literature, in theory and in teaching, and to reframe a discussion that has pretty much depended on ideas about how composition *should* be taught, rather than on recognition of the institutional conditions under which many composition courses *are* taught. The influence of literary studies in composition classrooms, whether it is a problem or not, can be examined only by being brought into the open. Unless writing programs separate themselves from English departments (which may or may not be a good idea), it is reasonable to expect that literature faculty will exert a significant influence over how they teach composition in their own classrooms. Although composition faculty have by and large managed to gain and maintain professional direction over the first-year composition curriculum, most English departments are still outnumbered by faculty and students educated in literary studies, who, as John Heyda's chapter illustrates, may have only a limited understanding of what compositionists are asking them to do in their writing courses, or why.[2] Thus, even when composition courses and programs in English departments are *designed* by compositionists, a great many of the courses are actually *taught* by faculty and graduate students steeped in literary studies. The consensus that might emerge while a writing program is being created can soon dissipate because of the marginal institutional position of much composition instruction. Moreover, because so many writing programs rely heavily on temporary faculty (Stygall 379), and because even under the best circumstances students and faculty move from institution to institution, current instructors in a program may not completely understand the reasoning behind course structures and policies, and over time few will remember the (often heated) discussions behind those decisions. One of the points Sharon Crowley makes in *Composition in the University* concerns how little time for composition or pedagogical theory many adjunct writing teachers have (5), a disengagement exacerbated by the fact that much composition is taught by underemployed PhDs and by graduate students who have been educated in or who are currently being educated in literature and literary theory and see that as their "real work."

The dichotomy between composition and literature, however, is hardly absolute, because so many instructors teach in both areas. At many smaller institutions without graduate programs, composition courses are the bread and butter of English departments, and even tenure-line literature faculty teach more writing than literature in their normal course load. Thus, it is also distressing that effective uses of literature to teach composition seldom receive more than local notice within an institution or a department, if that much. Because of this failure to communicate, the possibilities for a genuine complementary relationship are not fully explored in many institutions and may be undermined by factional differences if they are proposed. For example, well over a decade ago James Berlin called for a reintegration of the English studies curriculum around critical and cultural studies. More recently, Thomas Miller has posited the practical necessity for department-wide collaboration ("What's") in the face of the decline of numbers of English majors over the past decades. The chapter by Katherine Fischer, Donna Reiss, and Art Young and the chapter by Edith M. Baker make clear cases for the value of bringing literature into composition through the front door, openly using it to foster and polish critical thinking and self-reflective writing.

Cooperation and collaboration between composition and literary studies is not easy to achieve because the differences between them are material as well as theoretical. The relationship between these historically connected disciplines is complicated by changes in the university, some of which were outlined in Bill Readings's *The University in Ruins*. Given the financial stresses and external demands made on universities, it is hardly surprising that the tweedy old English department that at least some of us remember has become contested territory. In all but the most elite universities, literature faculty can feel (and with some reason) threatened, as the job market for literary scholars has dwindled while the job market for compositionists has expanded. Faced with rising tuition and a fear of not finding jobs, contemporary students tend to favor courses that offer clear preparation for future careers. Occasionally literature teachers admit how appalled they are at their students' apparent lack of experience and interest in literary studies, a response so heartbreakingly described in Daniel Green's "Abandoning the Ruins." At the same time, as James Sosnoski points out, there is still considerable pressure on faculty at all colleges and universities to adapt their academic expectations to those at elite institutions, which are then used to measure their success or failure.

For compositionists, granting literature a place in the writing curriculum can seem risky as well, particularly in departments where there has been acrimony between literature and composition, or where compositionists feel they have been treated as second-class members of the profession. Over the past generation, composition has developed an intellectual base and professional identity of its own, rooted in its growing body of composition theory, research, and lore. Nonetheless, in many departments, literature faculty not only continue to maintain numerical superiority in tenure-track faculty positions but also assert superiority over composition faculty on aesthetic, moral, or political grounds, claiming to eschew "service," to rise above workplace skills, or to foment opposition to corporate values.[3] For example, even Daniel Green assumes that teaching literature—rather than teaching writing—is the proper work of English professors at his institution. Robert Scholes admits that "most English departments would not even accept writing courses as the equal of reading courses in their curricula, because reading is actually called literature, while writing is just writing" (160). And Richard Enos notes that because of the "ethos that Scholes has earned in literature," he has the authority to argue for the reinstatement of rhetoric to a position of importance in English departments (337)—an authority few literature scholars will recognize in compositionists. A similar ethos can be seen supporting Gerald Graff's more recent demand for writing instruction that enables students to understand and participate in academic discussions. Thomas Miller (*Formation*) and Sharon Crowley (*Composition*) call attention to how class biases result in the privileging of literature, and other compositionists note how class structure tends to be reenacted in departmental hierarchies (Fetterly; Harris; Alberti), strengthening the dominance of literary studies over composition. Barry Maid's essay in this collection takes on this class issue to engage his defense of separating writing programs from English departments.

A complicating factor in the position of composition faculty may come from the ongoing disagreements among compositionists about the goals of first-year composition and the best way to teach it. The first-year composition course has, at various times and places, worked to implement service learning (Schutz and Gere), learning communities (Williams), multicultural studies, genre theory, ethical and philosophical studies, and cultural studies. It has served as a site of the ongoing debate between the expressivists and the social contructivists, and as the target of the New Abolitionists, that is, compositionists who argue that the first-year composition requirement should be dropped because it is ineffective for students and detrimental to the profession (Petraglia; Crowley, *Composition*). For several years in the late 1990s, a subcommittee of the Council of Writing Program Administrators worked on a statement to document what "everyone (in the field) knows" to be the goals of first-year composition. This group produced the *WPA Outcomes Statement for First-Year Composition*, which was adopted by the council in 2000. However, although the Outcomes Statement has been used effectively in some sixty-eight universities and programs across the country, as Patricia Ericsson has established, the outcomes it defines are necessarily quite general. The statement was constructed to document broad consensus among writing programs, and to achieve that consensus its creators smoothed over the deep divides in the field, particularly the serious rift between expressivists and social constructivists and the arguments between faculty who at that time believed that computer applications are central to teaching writing and those who believed that writing transcends technology (Rhodes et al.).

Given these various pressures on faculty in both literature and composition, it is hardly surprising that in the classroom, as Sharon Crowley ("Around 1971") and others have noted, composition theory often tends to melt into current-traditional practices. Literature specialists teaching writing may ignore or subvert the designs of composition programs, and overworked adjuncts may not have the time, resources, or power to make much of a dent in the practices of their departments—even if they wanted to take on such thankless work. Many literature faculty who teach composition adhere to a genially conservative expressivism, a view of writing that W. Ross Winterowd attributes to the romantic ideal of individual inspiration that lingers in the teaching of literature even after the postmodern death of the author. This expressivism shares with literary studies the privileging of texts that are free from the demands and constraints of the workplace. It is easy to use expressivism to move from a focus on writing to a focus on reading and interpreting, a move that can lead to questionable classroom practices or degenerate into intra-departmental acrimony if it is not openly discussed among the various groups teaching composition.

Many of the chapters in *Composition and/or Literature: The End(s) of Education* have been provoked by Bill Readings's call in *The University in Ruins* to rethink our assumptions about the shape and purpose of the university. Eve Wiederhold advocates bringing literature back into composition in order to counter the replacement of culture by excellence as the focus of university education; Dominic DelliCarpini and Edward A. Kearns offer theoretical justifications and historical precedents for retaining or returning aesthetic understanding to composition instruction, although they differ greatly in their understanding of how that value should be identified and where it should be placed. Because of the contributors' experience as teachers and writing program administrators, however, even the most theoretically informed chapters situate composition theory in particular classrooms, departments, and institutions that have had to resolve or at least face relations between literature and composition. The articles in the first two sections in particular focus on institutional politics and in the last section on classroom applications, but every essay touches on aspects of theory, institutional politics, and teaching practices.

The experiences of program-builders such as Dominic DelliCarpini, Barry Maid, Tim Doherty, and John Heyda bring to the collection a high degree of practical experience in writing program administration as they examine the intersections between theory and institutional practices. The thoughtful, student- and teacher-oriented contribution of Katherine Fischer, Donna Reiss, and Art Young demonstrates how computer applications to writing about and producing literary texts reflect important present and future directions of composition studies. In another approach to teaching composition, Edith M. Baker describes a course in which reading and writing about literary texts focuses on fostering students' growth as writers as they grow as human beings. Mary T. Segall brings students into the conversation by reporting the results of a survey of students' responses to literature in composition courses. And Dennis Ciesielski argues for the value to composition faculty of teaching literature, making the case for a "whole-language" approach to reading and writing for both students and teachers.

The argument that underlies this collection is that because so many composition courses are taught in English departments (and heavily staffed by literature scholars), the relationships between reading and writing, literature and composition, must be continually reexamined and redrawn in order to maintain a vital curriculum. Freestanding writing programs may be able to maintain their coherence because of their separation from literature, but writing programs in English departments are the sites of ongoing collaborations and compromises that derive from the expertise of the people who teach in them. When the conversation stops, as John Heyda's chapter illustrates, a writing curriculum can very easily revert to an introduction to literature, a course that may have some value, but not the value intended by specialists in writing instruction or writing program administration. The goal of this collection, then, is to raise issues that need to be discussed in an ongoing, recursive conversation and to document some of the compromises that have been reached by a variety of institutions over the years during which rhetoric and composition has emerged as a discipline. While it may not give a definitive answer to the question with which this chapter began, it offers an opportunity for those of us who care about writing instruction to raise it once again.

## Notes

1. Kathleen Blake Yancey is currently leading a nationwide project to ascertain how composition is taught, but the preliminary results were not yet available at the time this was written.
2. Shirley Rose has reminded me that many of the students and faculty in literature who teach composition teach excellent courses based on what they have learned and internalized from composition studies over the years. I must also acknowledge the significant number of current compositionists—myself included—who began their careers in literary studies.
3. I would also suggest that the divide between pedagogies of writing and literature may have been instrumental in nurturing Writing Across the Curriculum programs, which promise to give students the professional communication skills they need, while freeing literature faculty from having to teach them.

## Works Cited

Alberti, John. "Returning to Class: Creating Opportunities for Multicultural Reform at Majority Second-Tier Schools." *College English* 63.5 (May 2001): 561–84.

Berlin, James. *Rhetorics, Poetics, Cultures: Refiguring College English Studies.* Urbana, IL: National Council of Teachers of English, 1996.

Crowley, Sharon. "Around 1971: Current-Traditional Rhetoric and Process Models of Composing." *Composition in the Twenty-first Century: Crisis and Change.* Ed. Lynn Z. Bloom, Donald A. Daiker, and Ed White. Carbondale: Southern Illinois UP, 1994. 64–74.

———. *Composition in the University: Historical and Polemical Essays.* Pittsburgh: U of Pittsburgh P, 1998.

Enos, Richard Leo. Review of *The Rise and Fall of English: Reconstructing English as a Discipline,* by Robert Scholes. *Rhetoric Review* 17.2 (Spring 1999): 337–39.

Ericsson, Patricia Freitag. Outcomes Use Table. January 2005. http://www.wsu.edu/~ericsson/OS_table.html (accessed 13 February 2005).

Fetterly, Judith. "Dreaming the Future of English." *College English* 61.6 (July 1999): 702–11.

Graff, Gerald. *Clueless in Academe: How Schooling Obscures the Life of the Mind.* New Haven, CT: Yale UP, 2003.

Green, Daniel. "Opinion: Abandoning the Ruins." *College English* 63.3 (January 2001): 273–87.

Harrington, Susanmarie, Keith Rhodes, Ruth Overman Fischer, and Rita Malenczyk, eds. *The Outcomes Book: Debate and Consensus after the WPA Outcomes Statement.* Logan: Utah State UP, 2005.

Harris, Joseph. "Meet the New Boss, Same as the Old Boss: Class Consciousness in Composition." *College Composition and Communication* 52.1 (September 2000): 43–68.

Horner, Winifred Bryan, ed. *Composition and Literature: Bridging the Gap.* Chicago: U of Chicago P, 1983.

Lindemann, Erika. "Freshman Composition: No Place for Literature." *College English* 55.3 (March 1993): 311–16.

Miller, Thomas P. *The Formation of College English: Rhetoric and Belles Lettres in the British Cultural Provinces.* Pittsburgh: U of Pittsburgh P, 1997.

———. "What's Going On with English Majors? Historical Contexts and National Trends in Undergraduate Curricula." Conference on College Composition and Communications Annual Convention. San Antonio, TX. March 2004. Updated 20 May 2004. http://www.gened.arizona.edu/tmiller/ccc.htm (accessed 13 February 2005).

Petraglia, Joseph, ed. *Reconceiving Writing, Rethinking Writing Instruction.* Mahwah, NJ: Erlbaum, 1995.

Readings, Bill. *The University in Ruins.* Cambridge, MA: Harvard UP, 1996.

Rhodes, Keith, Irvin Peckham, Linda S. Bergmann, and William Condon. "The Outcomes Project: The Insiders' History." *The Outcomes Book: Debate and Consensus after the WPA Outcomes Statement.* Ed. Susanmarie Harrington, Keith Rhodes, Ruth Overman Fischer, and Rita Malenczyk. Logan: Utah State UP, 2005.

*Introduction: "What Do You Folks Teach over There, Anyway?"*

Russell, David R. "Rethinking Genre in School and Society: An Activity Theory Analysis." *Written Communication* 14 (1997): 504–54.

Scholes, Robert. *The Rise and Fall of English: Reconstructing English as a Discipline.* New Haven, CT: Yale UP, 1998.

Schutz, Aaron, and Anne Ruggles Gere. "Service Learning and English Studies." *College English* 60.2 (February 1998): 129–49.

Sosnoski, James. *Token Professionals and Master Critics: A Critique of Orthodoxy in Literary Studies.* Albany: State U of New York P, 1994.

Stygall, Gail. "At the Century's End: The Job Market in Rhetoric and Composition." *Rhetoric Review* 18.2 (Spring 2000): 375–89.

Tate, Gary. "A Place for Literature in Freshman Composition." *College English* 55.3 (March 1993): 317–21.

Williams, Ashley. "Integrative Writing and Ways of Knowing Across Four Courses." Fifth National Writing Across the Curriculum Conference. Bloomington, IN. 1 June 2001.

Winterowd, W. Ross. *The English Department: A Personal and Institutional History.* Carbondale: Southern Illinois UP, 1998.

*WPA Outcomes Statement for First-Year Composition.* April 2000. http://www.wpacouncil.org/positions/outcomes.html (accessed 21 July 2005).

# I

# INSTITUTIONAL CONTEXTS

CHAPTER TWO

# *Composition, Literary Studies, and the End(s) of Civic Education*

DOMINIC DELLICARPINI
*York College of Pennsylvania*

This essay explores the topic of composition and literature within a specific context: the need to prepare students as active citizens within a democratic society. This civic goal, of course, has a long history within composition studies, and an even longer history within the rhetorical tradition. Yet, the same can be said about the teaching of literature. From Plato's half-hearted banning of the poets from his ideal Republic, through discussions of the power of literary discourse as a rhetorical tool in Isocrates, Aristotle, Cicero, and Quintilian, and into ongoing discussions about the use of literature in the writing classroom (which are continued in this collection), rhetoric, literature, and civic education have been linked in an intimate, if uneasy, dance. In this essay, I first outline current circumstances that suggest that composition classrooms should remain committed to civic education. I then recontextualize literature within the rhetorical tradition, recalling ways that poetic texts were used toward the ends of civic education. I go on to explore reasons why the teaching of literature and the teaching of civic responsibility—even within the composition classroom—grew apart under the sway of formalism. I conclude by suggesting how recent literary theories and attention to the democratic goals of education suggested by the American pragmatists might return literature to its place in the rich rhetorical tradition of civic education—while acknowledging the tangible exigencies that stand in the way of a solution that otherwise might bring the two together.

## Composition and the Exigencies of Civic Education

The fields of rhetoric and composition have consistently advocated for the preparation of youth for active civic engagement; however, recent shifts toward service learning and voluntarism as measures of civic engagement—in our culture more generally as well as in composition studies—represent a troubling trend for rhetorical education within a democratic culture. Although volunteerism and service learning are admirable activities, they do not seem to have increased *deliberative* action—engagement not just in civic programs but also in civic conversations.[1] To the contrary, political engagement continues to wane among the youth we are educating. Demographics suggest that social energy has found a new outlet, shifting toward volunteer programs and away from other forms of civic engagement: in 2002, the Center for Information and Research on Civic Learning and Engagement (CIRCLE) reported that four times as many young adults see volunteering in the local community as important (49 percent) as those who see getting involved in politics and government as important (12 percent). In comparison, fewer than a fifth have participated in an online discussion or visited a politically oriented Web site (18 percent). About a tenth have participated in a political march or demonstration (12 percent), volunteered in a political campaign (13 percent), joined a political club (13 percent), or worked for a political party (9 percent).

At the same time, there are clear declines in what we might term deliberative political participation, especially in the age groups we see most frequently in first-year writing. In 1990, Cheryl Russell reported in *American Demographics* that "41% of [college] respondents wanted to influence social norms and 20% wanted to influence the political structure," while "37% of college freshmen are likely to have participated in a demonstration in the previous year." This, according to that publication, was the highest rate of activism since the 1960s. In its 2002 study, conversely, CIRCLE reported that "young adults see politics and elections more as the business of elites than avenues for democratic participation, and do not see themselves and their generation as particularly significant in the political process." It also reported the following:

> More than half of DotNets [15 to 25-year-olds] (57%) are completely disengaged from civic life
>
> Only about one-third of DotNets regularly follow the news through newspapers (30%), the radio (33%), or television (38%)
>
> Only 38% of DotNets say that citizenship entails special obligations, while 58% say simply being a good person is enough. This is markedly different than the responses provided by GenXers (48% special obligations, 48% being a good person enough), Baby Boomers (60%, 34%) and Matures (59%, 32%).

Thus, though there are signs that young people are willing to perform civic duties as volunteers, there seems to be no demonstrable correlation between civic engagement defined as volunteering and civic engagement defined as political deliberation. And why would there be? As Jeffrey A. McLellan and James Youniss remind us, "one can reasonably ask why participation in single events, such as car washes or walkathons, or tutoring of peers, should instill fervor for political processes" (48).

Rather than fervor, our students are more likely to tell us just how unequipped they feel to discourse upon political matters—as did students in a writing course I taught with the theme of "Writing as Good Citizenship"[2]:

> "I don't consider myself to be politically active or aware; but if I was, I'm sure that I'd be liberal."
>
> "Political debate in our country has become very technical and complicated; that's why I try to stay away from politics."
>
> "I am neither conservative nor liberal. I have no point of view. I guess my country's condition is o.k. I am happy with my life and where I live."
>
> "I do not believe that citizens have a true voice in the current political system. The existing system is controlled by money and what I call 'just talk.'"

As the demographics and typical student responses above suggest, the problem may go beyond the lack of political knowledge. Students seem to lack the will to embrace politics. They *know* that they do not understand politics, and they wear that ignorance like a badge of decency and truth. But what looks to them like detachment from the tainted world of politics should look to a democracy like a harbinger of disaster.

Within our composition studies, the crucial necessity of civic education has been asserted frequently (though, as with all ideals, followed less frequently). James Berlin, for example, has noted that

> a literacy that is without this commitment to active participation in decision making in the public sphere . . . cannot possibly serve the interests of egalitarian political arrangements. For democracy to function . . . citizens must actively engage in public debate, applying reading and writing practices in the service of articulating their positions and their critiques of positions of others. To have citizens who are unable to write and read for the public forum thus defeats the central purpose of democracy. (101)

If we are to remain true to this tradition—as I am asserting the occasion demands—we must also ask whether literature is an efficacious means to this end. In effect, we must ask a question that is similar to one that was asked by Socrates in Plato's *Republic*: should literature and what he calls "the lovers of literature" be admitted to *our* republic? We might begin that discussion by reminding ourselves that they have been here all along.

## The Rhetorical Tradition's Use of Literature toward Civic Education

The uneasy relationship between the ends of civic education and the uses of literature is far from new. The banning of the poets by Socrates in Book 10 of Plato's *Republic* participates in this very question. Socrates exiled the poets from his Republic for specifically civic reasons and agreed to welcome them back under the same criteria:

> If poetry directed to pleasure and imitation has any argument to give showing that they should be in a city with good laws, we should be delighted to receive them back from exile, since we are aware that we ourselves are charmed by them. . . . For surely we shall gain if it should turn out to be not only pleasant but also beneficial. (607c,e)

Plato here contextualizes his banning of the poets within a wider set of specifically civic and political concerns—concerns with learning that is "not only pleasant but also beneficial," and the creation of "a city with good laws." And though Socrates' *polis* is self-consciously utopian in scope ("It doesn't make any difference whether it is or will be somewhere" [592b]), it is a city nonetheless.

Despite Socrates' belief that the tragic poets "maim the thought of those who hear them," he admits his reticence to betray an affection that has "possessed me since childhood"—and with it, the master narrative of poet/teacher. Socrates worries about being "denounced" among the poets (who, after all, control the way we are remembered by the future). And he holds a "certain friendship for Homer" as the *seeming* "first teacher." Yet, he concludes, "a man must not be honored before the truth, but, as I say, it must be told" (595b–c). And that "truth" is specifically related to the needs of the polis.

Within the literary tradition, of course, Socrates (in his role as scourge of the poets) has been treated largely as the straight man for the defenses of poetry that followed, especially the most famous ones by Sir Philip Sidney and Percy Shelley. But from a rhetorical perspective, Socrates' banning of the poets, and his suspicions of the "lovers of poetry" who argue for its importance for educating youth, are much more substantive. The question posed by Socrates about literature's use in a good society is not an isolated attack but participates in a wider discussion about the political uses of literature within the rhetorical tradition. (After all, treating this moment as a challenge to a *literary* tradition that did not yet exist is more than a little anachronistic.) Socrates banned poetry "directed to pleasure and imitation" only until the poets and lovers of poetry could successfully argue that "they should be in a city with good laws." As such, this moment participates in discussion about the uses of language, which treated literary discourse as a means to the more crucial goals of civic education (as does Sidney as well—if we read his defense as the rhetorical treatise that it is, rather than as a defense of poetry in and of itself). And though Socrates' answer to the question "Can the poets benefit a city with good laws" is no, or at least "not yet," other classical rhetors did find a place of value for literature—if used for the good of the polis.

Isocrates consistently advocated for a liberal education that serves the public rather than the individual good. In laying out his educational program, he recognized the special charm of poetic language. But his greatest praise was for deliberative discourses that drew upon the *techniques* of poetic language—the public discourses that "are more akin to works composed in rhythm and set to music than to the speeches made in court" (*Antidosis* 46). For Isocrates, the best models for students are public discourses (which may themselves use poetic techniques): "I do think that the study of political discourse can help more than any other thing to stimulate and form such qualities of character [sobriety and justice]" (*Against the Sophists* 21).

Likewise, Cicero's program of education in *De Oratore* includes a wide variety of genres, including but not limited to what we would call *literary texts*:

> We must also read the poets, acquaint ourselves with histories, study and peruse the masters and authors in every excellent art, and by way of practice praise, expound, emend, criticize, and confute them; we must argue every question on both sides, and bring out on every topic whatever points can be deemed plausible. (1.34.158)

For Cicero, poetry and oratory are not different in kind, but in technique: "The truth is that the poet is a very near kinsman of the orator, rather more heavily fettered as regards rhythm, but with ampler freedom in his choice of words" (1.15.70). Cicero goes on to suggest that poetic language can prove a useful training ground for the larger ends of civic discourse, "just as ballplayers do not in their game itself employ the characteristic dexterity of the gymnasium, and yet their very movements show whether they have had such training" (1.16.73). For Cicero, reading of literature is useful for practicing stylistic techniques; game day, however, takes place in the public sphere.

Literature has an even more central role within the writings of Quintilian, though the civic goals shift rather dramatically during this time of imperial rule and censorship. As Bizzell and Herzberg note, there was a tendency "to produce rhetoric with more literary than political implications" and a focus upon declamation rather than actual civic activism, which would have been very dangerous (38). And though the uses of poetry for Quintilian still included its utility in providing stylistic *copia*, during the Second Sophistic, those uses were limited to a private, rather than public, deliberation; under the oppressive political climate, judgments about the value of language uses shifted from social utility to stylistic flourishes in declamation. As noted below, Quintilian's apolitical uses of literary discourse make him an apt hero for formalist uses of literary texts, both in the literature and the composition classroom. After all, New Criticism eschewed political contexts (along with other external interpretations), valuing literary texts as well-wrought stylistic urns, rather than as exercises of power.

So, though Sharon Crowley makes a compelling—and in many ways, accurate—case for the institutional marriage of literature and composition to form English departments,[3] we might also recall that literature and rhetoric, or more accurately, literature *as a form of rhetoric*, has a long history. This relationship has been troubled from the start, as early teachers of rhetoric attempted to keep literary discourse in its place—for the education of youth and toward figurative language's use in civic prose.[4] Even aesthetic judgments included measures of civic utility and occasion. Cicero's words on this topic echo those of Isocrates: "Can any music be composed that is sweeter to the ear than a well-balanced speech? Is any poem better rounded than an artistic period in prose? What actor gives keener pleasure by his imitation of real life than your orator affords in the conduct of some real case?" (*De Oratore* 2.8.34). No art for art's sake here; instead, art is valued for its utility in the context of "some real case." However, just the fact that Cicero's characters felt compelled to debate this issue in his dialogue suggests that a debate about the value and uses of literary discourse was already evident. If we historicize this moment, or as Mikhail Bakhtin would suggest, hear the words of Isocrates and Cicero as rejoinders to those who argued for the value of poetry in its own right, we might better understand that the uneasy relationship among civic education, the uses of literature, and rhetoric has a long history indeed.[5]

## Composition's Uses (and Misuses) of Literature as a Basis for Civic Education

While classical rhetors clearly valued literary discourse for its stylistic charms and as a part of the tradition of the *progymnasmata*, composition studies has not always functioned within that tradition that treats literature as a useful form of rhetoric. Composition programs, after all, serve many masters: literature-driven English departments, liberal arts divisions, general education programs, and so on. They also comprise both those who teach composition from a position of commitment and expertise and those who teach composition as the price they pay to work in their areas of "real" expertise.[6]

Further, until relatively recently, literary studies was at the center of English departments—and the heyday of literary studies was based upon a mimetic and formalist model advanced by the New Critics. This acontextual study of literature was clearly at odds with the rhetorical tradition's treatment of literary discourse; still, composition and English education programs bowed to that dominant paradigm, establishing their own formalist versions of the rhetorical tradition. The sophist became the evil Other, and a convenient version of Quintilian emerged as the good rhetorician, defined as a type of anti-sophist who had the moral center to demand of rhetoric a "good man speaking well."

In 1974, for example, Frederick Wheelock excerpted Quintilian's *Institutes of Oratory* for his edition, *Quintilian as Educator*. This edition, compiled for prospective and current English teachers, adopts Quintilian into the literary tradition's cult of the author by forwarding Quintilian's ideas as "the best thinking of the ancient world concerning education and culture" (1). Wheelock cites the work of Elmer H. Wilds and Kenneth V. Lottich, who in their 1961 work *The Foundations of Modern Education* claim that in Quintilian can be found "many of the eternal principles of a sound education" (qtd. in Wheelock 1). Wheelock also clearly separates Quintilian from the Sophists who were "itinerant professors" and who, "since their prime aim was to teach how to succeed at all costs . . . were not concerned about standards of right and wrong (i.e., they were amoral)" (7). Quintilian, as constructed by Wheelock and the tradition of English studies that he represents, is closer to "the great Socrates" who "though sometimes linked superficially with the Sophists, differed from them fundamentally in that he was concerned with positive (not relative) virtue and right action and moral responsibility rather than merely selfish, expedient, practical, successful conduct and action" (7). Even Isocrates is baptized into the formalist camp; Wheelock praises Isocrates not for the democratic impulses that give him his place in the rhetorical tradition, but for his attention to form and ideals: "He taught elegant rhetorical composition in all styles, and like Quintilian, he stressed the improvement of natural ability through training, hard work, perseverance, and good character" (8). In this way, a formalist-friendly version of the rhetorical tradition was developed to support the literature-centered English departments, drawing upon passages from Quintilian that claimed this Roman rhetorician much in the same way the Calvin and other Reformation theologians claimed St. Paul for their own camp.

It is not surprising that this Quintilian became a central figure, since Wheelock is able to excerpt lines from *The Institutes* such as these: "The study of literature is a necessity for boys and the delight of old age, the sweet companion of our privacy and the sole branch. . . . Unless the foundations of oratory are well and truly laid by the teaching of literature, the superstructure will collapse" (47–48).

The fear of the collapsing superstructure that Quintilian posits should not sound unfamiliar to those who have read the defenses of traditional literature by Harold Bloom, William Bennett, and other defenders of the canon. This defensive attitude toward the liberal arts as a keeper of a foundational truth, *including the truth about writing*, goes a long way to explain why writing programs have been reticent to abandon literature as the basis for composition. What might happen if we do so? Would culture decline? Would students become mere sophists (in the most negative connotations of the term)?

However, historicized within the rhetorical tradition, other conclusions about acontextual uses of literature might be drawn. For example, we might recall that Quintilian's work, which has been used as a model for formalist uses of literary language, was written during a time of when political uses of language were suppressed. Such uses of literary language carry with them, a cultural critic or New Historicist might suggest, the traces of their time: a learned helplessness about language and the possibility for its actual civic uses under an oppressive regime. Focusing as this use of language did upon declamation and forensic rhetoric, deliberation (and hence actual political uses of language) becomes secondary to the formal techniques of language as display. Further, not only language but also its author—the "good man speaking well"—are given a type of moral status that was easily adapted to the cult of the author in the period before Roland Barthes proclaimed his death. However, we might question whether this moral status, which exists outside the vicissitudes of the political realm, serves any real purpose for civic education.

Hence, the alliance between current-traditional practices of teaching composition and its formalist roots in literary studies (detailed by Crowley and other historians of composition) tended to teach students something like this: The real world of politics is oppressive and dangerous, but in the English classroom, language functions within universal moral boundaries. The language of literature, which the rhetorical tradition viewed as having a natural relationship with the public sphere, was instead given the mantle of high culture. At the same time, however, the removal of literary language from the larger sphere of discourse studies undermined the potential of literature to serve the ends of civic education. Sophism became "mere rhetoric," the derogatory moniker used as weapons for politicians against one another, and for citizens against politicians.

This use of literature helped to partially erase the rhetorical tradition's central role in the classroom and to replace it with the literary tradition's version of history. It also tended to teach students that "political rhetoric" was depraved language. In the formalist literary tradition, for example, Sidney's *Apology*—an argument for the civic uses of literature that was itself written in a classic rhetorical structure—was reduced to sound bites about poetry's ability to "teach and delight," and a defense against charges that the writing of fiction amounts to lying: "But the poet nothing affirmeth, and therefore never lieth." However, this interpretation of Sidney's work goes against the grain of its message, which consistently argues that the "highest" end of literature is "the knowledge of a man's self in his ethic and politic consideration, with the end of well-doing and not well-knowing only."

What Sidney calls "ethic and politic consideration" is what the rhetorical tradition calls deliberation. In fact, in the *Apology*, Sidney himself of necessity "strayed from poetry to oratory"—acknowledging this key connection between the two arts and echoing Cicero's claim that the "poet is a very near kinsman of the orator." It is deeply ironic (and illustrative of the effects of the formalist era's treatment of both the rhetorical and literary traditions) that Sidney's rhetorical purpose has been so badly misread as to suggest that the poet is *above* the civic realm. But by focusing upon Sidney's claim that the poet "never lieth" because he "affirmeth nothing," Sidney's *Apology* was used to give literary discourse a higher status than nonfiction—including the nonfiction that is crucial to civic engagement. Further, this view of language caused English programs to focus heavily upon literary genres, neglecting and even denigrating what Bakhtin called "speech genres." Hence English programs, even within general education programs, tended to create quasi-literary critics rather than social critics and functioned within closed literary spheres rather than Jurgen Habermas's literary *public* spheres.

Literary studies, of course, has changed drastically in the last four decades, largely in ways that can better mesh with the rhetorical understandings of language and with the goals of composition programs. Teaching universals or aesthetics has been usefully tempered by attempts to resituate texts historically, socially, and culturally; literary texts no longer need to be treated as a form of discourse different in kind, or in value, from other types of texts. And postmodernism has asked us to acknowledge the meta-narratives under which we function—including the meta-narrative that privileges literary language over other forms. In many ways, the study of literature has become, like rhetoric, more of a social science.

New Historicism, in particular, has reconnected literary language to other types of discourse. Based as it is in the cultural anthropology of Clifford Geertz, New Historicist methodologies use "thick description" to show how social energies circulate throughout a wide variety of genres. A typical New Historicist analysis shows how texts as widely divergent as plays, journals, shopping lists, sermons, and political speeches all contribute to an epoch's politico-discursive environs. This critical methodology might enrich the use of literary texts in a composition classroom by asking students to see connections, rather than hierarchies, among literary and other texts. And due to the influence of Michel Foucault, New Historicism also asks students to be aware of the ways in which texts transmit power through their discourses—both purposely and through the cultural influences that are as much creators of a text as is the "author." Such attention to the rhetorical occasion and social influences on the creation of a text could be beneficially tied to the teaching of kairos and social-epistemic rhetoric.

Other sociocultural types of literary critique—feminisms, Marxism (or cultural materialism), queer studies, and so on—also participate in the anthropological bases that inform New Historicism, and so have potential to break down the boundaries between literary language and the language necessary for civic participation. Though detailing all the ways that these theoretical bases might be used to create a more civically aware writing classroom is beyond the scope of this essay, it is not hard to imagine how the concerns of each in literary texts—and the creative language used to discuss those concerns—might be used to involve students in contemporary issues.[7] Further, if the "texts" that are used as sites of analysis and stylistic study are expanded to include not only literature, but also nonfiction, political speeches, television, film, talk radio, visual rhetoric, and cultural artifacts—*and if none of these texts are privileged*—then the use of literature in the writing classroom might once again be seen as a means to the development of language abilities crucial to citizenship skills.

But what is possible in theory may not be as easily accomplished in practice, as the many attempts to create a type of "comp lit" suggest.[8] As literary studies continues to separate itself from formalism and to specialize more and more within esoteric areas of theory for the benefit of literature specialists, writing programs have often been left holding the formalist bag. And despite good faith efforts to rehabilitate the relationship between composition and literature in ways that reflect both rhetoric's civic bases and literary studies' changing methodologies, we are still faced with many obstacles.

First, the literary theories that I have oversimplified above are anything but easily accessible. Though they can be presented in less intimidating ways, whether they successfully capture the key theoretical bases in those watered-down forms is still a matter of question. And even if we are to find useful and palatable ways to present these theories in the undergraduate classroom, that would assume that "we" (compositionists) are at least ourselves conversant in these literary theories. But many material conditions work against that. As John Schilb has noted, writing programs that are housed in English departments have been reticent to make the leap toward the sociocultural concerns that might mesh well with more recent literary theories, since "although many teachers of writing have pursued other goals, including civic education, they always have felt pressed to concentrate on polishing students' language" (157–58).

Further, composition programs face a great many staffing constraints: a reliance upon adjunct faculty, who may not have studied literature on the graduate level, or recently; a reliance upon teaching assistants, who may have more of an interest in their own area of literary study than about the teaching of writing, or in the case of rhetoric and composition experts, who may not have studied recent literary theory; a reliance upon teachers of literature, who are more interested in working with advanced English majors and graduate students than with first-year writers.

Of course, even if teachers are prepared in, and committed to, both literary theory and teaching composition, that does not change the audience: undergraduates who may or may not be prepared for, or interested in, literary theory. And even if they were interested, could this type of complex disciplinary study be accomplished in one or two semesters, considering that the study of literature on the secondary level rarely includes more recent literary theories? For most incoming students, calling the works read in the writing classroom "Literature" is always already an implicit statement about their higher value. As a result, literature leads students to retreat to the standard epideictic mode of literary analysis, praising and blaming (but mostly praising) the works for their formal and moral value.

Civic education, conversely, requires attention to the *deliberative* realm, a realm that is largely muted by formalist literary analysis, and which may be better served by the educational program suggested by American pragmatism. In his discussions of "What Pragmatism Means by the Practical," John Dewey builds upon the work of William James. James suggested that "I was primarily concerned in my lectures with contrasting the belief that the world is still in the process of making with the belief that there is an external edition of it ready-made and complete" (qtd. in *Essays* 99). This version of education looks to *future* action—and so by definition centers upon deliberation.

Dewey's pragmatic impulses also lead him to a set of educational goals based upon real, not simulated, inquiry. Dewey seeks to extend Charles Peirce's "laboratory habit of mind" to "every area where inquiry may be fruitfully carried on" (*Essays on Pragmatism* 100). Such inquiry changes the meaning of seeking *meaning* in a text from the uncovering of universal morals to the more pragmatic goal of inspiring deliberation and action. Under such a program of study, education means giving students the ability to make the informed civic decisions that are crucial for a democratic culture. As such, reading and writing are consistently oriented toward future action: "meaning signifies its *conceptual content or connotation, and 'practical' means the future responses which an object requires of us or commits us to*" (102). As such, according to Dewey, "the chief function of philosophy is not to find out what difference ready-made formulae make, *if true*, but to arrive at and to clarify their *meaning as programs of behavior for modifying the existent world*" (104).

Dewey's deliberative impulses lead him to question, not literature, but the *use of literature* as a type of exclusive and purified moral training ground that remains separate from the world outside of the classroom. Though a strong advocate for the use of literature in training the ethical facility of children, Dewey suggested that literary genres had been "overused," perhaps at the expense of other subject areas that could serve the moral and civic education of our youth: "Art, of which literature is only one branch, though the one most readily available for school uses, is perhaps the most unmixed and simplest record of human endeavor. For this reason, it has been overused in the schools as a moral force compared with other subjects" (*Essays* 206).

According to Dewey, this overuse has further separated the uses of language in our writing classroom from civic concerns, creating a "museum conception" of this art that separates literary language from the language of active democracy (*Art* 14–18). At the same time, we might note, it creates a hierarchy of language uses, suggesting that its "pure form" in great literature is in and of itself superior to the civic language of politics, especially as moral training. But Dewey reminds us that

> "Literature" has no magical automatic efficacy simply because it is called literature. Its importance measures also the dangers of its use, and hence while it cannot be said that current pedagogical traditions exaggerate the moral value of literature, it is nevertheless true that they are highly misleading so far as they create the belief that literature is the chief conscious moral resource of the teacher with respect to the various branches of subject matter. (*Essays* 208)

Not only does this compartmentalization of literature as a unique form of discourse undermine students' confidence in their own ideas and words, but it also exacerbates the liberal arts' perceived detachment from actual concerns of day-to-day life. Conversely, Dewey's concept of democratic education decries the separation of art from experience and suggests uses of art (including literature) that mesh more closely with the civic pragmatism of Isocrates and others in the rhetorical tradition.

In the end, my questions about literature are also pragmatic ones, not unlike the one asked by Socrates: Can the use of literature in the writing classroom serve a city with good laws? Or perhaps the questions should be a bit wider: Should literary discourse be privileged? Does it form a better stylistic and generative text for preparing citizens than those found in political philosophy, the rhetorical tradition, film, media studies, visual and electronic rhetorics, world cultures, political science, history, or science?

Rather than keep literature isolated in what Dewey called a "museum" of high culture, literature may best serve the ends of civic education if it is restored to its place among other texts. Such a program would treat rhetoric as what Sidney called an *architectonike*—an overarching method of reading culture and its texts. Its mode would be deliberative and historical, engaging students in the critical study of past and present politics and applying rhetorical critiques to current events.[9] It would demand knowledge of American government, both as a theoretical base and as a prerequisite for understanding the civic environment within which rhetoric functions. In such a program, all texts—including literary texts—would be read within their historical or contemporary contexts, encouraging students to ask questions about efficacy, about ethics, and, ultimately, about ways that figurative language can be used to assume their place in the civic conversation. Such a program would treat rhetoric not as "mere talk," but as the mode within which democracy must function, and so see every word as political, and all politics as rhetorical. Perhaps most importantly, such a program would resist any attempt to cordon language off from its civic uses and any attempt to foreground any type of text—including the literary—as primary, as pure, or as venerable. Instead, it would nurture a *healthy* skepticism about civics as an alternative to the *unhealthy* cynicism about the brazen world of politics that now undermines our citizenry's ability to engage in civil discourse. In such a republic, if they serve a city with good laws, the poets might once again be welcome.

## Notes

1. While service learning components of composition courses have become commonplace, there are still many debates about their ultimate learning goals and their effect upon civic participation. See, for example, Cushman ("Sustainable"); Deans and Meyer-Goncalves; Hutchinson; and Schutz and Gere.

2. I devoted an upper-division writing course to this theme in 1996 and subsequently reported on its results at the Conference on College Composition and Communication annual convention, Chicago, 1997.

3. See "The Invention of Freshman English" and "Literature and Composition: Not Separate but Certainly Unequal" in *Composition in the University*.

4. Even in the "Renaissance," early modern educators and poets followed Virgil in tending to think of any poetry other than that which served political purposes to be largely the domain of the young—something to be put aside when one matured enough to involve oneself in political writings (including, but not limited to, national epic). For example, John Milton spent the better part of his career writing nonfiction political tracts, and Spenser proceeded from youthful pastorals to national epic.

5. Cicero addresses what he calls the "cult of the Muses," insisting that praiseworthy poetry involves not only stylistic prowess but also content knowledge, bringing "within the compass of his knowledge and observation the almost boundless range and subject-matter of those arts" (1.2.10).

6. As I discuss in an article published in *Composition Studies* ("Must Be Willing"), even the job advertisements for teaching positions in English departments often follow the area of "real" expertise—usually literary—with an added line something like this: "Must be willing to teach composition."

7. See John Schilb's *Between the Lines* for one attempt to show the potential of postmodern literary theories to impact the composition classroom.

8. See, for example, Winifred Bryan Horner's edited collection *Composition and Literature* (1983); James A. Berlin's *Rhetorics, Poetics, and Cultures* (1996); John Schilb's *Between the Lines* (1996); and Gary Tate's "A Place for Literature in Freshman Composition" (1993) as well as Sharon Crowley's 1998 historical overview of the uneasy relationship between composition and literature in Chapter 5 of *Composition in the University*, "Literature and Composition: Not Separate but Certainly Unequal." Wayne Booth, in his chapter of Horner's collection, pointed out that though "we have produced many a 'defense of poesie' showing that the advanced study of literature is as important as—maybe even more important than—all other studies," we have not fulfilled the larger purpose: "What we must seek are programs likely to educate bachelors of arts who can read, think, and write in educated ways—B.A.'s whose critical capacities will not shame us" (59–60).

9. See Fleming for a discussion of one model for rhetoric as a course of study.

# Works Consulted

Berlin, James. *Rhetorics, Poetics, and Cultures: Refiguring College English Studies*. Urbana, IL: National Council of Teachers of English, 1996.

Boisvert, Raymond D. *John Dewey: Rethinking Our Time*. Albany: State U of New York P, 1998.

Booth, Wayne. "'LITCOMP': Some Rhetoric Addressed to Cryptorhetoricians about a Rhetorical Solution to a Rhetorical Problem." Horner 57–80.

The Center for Information and Research on Civic Learning and Engagement. School of Public Affairs, University of Maryland. "Volunteering among Young People." http://www.civicyouth.org/quick/volunteer.htm (accessed 20 January 2003).

Corbett, Edward P. J. "Literature and Composition: Allies or Rivals in the Classroom?" Horner 168–84.

Crowley, Sharon. *Composition in the University: Historical and Polemical Essays*. Pittsburgh: U of Pittsburgh P, 1998.

Cushman, Ellen. "The Rhetorician as an Agent of Social Change." CCC 47.1 (1996): 7–28.

———. "Sustainable Service Learning Programs." CCC 54.1 (2002): 40–65.

Deans, Thomas, and Zan Meyer-Goncalves. "Service-Learning Projects in Composition and Beyond." *College Teaching* 46.1 (1998): 12–16.

DelliCarpini, Dominic. "'Must Be Willing to Teach Composition': The Rhetoric and Practices of the Small College Job Search." *Composition Studies* 32.2 (Fall 2004): 31–52.

Dewey, John. *Art as Experience. The Later Works of John Dewey, 1925–1953*. Vol. 10, 1934. Ed. Jo Ann Boydston. Carbondale: Southern Illinois UP, 1987.

———. *Essays on Pragmatism and Truth. The Middle Works of John Dewey, 1899–1924*. Vol. 4, 1907–1909. Ed. Jo Ann Boydston. Carbondale: Southern Illinois UP, 1977.

———. *The School and Society*. Chicago: U of Chicago P, 1943.

Elbow, Peter. "The Cultures of Literature and Composition: What Could Each Learn from the Other?" *College English* 64.5 (2002): 533–46.

Fleming, David. "Rhetoric as a Course of Study." *College English* 61.2 (1998): 169–91.

Horner, Winifred Bryan. *Composition and Literature: Bridging the Gap*. Chicago: U of Chicago P, 1983.

Hutchinson, Glenn. "Service-Learning: Vygotsky, Dewey, and Teaching Writing." *Academic Exchange Quarterly* 4.4 (2000): 73+.

Isocrates. *Isocrates*. Ed. and trans. George Norlin. Vol. 2. Cambridge, MA: Harvard UP, 1962.

Keeter, Scott, Cliff Zukin, Molly Andolina, and Krista Jenkins. "The Civic and Political Health of the Nation: A Generational Portrait." Center for Information and Research on Civic Learning and Engagement. 19 September 2002. http://www.civicyouth.org/research/products/Civic_Political_Health.pdf (accessed 3 December 2002).

McLellan, Jeffrey A., and James Youniss. "Two Systems of Youth Service: Determinants of Voluntary and Required Youth Community Service." *Journal of Youth and Adolescence* 32.1 (2003): 47–58.

Plato. *The Republic of Plato*. Ed. and trans. Allan Bloom. New York: Basic Books, 1968.

Russell, Cheryl. "Meet the Next Generation." *American Demographics* 12.4 (April 1990): 2.

Schilb, John. *Between the Lines: Relating Composition Theory and Literary Theory*. Portsmouth, NH: Boynton/Cook, 1996.

Schutz, Aaron, and Ann Ruggles Gere. "Service Learning and English Studies: Rethinking the Public Sphere." *College English* 60.2 (1998): 129–49.

Tate, Gary. "A Place for Literature in Freshman Composition." *College English* 53.3 (March 1993): 317–21.

Wheelock, Frederick M., ed. *Quintilian as Educator: Selections from the Institutio Oratorio of Marcus Fabius Quintilianus*. Trans. H. E. Butler. New York: Twayne, 1974.

CHAPTER THREE

# Restructuring in Higher Education and the Relationship between Literature and Composition

TIMOTHY J. DOHERTY
*Rivier College*

This chapter analyzes a dynamic process as a writing program moved from its traditional location in an English department. Through a narrative of changes at a mid-sized state university (henceforth referred to as "the University"), I examine the forces leading to the eventual split between the Writing Program and the English Department, the structures for deliberation that were used or thwarted, the theoretical positions involved, the proposals that were considered or not considered, the personnel relationships that were affected, and, in the luxury of hindsight, the kind of conversations that might have happened, or indeed could happen at any institution facing similar pressures.

The central claim of this chapter is that it is possible for departments of English to lead change, rather than react to it, if they can foster focused, informed, and ample discussion of literacy and its aims on campus. Ultimately, local circumstances will dictate whether literature and composition are housed together, fracture in animosity, or somehow collaboratively link through a separate Writing Across the Curriculum program or a bolder reorganization. I believe, however, that literature and composition faculty *can* maintain their ties by embracing an approach to culture and language that ranges beyond the traditionally textual and literary. What is most crucial is that all parties in the discussion be given ample time at the table. All stakeholders need time to build trust and contemplate essential questions—What is literacy becoming? What organizational structures can best help students become literate? What attitudes and structures impede a wide orientation to literacy? And how can faculty be persuaded to participate in an expanded agenda of literacy instruction?

In proposing the topics and terms of discussion, I openly admit to a particular stance: that change *is* needed when literacy instruction is constrained because of a prevailing belletristic tradition, which can result from location in an English department. We should more broadly define literacy as the development of rhetorical habits of mind, a process that should expose writers to multiple discourses and audiences. Even more boldly, as Thomas P. Miller suggests, English departments should root themselves in "[a] civic philosophy of rhetoric [that] can enable us to bring our work with service learning, new technologies, and political controversies into a unified project that challenges hierarchies of research, teaching, and service that limits the social implications of academic work and devalues the work of the humanities" ("Rhetoric" 34). If such a revaluation of rhetoric cannot happen in an English department, then universities must seek other more effective locations for literacy instruction.

## Forces Leading to Change: A Case Study

Writing programs separate from English departments for different reasons. Many universities restructure their general education programs, a process that may affect the way in which writing requirements are fulfilled. Some institutions create more streamlined instruction through learning communities, and such new relationships may stress existing ties between a writing program and an English department. Others establish separate writing programs because a critical mass of constituencies accept the claim that the field of rhetoric and composition has its own theoretical traditions, canons, aims of inquiry, fields of application, and so on. In still other cases, the burden of launching large WAC initiatives also creates a rationale for separation based upon efficiencies of scale and the need for resources. And finally, administrators may question the lack of composition teaching by tenure-track literature faculty, initiating a process of organizational inquiry (Royer and Gilles 24). Whatever the forces prompting separation, an independent writing program may communicate a broad definition of the aims of language instruction, especially if WAC is involved, as it often is. Independence may finally bring to rhetoric and composition the material benefits historically enjoyed by literature, providing new resources that enable scholarly research and curriculum development.

However, as Angela Crow and Peggy O'Neill caution in their introduction to *A Field of Dreams: Independent Writing Programs and the Future of Composition Studies*, "independence, particularly within the traditional institution of the university, is perhaps a fantasy, as we always function in dependent ways within institutional systems. . . . Independence takes on multiple meanings, none of which may accurately reflect individuals' ideals and all of which demonstrate the complexities of attempting to establish a department or program" (4, 12). Indeed, regardless of what we may think is the best location for composition instruction, when composition splits from English, independence may prove ambiguous and, for the unprepared, turbulent and precarious. The relocation of composition may bring unforeseen effects, potentially altering budgets and reporting lines, faculty lines, theoretical positions about literacy, personal relationships among faculty, intra- and interdepartmental politics, and the nature of writing instruction experienced by students.

I first provide a context and chronology of institutional change at the University, showing how its efforts to reform general education, and the particular personal dynamics and histories at play throughout the reform effort, prompted the split between the Writing Program and the English Department. My narrative is meant to expose the complex local political conditions affecting institutional reform.

In the late 1990s, the University attempted to restructure its general education program. The new program was defined less by discipline-specific, credit-hour requirements and more by "outcomes" pursued in an ostensibly interdisciplinary fashion. Common to such reform endeavors is a critique of organizing curriculum by specific disciplinary knowledge, canons, terms, people, and so forth. Instead, faculty are asked not only to provide traditional curricular content but also to emphasize and assess skill outcomes. The reasons for the University's reform were articulated in official memos, stating that distribution requirements, as a model, fragment learning, thwart retention, and offer little basis for life-long learning. To promote "continued learning," faculty were admonished to break traditional disciplinary boundaries by "clustering."

The University accordingly replaced its previous Liberal Studies program, which left curricular decisions in the hands of faculty and departments, with a new general education program stewarded by a new dean. In the new program, instead of choosing from large numbers of different courses to satisfy a requirement in, say, U.S. culture, now students would have to choose from a limited number of predetermined paths within specific "clusters" of study. In the reformed program, students must complete five General Education clusters (such as "The Natural World," "Social and Cultural Processes"). Within each of these five clusters, students choose a set of courses called a "package." There are, however, only two or three packages of courses in a given cluster. Within a particular package, usually three courses from different disciplines participate, and the courses are supposed to help students make connections among disciplines. Because every package purports to form a locus of content pursued in interdisciplinary ways, students must take only one package of courses and may not pick and choose courses from different packages.

Students and faculty alike were vocal critics. In the university's newspaper, students clearly opposed their restricted choices. Faculty objected to packages designed to interrelate instruction based on measurable objectives, preoccupied merely with functional skills. For example, the Writing Program at the University, then housed within the English Department, found itself suddenly thrust into new partnerships through participation in several "packages" with business, philosophy, and media arts and design, creating new pressures upon how writing might be valued and conceived (as a measurable product, for example). Indeed, "Cluster One," the umbrella containing all of these packages, was entitled "Skills for the Twenty-first Century," the sole location for all speech and writing courses. Yet, literate behavior is fundamental to all learning *and* marked by disciplinary differences. Thus, although driven by a critique of self-enclosed, discipline-based structures, the University's general education plan seemed paradoxically to commit the very offense it aimed to eliminate: partitioning learning into a separate cluster, "Skills for the Twenty-first Century." In effect, writing was always in danger of being reductively construed as a mere skill. Ultimately, despite its support of two WAC workshops, the General Education program's outcomes-based paradigm of skills instruction actually undermined its own purported values of interdisciplinarity and writing across the curriculum.

Conceptual inconsistencies aside, the General Education program's interdisciplinary aims created an ambiguous overlap of faculty in English, speech communication, and general education. This confusion, further compounded by the concurrent and sudden formation of a new Institute for Technical Communication that splintered off from the English Department, prompted the dean of arts and letters to call for further organizational study of all communication instruction, "written, oral, and mediated." The dean charged the Task Force on Communication to examine the organizational structure through which all communication instruction at the university should be provided. At this point theoretical positions about literacy, debates about organizational structure, and institutional politics began to collide. Moreover, the task force selection process crippled the possibility for focused, informed, and ample discussion of literacy and its aims on campus.

All positions on the task force were appointed by the dean. It was chaired by an assistant dean, formerly chair of the English Department, whose relationships had become strained with others in that department. It contained several newly hired, untenured members and no tenured faculty members with specialization in literature (aside from the former chair himself). The untenured director of the Writing Program was also a member, and throughout the process she was virtually silent. I was a newly hired and untenured rhetoric and composition specialist with a strong background in English Renaissance drama, asked by the dean to join the committee. I reluctantly agreed, with a sense of great foreboding and divided loyalty.

Thus, from the start, the task force was ill equipped to function in a way that was open, not merely to difference and negotiation, but to the unpredictable benefits of that process, potentially leading to an innovative and effective program. As its investigation unfolded, it addressed the organizational structure for teaching communication on campus but ignored the deeper, more vexing questions: What is literacy? How should it be taught, and for what ends? How does literature—its reception *and* production—figure into its education?

The preceding narrative suggests how discussions of theory and organizational possibility can be muted by personal agendas, and how the roiling micropolitics of institutions can bring unforeseen theoretical implications. It may be tempting to see this narrative as an isolated instance. Yet, the troubled "wedlock" of composition and literature at this institution is not isolated from larger, national forces impinging upon all universities of its size—global pressures to compete in an information economy, national movements toward educational accountability, increased competition among colleges and universities, the perceived crises in literacy ability, new definitions of literacy shaped by new technologies, the now generally accepted ideology of WAC, and the rising institutional and professional recognition of rhetoric and composition.[1] These forces operated on this university, heating up the climate in which the task force tried to function. With change suddenly thrust upon them, the English Department and the Writing Program were not adequately poised to negotiate such external pressures. A newly hired chair of the English Department had just arrived as the Task Force on Communication was forming, and with so many other challenges, the department seemed to have no solidified front.

The department's lack of dialogue about how and why composition and literature relate forced it to succumb to change. Prior to and during the Writing Program's coordination with General Education, the literature faculty of the English Department had little interest in teaching first-year writing courses. The former chair and current leader of the task force had hired more adjunct faculty so that literature faculty could meet student demand in upper-division literature courses. Thus, before the task force, to return to the marriage metaphor, composition and literature had an amicable union but slept in separate rooms. This lack of communication between faculty members in the department, however, helped contribute to the eventual divorce of literature from composition at the university.

## The Personal Toll of Institutional Change

Against this backdrop of institutional change, my narrative now turns to the moment of truth—the task force recommendation that the Writing Program split from the English Department—and the possibilities that "divorce" might create for the new program.

When the dean's task force formed, several vocal members of the English Department considered it mere window dressing to cover up a biased process with a predetermined outcome. The new chair of the English Department was invited to present the case for the status quo to the task force, but only a part of the task force was present for her presentation, and there was no serious consideration of the relationship of literary study to a comprehensive vision of academic and civic literacy. To his credit, the chair of the task force did hold a meeting with all English Department faculty, where they could have claimed that the task force membership was biased against them from the start. They did not, perhaps because they did not want to trouble the waters for the new chair, and perhaps because they did not want to teach first-year composition courses. In any event, lengthy, well-informed discussions never occurred, and, as I hope this essay makes clear, the reasons were local *and* global, personal *and* institutional. I am not sure any cooperative, *scholarly* dialogue could have directed the changes at the University (and that was a difficult paradox to endure). That need not be true for similar institutions.

What this narrative shows is that powerful constituencies can derail deliberative processes, and that when unjust proceedings ensue, theoretical positions, personal fortunes and relationships, and institutional politics tangle. My own case is an example of these forces. A few seasoned colleagues told me to abstain from voting on the task force recommendation to split the Writing Program from the English Department, or to ask that I be removed from the task force altogether. However, I firmly believe in participating in my community's dialogue about its fate. These issues fascinate me, hence my attempt to use this essay to gain clarity. I was also uncertain how *any* of my actions might be construed, by either a dean noting my unwillingness to support what others thought a foregone conclusion, or by a department rife with historic animosities. Another English Department colleague told me that I should tuck my chin down and resist, insisting that the conversations I so desired should happen.

However, for political and personal reasons, I was reluctant to make bold *demands* for discussion, and three events gave me warrant: first and foremost, when the chair of the task force responded to my private admission of feeling vulnerable by saying, "Tim, it's time to get on the side of the big boys"; second, when a tenured English Department "mentor" betrayed my confidence, publicly impugning my character; and finally, when a faculty member from the Foreign Languages Department, confirming my vulnerability, publicly responded to the task force recommendation that, because non-tenured English faculty on the task force would be victimized by the English Department at tenure time, the Writing Program's split from English was now beyond question.

Indeed, after a rancorous public forum for "feedback" on the task force recommendations, the dean issued his edict separating the Writing Program from the English Department. The Writing Program became a separate unit, eventually aspiring to become a department that would construct an entire major. I reluctantly endorsed this proposal, driven by a sense of survival and practicality, but also cowardice. The assistant dean, the chair of the task force, became one of three members on my new personnel committee. In *A Field of Dreams,* Crow and O'Neill caution those contemplating the creation of an independent writing unit to be sure that the new unit is able to "establish the means by which it can protect its faculty" (14). Ideally, the assistant dean's presence on my personnel committee could be construed as protection—an alliance that might sustain a new program and its faculty by ensuring relevant criteria for promotion and tenure. However, from a political perspective attentive to local history, the assistant dean's past and current behavior raised many "general climate questions" (14), casting doubt on exactly how stable the relationship would prove to be. Worried that I would simply be "shacking up with another 'oppressor'" (3), I found a chilling message in my new personnel committee: don't rock the boat. I quickly unfurled my curriculum vitae and sailed for calmer seas.

The new Writing Program began to take root as I left, first relying upon three-year, renewable contracts for the majority of its positions, then turning some of those into tenure-track positions after general complaint arose that non-tenure contracts institutionally inscribe second-class citizenship for the program's faculty. Despite that effort, significant faculty turnover has marked the program's inception, including the departure of the Writing Program's director.

Has the separation of the Writing Program at the University, then, been a bad thing? The process was horrendous for the University's collegial culture, certainly. To judge by how easily old scars opened during the task force proceedings, the new wounds perhaps will always vex particular people and departments. However, if the new Writing Program indeed pursues an expanded agenda of rhetorical education that helps students to deliberate values and controversies and to engage in a variety of rhetorical settings, that effort will benefit students and composition faculty. What has been lost forever, I fear, is the possibility of a healthy, warm, trusting, and collaborative linkage with the English Department, whose faculty missed the opportunity to "reassess the modern distinction between the arts and sciences that underlies the reduction of literature to nonutilitarian, nonfactual discourse" (Miller, "Rhetoric" 41), enabling them to have a more powerful voice on campus about the breadth of literacy education and its relationship to literary study.

## The Conversation We Should Have Had

The moral of my story is that in times of institutional change, fair and full discussions are needed, contemplating different institutional models of literacy instruction. No doubt, institutional change is often sluggish or, if spurred, wounding. In most cases, institutional change is constrained by the existing inclinations, expertise, and relationships of faculty, and by local matters of institutional size, mission, and tradition. Every university has personnel differences, and many have fractured cultures, vying for different orientations to the university's mission. However, regardless of local circumstances, most institutions would benefit from pursuing open conversations about change, focused on particular issues and prompted by particular published texts. Reasonable people should be able to discuss the following important questions as they deliberate institutional restructuring:

> What is *literacy* becoming, and what organizational entities can best help students become literate?
>
> What organizational structures would help the entire university pursue literacy instruction without inordinate disadvantage to particular constituencies?
>
> What attitudes and structures impede a wider orientation to literacy?
>
> How can faculty be persuaded to participate in an expanded agenda of literacy instruction?

First, what is literacy? What is the aim of literacy instruction at the university? As Robert Scholes, James Berlin, and Thomas P. Miller, to name but a few, have argued, developments in both composition and literary theory should inspire us to widen our definition of *text*, to assert the centrality of rhetoric as an orienting principle for English studies, to acknowledge the specificity of disciplinary discourses and the value of interdisciplinary learning, and to embrace the way in which new technologies are altering conceptions of reading, writing, and research.

If we accept a broader definition of *literacy* that serves the entire university's interest, then what structure for literacy education works best, within the local limitations of faculty and student abilities and interests? The first matter of discussion, then, is whether or not to separate a writing program from an English department, if that is the status quo. In either case, what hangs in the balance is the power to decide what aims are worth pursuing and to pursue them.

It may be possible for an English department to design and lead a campuswide writing program pursuing broad civic and rhetorical education.[2] Why bother? Department chairs often see the need quite clearly: the department's size, hiring options, and prestige are at stake in how it handles the centrality of composition. Yet, why should a department's specialist in twentieth-century poetry care about this discussion? How is she a stakeholder? First, at the least, she should be given the opportunity to have a voice in the matter, rather than have it decided without her participation. When in the midst of institutional change you do nothing, things happen *to* you. She may find that it is better to lead change than to react defensively to it. What hangs in the balance is the English department's long and, for the public, continuing association with instruction in reading and writing. Second, she may assert that teaching composition is not a chore, but a central activity for a liberal education. Third, she may discover that her department's central role in shaping literacy education on campus will help to reinvigorate the importance of literary study in the institution's mission. Opportunities may emerge through these discussions for the department to rethink the public role of literary study. She may be surprised by the personal and professional growth that usually attends pivotal involvement in WAC efforts.

For any department of English facing institutional reorganization of a writing program, the question is, *Are you able to make composition a central part of your disciplinary identity and to direct change*, not fearing connection with the nonliterary but instead pursuing curricular innovation in which, among many other projects, the literary makes a vital contribution? English departments could indeed lead WAC programs, and the collaboration with other disciplines could lead to exciting courses engaging students in a range of literacy practices.

Maintaining the tie between an English department and a writing program may also benefit specialists in rhetoric and composition as well, providing intellectual historical rootedness, possibly stable budgets, and established processes for promotion and tenure. For rhetoric and composition specialists and adjunct writing faculty, the question must be, Will the change lead to improved labor conditions, expanded curriculum, and fair rewards for service and scholarship? To what degree should the literary be included in, say, first-year composition courses? At what cost? To what degree of advantage or disadvantage?

Separation is, of course, an option. Facing new pressures to rethink how we navigate disciplinary boundaries, isolationists such as George Levine claim that "Literature" departments should stick to literature (14). If we accept the separation of the literary and nonliterary, then English can't lay claim to *all* writing,[3] and a separate writing (or WAC) program makes sense: literature is only one species of writing (and the literary explication its parasite?). Furthermore, for some literature faculty, losing a writing program does not matter as long as there is no deterioration of their graduate program, which often rests upon the lure of teaching assistantships and upon upper-level instruction enabled by lower-tier writing courses taught by poorly paid adjuncts.

Indeed, a separate writing program may be best for the entire university. Especially if it is WAC-based, it has the potential of serving wider civic and rhetorical aims of language instruction, open to a variety of discourses and academic communities. Coordinating WAC efforts, such a program can offer more freedom for expanded curriculum development and scholarly projects. Katherine Gottschalk describes the inception and growth of Cornell University's Writing Program, an independent entity, the success of which has come from clear leadership, budgetary independence, and an openness to faculty interests in language in all of the disciplines. Daniel Royer and Roger Gilles also describe the benefits of their independent department at Grand Valley State University. Thus, certain institutions, *with local conditions ripe for such change*, can make a more confident step toward an expanded orientation to literacy, involving not a separate "cluster" of communication skills courses as in some general education programs, but a university WAC framework similar to Cornell's. For Gottschalk, independence from English per se isn't the issue for a writing program, but rather the mechanisms of fostering and guiding collaboration across the university in pursuing wider literacy education. At Grand Valley State University, the English Department established a task force to investigate organizational possibilities for the writing program, and at least all departmental stakeholders had a voice. All members of an English department would benefit from reading the story Royer and Gilles tell, for it exposes the cultural tensions that exist within such departments and the costs and benefits of separation.

My concern in this essay is not to advocate for separation or union between literature and composition, but to underscore the need for all stakeholders to participate in an open and thoughtful dialogue, considering how the department might change so that separation becomes unnecessary. How can an English department widen students' exposure to, and application of, a range of literate strategies? Certain attitudes and structures impede the pursuit of the new orientations to literacy I've described. How can a departmental culture be encouraged so that an expanded agenda of literacy instruction becomes possible? If all constituencies can agree that a wider definition of literacy is the aim, then *all* faculty interested in literacy need to seize the moment and strengthen arguments for an interdisciplinary, campuswide literacy initiative. But, how?

First, if department members decide that a writing program can indeed expand within the department, *without exploitation and hindrance*, then that department should charge its curriculum committee with the ongoing task of exploring new curricula and pedagogy, specifically with the aims of strengthening the department's commitment to composition and its leadership role in a universitywide program that enables many disciplines to offer writing-intensive courses. Second, English departments should hire candidates who think beyond the simplistic divide of literature and composition; or more radically, they should hire individuals with multidisciplinary expertise, able to begin developing courses that help students pursue a variety of literacy interests.

Third, ongoing conversation within the department should be fostered, fueled by readings of Thomas Miller's *The Formation of College English*, David Damrosch's *We Scholars* and *Meeting of the Minds*, Cynthia Selfe's *Technology and Literacy in the Twenty-first Century*, Susan Miller's *Textual Carnivals*, Robert Scholes's *The Rise and Fall of English*, James Berlin's *Rhetorics, Poetics, and Cultures*, and Ross Winterowd's *The English Department*, especially his explanation of the development of rhetoric and composition from the vantage of both the institutional history of English studies and literary theory. We need to discuss seriously "the literature side," deciding how literary education matters within the institution's mission. We also need constructive brainstorming about disciplinary boundaries, perhaps based on Gerald Graff's stance that some institutional framework must be sought, not so much to achieve coherence in defining and teaching literacy, but to put various specialties into dialogue (Graff, "Conversation" 24). Elsewhere, Graff writes, "it is not specialization itself that occasions problems so much as the failure to bring specializations into relation with one another in any planned way. Specialization becomes self-enclosure only when there is no institutionalized correlation of specialties" (Graff, "University" 65; qtd. in Nelson 6).

Finally, from the most obvious, pragmatic perspective, if composition and literature are to remain together in an institution, a department should do all it can to ensure that literature faculty teach first-year writing courses in a well-directed program aimed, more broadly, at fostering writing across the curriculum. More and more, administrations seek justification for the size of English departments where tenure-track literature faculty do not assume responsibility for first-year composition. Further, where specialization and expertise warrant, composition faculty should teach literature. A culture of cross-disciplinary conversation needs to emerge. In addition to the personal and professional growth all faculty can realize through the teaching of first-year composition, the funding, class size, hiring options, prestige, and traditions associated with a department of English hang in the balance.

I hope the terms of conversation I have thus far proposed will help *any* institution consider questions about the public purposes of literacy and literary education, about the most relevant and strong connection between composition and literature, and about how an existing department of English housing a writing program may lead change, not defensively react to it. These suggestions comprise the sort of "marriage counseling" advocated by Edward White that might mend the split between literature and composition (37). If, on the other hand, traditional English departments are divided, with all "bridges" between literature and composition collapsed from disuse or from past ideological detonations, then institutions are warranted in seeking other structural alternatives for the "place" of literacy instruction in a university. Crow and O'Neill ask, "[A]re independent writing departments more able to address changing conceptions of disciplinarity because they are separated from English departments? Is it possible to create more radical change than we would have heretofore imagined because we are situated outside English departments?" (14). Their answer is a definitive "perhaps," with a strong caution that any relocation may bring dislocation. The success of any change rests upon a savvy grasp of "family systems, of the local situation, of the institutional system one attempts to shift" (3).

## The End(s) of Literate Conversation

At the university whose story I have told, change left many suspicious and torn. Rather than accept the death of collegial, collaborative problem solving and decision making, universities can conduct better conversations about the structures that serve all stakeholders in literacy education and imagine several ends of literate life. Change should be based upon the premise that all students, faculty, and administration, and not just composition and literature "departments," are stakeholders in the matter of literacy. Leadership—typically from deans—must ensure that the conversation happens, and that it is as transparent, representative, and informed as possible. If faculty do embrace the need for expanded literacy education, how can we transform or supplement concepts such as *the major, required courses, departments, electives, FTE,* and so forth, in order to create new structures for writing-intensive and linked courses, co-teaching, and interdisciplinary paths of study, producing undergraduates with a range of abilities—creative, critical, and practical? In the midst of yet further pressures for change, pressures particularly focused upon composition, new tensions are apt to arise between composition and literature. The "conversation" I envision can offer a medium through which all stakeholders may continue to shape how literacy matters in the university and in public life.

In the end, the specific local conditions of an institution will determine whether literature and composition remain in the same department, "divorce," or somehow collaborate in a bolder reorganization. For some institutions, such collaborations could happen without radical restructuring of the status quo in English departments. With vocal, activist members, eager to shape the university's ability to address a broader range of rhetorical activity, the English department could be uniquely positioned to develop rhetorical learning and practice and to foster writing and interdisciplinary learning. Much depends on the level of morale and commitment among faculty, and the history of their community relative to administration. It takes a strong departmental culture to negotiate administrative interests in technology, market relevance, efficiency, and accountability. In the end, universities face many structural options for literacy, posing uncertain prospects for departments of English and writing programs. Through an open process, all stakeholders should direct this potentially anxious moment into occasions for innovation.

## Notes

1. For various perspectives on how domestic metaphors have been used to describe the relationship between literature and composition, see Crow and O'Neill; White; Slagle and Rose; and Schneider.
2. For example, Louise Z. Smith asks, why can't English "house" WAC? This was a fundamental institutional issue never quite openly confronted by the task force at the University.
3. For an overview of commentaries on the relationship between literature and composition, see Goggin and Varnum; for an argument that English doesn't "own" writing, see Blair.

## Works Cited

Berlin, James A. *Rhetorics, Poetics, and Cultures: Refiguring College English Studies*. Urbana, IL: National Council of Teachers of English, 1996.

Blair, Catherine Pastore. "Only One of the Voices: Dialogic Writing Across the Curriculum." *College English* 50 (April 1988): 383–89.

Crow, Angela, and Peggy O'Neill. "Introduction: Cautionary Tales about Change." O'Neill, Crow, and Burton 1–18.

Damrosch, David. *Meetings of the Mind*. Princeton, NJ: Princeton UP, 2000.

———. *We Scholars: Changing the Culture of the University.* Cambridge, MA: Harvard UP, 1995.

Goggin, Maureen. "Literature." *Keywords in Composition Studies.* Ed. Paul Heilker and Peter Vandenburg. Portsmouth, NH: Heinemann/Cook, 1996. 145–50.

Gottschalk, Katherine. "The Writing Program in the University." *ADE Bulletin* 112 (Winter 1995): 1–6.

Graff, Gerald. "Is There a Conversation in This Curriculum? Or, Coherence without Disciplinarity." *English as a Discipline: Or, Is There a Plot in This Play?* Ed. James C. Raymond. Tuscaloosa: UP of Alabama, 1996. 11–28.

———. "The University and the Prevention of Culture." *Criticism in the University.* Ed. Gerald Graff and Reginald Gibbons. Evanston, IL: Northwestern UP, 1985. 62–82.

Heilker, Paul, and Peter Vandenburg, eds. *Keywords in Composition Studies.* Portsmouth, NH: Heinemann/Cook, 1996.

Levine, George. "Putting the 'Literature' Back into Literature Departments." *ADE Bulletin* 113 (Spring 1996): 13–20.

Miller, Susan. *Textual Carnivals: The Politics of Composition.* Carbondale: Southern Illinois UP, 1993.

Miller, Thomas P. *The Formation of College English: Rhetoric and Belles Lettres in the British Cultural Provinces.* Pittsburgh: U of Pittsburgh P, 1997.

———. "Rhetoric within and without Composition: Reimagining the Civic." *Coming of Age: The Advanced Writing Curriculum.* Ed. Linda K. Shamoon et al. Portsmouth, NH: Boynton/Cook, 2000. 32–41.

Nelson, Cary. "Against English: Theory and the Limits of the Discipline." *ADE Bulletin* 85 (1986): 1–6.

O'Neill, Peggy, Angela Crow, and Larry W. Burton, eds. *A Field of Dreams: Independent Writing Programs and the Future of Composition Studies.* Logan: Utah State UP, 2002.

Royer, Daniel J., and Roger Gilles. "The Origins of a Department of Academic, Creative, and Professional Writing." O'Neill, Crow, and Burton. 21–37.

Schneider, Alison. "Bad Blood in the English Department: The Rift between Composition and Literature." *Chronicle of Higher Education,* 13 February 1998: A14.

Scholes, Robert. *The Rise and Fall of English: Reconstructing English as a Discipline.* New Haven, CT: Yale UP, 1998.

Selfe, Cynthia L. *Technology and Literacy in the Twenty-first Century: The Importance of Paying Attention.* Carbondale: Southern Illinois UP, 1999.

Slagle, Diane Buckles, and Shirley K. Rose. "Domesticating English Studies." *Journal of Teaching Writing* 13.1–2 (1994): 147–68.

Smith, Louise Z. "Why English Departments Should 'House' Writing Across the Curriculum." *College English* 50 (April 1988): 390–95.

Varnum, Robin. "Composition Studies." *Keywords in Composition Studies.* Ed. Paul Heilker and Peter Vandenburg. Portsmouth, NH: Heinemann/Cook, 1996. 44–48.

White, Edward M. *Developing Successful College Writing Programs.* San Francisco: Jossey-Bass, 1989.

Winterowd, W. Ross. *The English Department: A Personal and Institutional History.* Carbondale: Southern Illinois UP, 1998.

CHAPTER FOUR

## *Causes and Cures for Our Professional Schizophrenia*

EDWARD A. KEARNS
*University of Northern Colorado*

The twentieth century began with English departments suffering from a simple schizophrenia, what Robert Scholes calls the "invidious binary opposition between writing teachers and literary scholars" (35). Over the century, the profession became "too concerned with teaching the right ideas in the classroom and not concerned enough with teaching the most effective ways of speaking, listening, reading, and writing" (65). As a result, many compositionists fear including literature in first-year composition—taught on most campuses by graduate assistants whose undergraduate and graduate training is rooted in literary scholarship. For the odds are that including fiction, poetry, and drama in composition will *not* lead to producing better writers—any more than introductory and advanced literature courses aim at producing them. Rather, the odds favor FYC becoming yet another course in "right ideas": the ideas of theorists, interpreters, would-be historians, and latent social scientists.[1]

Toward the end of the century, our schizophrenia gave way to full-blown Multiple Personality Disorder. Peter Elbow titled his report on the 1987 English Coalition Conference *What Is English?* Conference participants—kindergarten through graduate school teachers—could not answer the question because, lacking a coherent identity for nearly a century, we had tried to become all things to everybody. The National Council of Teachers of English and the International Reading Association's (NCTE/IRA) *Standards for the English Language Arts*, for example, identified us as teachers of "diversity in language use, patterns, and dialects across cultures, ethnic groups, geographic regions, and social roles," teachers of "media techniques" and "graphics," of strategies for "personal fulfillment," teachers "of the cultures of the United States and the world," and—this is truly breathtaking—teachers "of the many dimensions (e.g., philosophical, ethical, aesthetic) of human experience" (3). Such pretensions would be merely comic were they not so obviously deluded.

Consequently, English is the only department devoted to an art in which making the art plays second fiddle to talking about it; indeed, in which many members actually snub "the language arts," and many of its self-styled critics avoid aesthetic judgment, "quality," and "taste." While fine arts departments have their historians and theorists, performance and studio courses dominate their curricula, just as issues of aesthetics govern their professional routines. These departments respect their painters, directors, composers, and other makers, and think their primary task is to produce more of them. Things are different in English departments.

In what follows I briefly trace the development of our malady and offer cures for it, but I must re-emphasize from the beginning Scholes's binary poles: *writing teachers* and *literary scholars*. Further splinterings among composition, creative writing, and, more recently, creative nonfiction are symptomatic of the larger disorder. The *creative* adjective is symptomatic as well. What writing isn't created by writers? What literature hasn't been created by them?

# I. Causes

Our schizophrenia began over a century ago when we abandoned Art for Science. Led by college faculties, the profession turned away from making and judging literature and from forthrightly dealing with matters of taste. As Gerald Graff's *Professing Literature* demonstrates, it turned toward description, analysis, and interpretation. Significantly, Graff limited his study to college departments and the Modern Language Association. He mentions neither the appearance of the NCTE early in the twentieth century, nor its impact on English education, nor its sponsorship of the Conference on College Composition and Communication. He ignores "creative writing." His omissions are symptomatic of the divisions in English departments up to and beyond 1987, and his admirable history reveals the sources of our nuttiness.

According to Graff, at the first meeting of the Modern Language Association in 1883, German professor H. C. G. Brandt spoke of all modern language instruction and affirmed that "our department *is* a science, and . . . its teaching must be carried on accordingly"; "a scientific basis dignifies our profession." Moreover:

> By basing our instruction and text-books upon a scientific groundwork, our department and our profession gain dignity and weight. . . . By introducing scientific methods, we shall show before very long that every body cannot [teach English], that the teacher must be as specially and as scientifically trained for his work in our department as well as in any other. (Brandt, qtd. in Graff 67–68)

It is difficult to imagine any professor of music, fine arts, theater, or dance saying such a thing. Nevertheless, Brandt's sentiments became the ethos for literary study throughout the twentieth century. Aristotle's "*arts* of language" were out. Value judgments were out. The non-normative, objectivist, professional ethos was in.

Novelist Frank Norris, who attended Berkeley from 1890 to 1894, noted that classification was in: of metaphors and similes, lyrics and ballads, with depressing consequences for students. By the senior year, the student's "enthusiasm is about dead," and he is "ashamed of his original thoughts and of those ideas of his own that he entertained as a Freshman and Sophomore." He has learned to write "'papers' in the true academic style." Norris believed the university's literary courses "do not develop literary instincts," and he doubted whether analytic study could ever prove useful: "the best way to study literature is to try to produce literature" (Norris, qtd. in Graff 103–4).

If we had to pick a time when literature split from writing, we could do no better than this. Brandt's scientific "dignity and weight" led "English" to become predominantly a literature curriculum, with little sense of purpose beyond observing, describing, and interpreting a relatively fixed canon. Consequently, the scientific approach also led professors to adopt the Latin definition of *critic*. The Greek *kritios* points to one who *judges*, who *decides*—to those who gave Sophocles his prizes. The Roman *criticus* was a descriptive term used in medicine, as in a patient's critical condition. Again, according to Graff, in the 1890s "scholar and critic emerge as antithetical terms, and the gulf further widens between fact and value, investigation and appreciation, scientific specialization and general culture" (122). Bliss Perry argued in 1896 that the low level of public taste made it all the more incumbent on colleges to "send into this public, to serve as leaven, men who know good work from bad and who know why they know it" (Graff 125). English departments have ignored Perry's urging.

Instead, by the beginning of the twentieth century, English had become the only art department that routinely snubbed artists, teachers of writing, and questions of taste. Schools of analysts and interpreters proliferated: Marxists, Freudians, mythologists, formalists, and, more recently, deconstructionists, feminists, and postmodernists. Little wonder, then, that throughout the twentieth century, college-level English departments offered only a spate of creative writing courses *and* few contemporary literature courses. The canon was established; the task was to analyze and interpret it, not add to it.

By the late 1950s, the interpretive, "meaning-making" bias became so dominant it prompted Susan Sontag's famous essay, "Against Interpretation." Sontag attacked interpretation as "the revenge of the intellect upon art." "Even more": "It is the revenge of the intellect upon the world. To interpret is to impoverish, to deplete the world—in order to set up a shadow world of 'meanings'" (7). In other words, interpretations, from whatever interpretive school, amount to little more than paraphrases or "retellings," usually in language notorious for its pretentious jargon. That poems, fictions, and dramas spawn multiple interpretations should tell us something: namely, that the artists who create them care little about the "meaning" of their work. When artists wish to share their thoughts on life, death, love, men, or women, they aim at clarity of meaning and write nonfiction. But in writing poems, stories, and plays, they strike at something else: clarity of image. By *image* I mean everything from a single metaphor to the whole of a novel, everything from Hamlet to *Hamlet*. Thus, the sharper the image, the more elusive its meaning, the more resonant its mystery. *And the more important our judgment of its worth becomes.*

Poetry, fiction, and drama are more than sociopolitical artifacts, and the work of both their creators and (normative) critics differs from that of historians, interpreters, sociologists, and scientists. Marya Mannes noted the difference in 1962 when she assailed critics' flight from value judgments:

> the fashion in criticism or appreciation of the arts has been to deny the existence of any valid criteria and to make the words "good" or "bad" irrelevant, immaterial, and inapplicable. . . . This has been a popular approach, for it relieves the critic of the responsibility of judgment and the public of the necessity of knowledge. It pleases those resentful of disciplines, it flatters the empty-minded by calling them open-minded, it comforts the confused. . . . If [the critic] has mastered the art of saying nothing with exquisite complexity, nobody can quote him later as saying anything.
> 
> But all these [forms of criticism] . . . are forms of abdication from the responsibility of judgment. In creating, the artist commits himself; in appreciating, you have a commitment of your own. . . . only a public ill-served by its critics could have accepted as art and as literature so much in these last years that has been neither. If anything goes, everything goes; and at the bottom of the junk pile lie the discarded standards too. (Mannes 347–48)

Of course, writing teachers judge good work and bad every day, and even literature professors evaluate their students' tests and papers. Their grading standards simply articulate their tastes, so I would add only this to Mannes's comments: we should teach students that creativity and a critical stance go hand in hand, that science without judgment is dangerous, and that there are such things as cant and drivel, much of it appearing in academic journals.

The pseudo-scientific bias supporting interpretation persisted, however, and by the 1980s the interpreters would raise themselves and their theories above artists and their creations; the parasite would become superior to the host. Some professors would eventually argue that theory and interpretation replace poetry, fiction, and drama altogether. On the final page of *Professing Literature*, Graff himself recommended James Kincaid's "new conception of literary studies": "We need to teach not the texts themselves but how we situate ourselves in reference to those texts" (Graff 262). And thus the revenge of intellect upon art might become complete.

In sum, the invidious binary opposition between literary scholars and writing teachers arose as English departments opted for Science over Art, description over judgment. The purposes for literary study in the "literature" classroom became twofold: to help students become more sophisticated interpreters of texts, and to help them learn something about human history and behavior. Both are legitimate purposes, but they became ends in themselves, ends so pervasive that we lost a major component of critical thinking along the way. That is, "critical thinking skills" as taught in English and other departments are essentially analytical, descriptive, and non-normative, tending toward "objectivity," "accuracy," "measurement," and the like. For example, the extended discussion of Standard Three on the NCTE/IRA list of standards emphasizes that students learn to "develop strategies for making meaning" (31) and then ends with this sentence: "One of the most important functions of English language arts education is to help students learn to interpret texts—that is, to reflect on textual meaning from their own perspectives—and to evaluate texts—that is, to use critical thinking to identify particular text elements, such as logic, emotional appeal, and purpose" (33). Notice: "evaluate" and "use critical thinking" here mean "to identify," not "to judge." Now notice how the meaning of "evaluate" and "critical" would shift to the Greek definition (decision making) were we to say, "use critical thinking *to judge* . . . logic, emotional appeal, and purpose." The statement as written contains a root fallacy, namely that identifying, descriptively analyzing, and interpreting texts equates to evaluating them.

No surprise, then, that so many people in and outside of academe hope to evaluate student writing with the "objective methods" of machine-scored tests. (Judging writing without looking at writing parallels studying literature without "the texts themselves.") We must understand a simple fact: *the purpose for applying "objective methods" to evaluating anything is to eliminate human judgment*. That is the great strength of Science, and it is all well and good in games (keeping score) and races (clocking times in hundredths of seconds), but it does not work in ice-skating competitions, in the Supreme Court, or in most serious problems confronting human beings: namely, problems involving competing goods and lesser evils, problems *inherently* based in values, and problems that require decision making.

Objectivity doesn't work in judging writing, first of all, because *evaluating the writing of either professionals or amateurs means working with a fundamental paradox: the material must be conventional and original at once*. The more one writer's work resembles another's, the more the first seems to be hackwork or worse, plagiarism. Yet the less resemblance, the less basis for comparison; standardization suffers. Negotiating the paradox means *hard* work for writers and evaluators. It is much easier, for example, to demand five-paragraph essays and eight-sentence paragraphs and to prohibit one-sentence paragraphs and legitimate, stylistically effective sentence fragments; doing so reduces the decision making for writers and judges, as does applying rigid grading standards for errors (e.g., a one-point grade reduction for three major errors). Some teachers may justify these and a host of similar practices in the names of objectivity, standardization, and fairness, but standardization, even under its most legitimate applications, masks simple convenience. I hope this behavior is dying out in the classroom. But its premises survive in large- and small-scale assessments that specify audiences, genres, rhetorical purposes, and topics: "Write a letter-to-the-editor of your local paper in which you argue for or against this proposed legislation." And what is the result of heightened standardization both inside and outside the classroom? Teacher critics gripe about how their students' writing all sounds the same.

Second, attempting to eliminate value judgments through objectivity does not work in writing because *writers necessarily choose what knowledge and skills to reveal at a given moment*. They choose vocabularies, sentence structures, paragraph strategies, and the like. Their degree of consciousness *and learning* account for differences among them and for differences in samples drawn from the same writer. Narrowing the range of choice in direct writing assessments—and especially narrowing it to four "multiple choices" in "objective" ones—increases standardization at the expense of genuine writing assessment: it narrows the range of learning writers may display, whereas the ability to make good, effective choices is what we are testing for in the first place.

Third, objectivity doesn't work in writing because *both creating and critiquing are personal acts and, in the present context, publicly performed*. That means, simply, they are done by persons exercising personal (subjective) judgment; the public context, as Mannes affirmed, lends an existential dimension to them. They are risky acts precisely because they lack the assurance, the predictability, of numbers and Science. This lack of a "scientific basis" for judgment seems to intimidate us, makes us fear using words like *personal, subjective*, and *taste*, as if such words equate to "arbitrary" or "capricious." Nonsense. Ice-skating judges, Supreme Court justices, and doctors all *subject* material (performances, law, symptoms) to their personal judgment and render decisions. But their judgment is professionally trained and, therefore, not at all arbitrary. Nor do the facts that judges frequently disagree and reach split decisions or doctors recommend seeking other opinions make the process capricious.

In sum, the objectivity offered by numbers and machines is perfectly appropriate in circumstances legitimately requiring measurement, such as races. But "scoring" writing simply disguises the human, fallible process of judgment. We can grant five points for "correctness," ten for "organization," seven for "style," or we can score holistically, by primary traits, what have you, but tallying up a series of professional, subjective value judgments does not make them objective.

To return to the primary thread of the argument: in the course of the twentieth century, description replaced judgment in literature courses and in professional academic literary organizations. Interpretation, "making meaning," became an end in itself, and interpreter-parasites declared themselves superior to artist-hosts. Works of art became no more than sociopolitical documents to be used as evidence for this or that theoretical bias, and the necessary balance between the Arts and Sciences was lost. Perhaps English professors forgot that the language arts are the only arts required of all citizens. So long as we ask only that students explain "how the figurative language contributes to the *meaning* of the poem," or how this theory can be applied to that text, then we have little business griping about sexist or racist expression, bemoaning the level of public taste, complaining about the shabby level of political discourse, or whining about any other abuses of our art.

## II. Cures

In proposing remedies I am tempted to pack up English departments and move them, bag and baggage, across campus to the College of Fine Arts. Rubbing elbows with painters, potters, musicians, actors, and dancers would do us a world of good and might not harm them very much. However, administrative proposals lead to more committees, reports, and even more conferences—activities certain to undermine the cause of sanity. For similar reasons I am reluctant to propose changes in departmental curriculum, so I will address colleagues directly and suggest ways in which we might improve our mental health. Perhaps in the long run the English ward will also improve.

Curing schizophrenia requires putting pieces back together: re-uniting Aristotle's Arts of Language (reading, writing, listening, and speaking), re-uniting the emotions with the intellect in literary experience, and drawing together descriptive and normative criticism. It requires root reforms, so let us begin by redefining literature and reexamining our critical vocabularies.

### *Redefining and Reexamining Our Language*

For decades we have hassled over what we mean by *literature*, as if literature is not "writing," not "creative writing," not the writing of historians, sociologists, what have you. Yet our literary anthologies include philosophical tracts, personal letters, sermons, journalistic pieces, and diary excerpts along with fiction, poetry, and scripts. Let us end this confusion by affirming simply that *Literature is the language societies decide to keep*. The definition includes oral as well as print material. The key word is *decide*, and it immediately gives focus to our professional purpose, which should be *to teach people how to create and judge language worth keeping.*

Certainly other disciplines do that through their own, specialized publications and generally keep various documents for equally varied purposes (e.g., legal and historical records). Insofar as English teachers teach expository writing and basic elements of research, logic, and argumentation, we contribute to the non-aesthetic values that determine what's worth writing and saving across the disciplines. What separates us first of all from other disciplines, then, is our special attention to fiction, poetry, drama. (As I have already hinted, we should eliminate the adjective *creative*; it is as unnecessary and foolish as "creative painting" or "creative pottery." "Fiction writing," "poetry writing," and "script writing" are sufficient.) More important, what separates us from other departments is our attention *to the aesthetic values on which all good writing depends.* Note: that's a present-tense, descriptive statement. The problem is that writing teachers are not always fully conscious of that attention, and many literature teachers think they are free of it.

Words and phrases such as *aesthetic values, taste,* and *subjectivity* needlessly frighten some teachers and irritate others. In fact, our grading criteria, rubrics, standards, what have you, are nothing more nor less than articulations of our own aesthetic values, which we daily apply to student work in writing and literature classes. Words such as *clarity, precise diction, sentence variety, cohesion, logic,* and *wordiness* form the basis for our judgments. We decide *how* clear, precise, varied, or cohesive a given paper is. We subject student work to our personal, professionally trained tastes, but as mentioned earlier, that does not mean we judge arbitrarily or unfairly.

Again the Standards Movement shows what happens when we deceive ourselves on this point. NCTE and IRA's Standard 6 declares, "Students apply knowledge of language structure, language conventions . . . to create, critique, and discuss print and nonprint texts." But of course students have always made such applications, often *badly*; that is, they can meet such standards and still write failing papers. Reexamining our vocabularies should produce distinctions between features present in any writing and the qualities necessary for *good* writing. For example, "knowledge of *effective* language structures," and "*appropriate* language conventions" might lead to *high-quality* creations and critiques and *interesting* or *insightful* discussions.

Thus, whether or not we are conscious of it, grading standards (our tastes articulated) constitute the central curriculum of all writing courses. Writing teachers should have little difficulty accepting that assertion and the professional purpose stated earlier. Portfolio assessment, for example, embodies creating and judging "what's worth keeping." By implication, those central "tastes articulated" deserve constant scrutiny, and this is no less true for courses in fiction, poetry, and script writing than for courses in composition and nonfiction writing. The tendency to "loosen up" grading standards in poetry writing, for example, to allow or even praise most anything, contradicts offering a course in the first place. Students fearful of having their creativity stifled or their souls abused by judgments of their work ought not to sign up for such courses; they are perfectly free to keep their work to themselves or share it only with those they trust to praise it. Presumably, they take writing courses to improve their writing, and this means both they and their teachers must accept the hard work involved in navigating between conventionality (clichés, banalities, etc.) and originality (freshness, uniqueness), in discriminating between quality and crap. The aim of this hard work is to help students become better writers by becoming their own best critics. They cannot do that in either composition courses or poetry writing if "anything goes."

W. David LeNoir of Western Kentucky University elaborates the point in "Grading Student Poetry: A Few Words from the Devil's Advocate." LeNoir also suggests strategies for heightening students' consciousness of the choices they make in writing: for example, by writing explications of their poems and formal, self-evaluations of collections. I would add that if teachers of poetry, fiction, and script writing feel insecure about their own standards, they should turn to the criteria publishers use to decide what gets into print today—to primary sources or to books on "how to get published," such as Sol Stein's *Stein on Writing*.

Reexamining our critical language—our rubrics, standards, criteria for judgment—both with students and colleagues should keep us honest and remind us of our fallibility *and purpose* as writing teachers. We might also prompt our professional associations and conferences, such as CCCC, to support publications and sessions forthrightly aimed at issues of Taste.

For literature teachers, reexamining our critical language means at least two things. First, it means acknowledging the value judgments behind our syllabi and the aesthetic criteria with which we judge student writing. Why have we chosen the texts we teach? If they offer examples of cultural or political behavior and attitudes, so be it (although administrators might justify eliminating literature departments on the grounds that they duplicate the work of trained social scientists). But why the *particular* examples? Why Maxine Hong Kingston rather than Amy Tan? Why this poem by Wordsworth rather than that one? What criteria did we use in constructing the "canon" of our own syllabi? In regard to our grading standards: Are we willing to risk having them critiqued? What values do they reflect? Where do these values come from? What values do we promote in both our reading assignments and grading practices?

Second, it means focusing attention on the aesthetic values evident in the literature we teach. For example, we might ask: What values determined what was written and kept in earlier periods or other languages (if we choose to teach literature in translation)? How have these values changed (if at all) over time? How do we account for the *ambiguities* in "great" or "classic" works of any culture—that is, for the numerous interpretations spawned by them? Is a play containing conflicting meanings *good*? Or was the author simply confused? How did writers of various periods and societies navigate between "standard conventions" and "originality" or "uniqueness"? How are student and professional writers expected to do so today? What elements of Romantic or Victorian taste remain with us? How did "realism" become praiseworthy? Is a "realistic treatment" sufficient reason for publication or inclusion in a syllabus? What elements of literary taste do we share with other cultures?

Finally, reexamining our critical language means introducing students to wider, more inclusive aesthetic vocabularies, to words that cut across artistic disciplines: *harmony, balance, symmetry, moderation, proportion, unity*. It means considering the opposites of these words and the extent to which they carry moral and political overtones. And it means considering how these values appear in the literature and other arts of other cultures. Clearly, there's ample material for literary scholars and writing teachers in reexamining our critical vocabularies, and restoring Taste to the center of our professional attention would do much to cure our schizophrenia.

## *Re-uniting the Language Arts: Emotion and Intellect*

One problem in limiting literary study to scholarly and theoretical concerns is that the senses and emotions get left behind. Aristotle alerted us to the emotional contents of drama (e.g., fear, pity, catharsis), and introductory anthologies usually mention tone and mood, but by and large the senses and emotions receive scant attention in writing and literature classes. I suspect this neglect stems from excluding *oral* interpretation from literary study—another sign of our schizophrenia as speech, theater, and English departments went their separate ways years ago. Few English teachers at any level pursue speaking and listening skills, even though many must teach both in the public schools. (I also suspect this neglect explains the dreary, uninspired readings of some conference papers.)

*Voice* is the primary bridge to sensual and emotional literary experience. It is the bridge to seeing frosty moors, tasting cold, delicious plums, and feeling the "damp, drizzly November" in Ishmael's soul. Peter Elbow's comments on voice notwithstanding (*Everyone Can Write* 168-72, 184–221), students cannot produce distinctive voices in their writing if they haven't heard others' literary voices or listened to their own, and surely no interpretation of literature is fully valid until we *hear* how its language might be spoken. Inflections and vocal emphasis have as much to do with "meanings" in literature as do the interpretive perspectives readers impose.

Again, some writing teachers are ahead of the game in this regard, as they require students to read their essays aloud in groups or to full classes. In my own experience, the practice prompts writers to listen to themselves—to whether or not they have left words out of sentences, to whether or not they have made sense, and especially to whether or not they have achieved the intended emotional aims. Likewise, some literature teachers may require oral interpretations of poetry and drama in their classes—a readers theater approach to passages from plays, for example. Even without formal instruction, students inevitably become involved in the moods of scenes, the tones of characters and lines, and therefore eventually in the emotional content of—and their reactions to—what they're hearing. Just as inevitably, the process heightens their other senses; they "see" the clothing or costumes of Margaret Atwood's characters, for example, much more clearly. Approaches to literature that ignore its sounds and emotional dimensions are ill-conceived, cannot produce good writers or good critics, and certainly will never improve public taste.

Indeed, when we ignore the emotional content of what we write and save, audiences' ability to discriminate between legitimate and bogus emotional experience declines. The media deluge us with candy sex, ever-more dazzling special effects, increasingly brutal scenes of violence; with acting styles that limit expressions of anger to shouting; with laugh tracks; with trash-talking, with *attitude*. Sentimental soundtrack music rises with the melodrama, telling audiences that they should weep. And they do. The camera comes on for the interview with "ordinary people," cuing them to express "deep remorse" over the death of a celebrity they have never known (e.g., Princess Diana). And they do. Are these emotional outpourings genuine or false? All artists manipulate our feelings. Knowing the difference between legitimate and bogus sentiment is just as important as knowing the difference between valid and fallacious arguments.

It has become popular to characterize ours as a "visual" society and to imagine that visual media have replaced print. But, in fact, what we see on computers, on television, and in film has been scripted for reading or listening. All four language arts (reading, writing, speaking, and listening) are very much alive and well in our world, as is their emotional impact on audiences. The question is whether or not their producers and audiences know good work from bad.

## Re-uniting Descriptive and Normative Criticism

Whether our students are writing fiction, poetry, drama, or expository prose, they cannot judge the originality or other merits of their work without knowing what has been written before, so I certainly favor using the writing that societies have kept as critical touchstones for what students create. For example, in poetry writing classes, as exercises, students might try emulating the formal elements and stylistic conventions of previous periods. In script writing, they might try following Aristotle's unities. In fiction, they might try reproducing the styles of Hemingway or Joyce. While composition should expose them to the academic styles in different disciplines, it should also expose them to non-academic styles, such as those found in newspapers or *Sports Illustrated*. And while writing workshops typically involve reading and critiquing each other's work, students might also read and discuss the best and worst of published writers. My point is that broadening student writers' scholarly background through history and various theoretical perspectives enlarges the rhetorical choices available to them and heightens their awareness as critics of their own writing.

Descriptive and normative criticism can re-unite in literature classes by following Frank Norris's advice: "the best way to study literature is to try to produce literature" (qtd. in Graff 104). No, I do not mean to eliminate all exams or scholarly papers, but I do suggest that trying to write a Shakespearean sonnet will greatly enhance our appreciation of Shakespeare. Or imagine trying to write the scene of Arthur Dimmesdale's first meeting with Hester Prynne—and emulating Hawthorne's style. Or writing character analyses based on how students would perform a given part— how they would deliver certain lines, what "body language" they would use. One good "test" of how well students have read and understood a text would be their ability to parody it, and writing satire might well demonstrate their understanding of Swift. Or given solid exposure to the tastes of one body of literature, such as Romantic poetry, we might ask students to critique a current work. Certainly they might write critical reviews of whatever they read. Such exercises require close reading, analytical skill, and scholarship and lead students to a greater appreciation of the literature they study. At the same time, critical reviews extend students' performance repertoire. Norris was right: requiring students to read drama, poetry, and fiction, but limiting their responses to "papers," does little to develop students' literary instincts.

Again, my aim is not to abandon scholarship or our various theoretical schools, and it certainly is not to replace one set of "right ideas" with another—theoretical categories with rhetorical or aesthetic ones. Rather, it is to engage our students and ourselves in the process of making value judgments, and it is to reveal to students and to remind ourselves that what societies decide to keep—and cast out—depends on values they hold dear in particular historical circumstances. Some of those values are moral or religious; some are political or cultural; but from the beginning or in the end, they translate into Taste. My aim, in other words, is simply to align descriptive analysis with evaluative goals. In sum, we should ask ourselves how our teaching practices, presentations, or publications contribute to helping people create and judge language worth keeping. Doing so will do much to establish a coherent identity for our discipline.

## III. Conclusion

Admittedly, I am not optimistic about our prognosis, even though many writing teachers and literary scholars may have already adopted the perspective and some of the practices recommended here. X. J. Kennedy and Dana Gioia's introductory anthology, *Literature,* includes chapters on evaluating fiction, poetry, and drama and offers wonderful samples of bad poems, but theirs remains an exceptional anthology. Job assignments in the public schools tend to integrate writing, literature, and speech; and political pressures for accountability, with all their pernicious effects, nevertheless prompt reappraisals of quality, standards, and value, and provide an existential edge to questions of literary merit. Unfortunately, however, the gulf between K–12 English teachers and college professors remains wide, offering still more evidence of our professional splintering.

I also have increasing doubts over trends among professors of rhetoric and composition. Compositionists began establishing academic respectability for ourselves in the 1980s essentially by playing the same game our literary colleagues began decades earlier. It is the PhD game, the research game. It is H. C. G. Brandt's game, based on the notion that "a scientific basis dignifies our profession" (qtd. in Graff 66–67), and it produces similar results. Professional journals and newsletters proliferate. Subspecialties (e.g., WAC, assessment, basic writing, feminist perspectives, writing program administration) proliferate. Through the 1980s and 1990s, new PhDs in rhetoric and composition increasingly sought and increasingly found faculty positions that reduced their teaching loads, increased research, and privileged teaching graduate students over first-year undergraduates. Composition scholarship seems increasingly sociopolitical rather than aesthetic, and theory seems to overwhelm practice.

A century's worth of scientific bias has become so ingrained that many of us seem unconscious of it. Two incidents in my own experience encapsulate our history. Just before the beginning of a new semester, our creative writing (poetry) teacher went on sick leave. Someone suggested that one of the literature faculty members step in and teach the course. One colleague vehemently opposed this solution, declaring that it would set a bad professional precedent, because "none of us is trained to teach poetry or judge creative writing." He seemed proud of this confession and marched off to teach a graduate seminar in Romantic literature.

The second incident occurred in a survey of American literature. I had returned a batch of papers and was summarizing their strengths and weaknesses; most were badly written. I could see one fellow in the second row grow increasingly angry as he leafed through his D- paper. After reading my comments at the end of the paper, he blurted out his protest: "I thought this was a literature class, not a writing class!"

Thus, I cannot be optimistic about the future of our mental health, at least at the college level. I hope that younger faculty find ways to return us to aesthetics, to the troubling and marvelous ambiguities of fiction, poetry, and drama, and to the ways in which research papers can be written to read like good detective stories, but asking one generation to reverse the mind-set of many is probably unfair. Yet pessimism over the future is no excuse, so I'll close with the following argument.

A scientific basis does not "dignify our profession." On the contrary, it mocks it. It mocks the ambiguity of Art, the uncertainties of value judgments, the vagueries (and vagaries) of Taste. It leads to preposterous assertions such as, "There's no accounting for Taste." Nonsense. The uncertainty, the tentativeness of values, is what calls us to account for them and lends our choices, our preferences, an existential edge. That values are "relative" is an excuse and consolation only for those who would retreat from humanity. Philip Thody, writing about Albert Camus, made the point clearly: "Accepting the absurdity of everything around us is one step, a necessary experience: it should not become a dead end" (346). Pretending that literature is not writing, that the readings we require and grades we assign have nothing to do with Taste, or that the issues dividing us are signs of healthy vigor are crazy behaviors, not dignified ones. No one looks very dignified in a psycho ward.

## Note

1. Ed Kearns completed revisions to this manuscript about a month before he passed away from cancer in July 2004. As is evident from his tone, he was passionate about these issues.

## Works Cited

Elbow, Peter. *Everyone Can Write: Essays toward a Hopeful Theory of Writing and Teaching Writing.* New York: Oxford UP, 2000.

———. *What Is English?* New York: Modern Language Association, 1990.

Graff, Gerald. *Professing Literature: An Institutional History.* Chicago: U of Chicago P, 1987.

Kennedy, X. J., and Dana Gioia, eds. *Literature: An Introduction to Fiction, Poetry, and Drama.* 7th ed. New York: Longman, 1999.

LeNoir, W. David. "Grading Student Poetry: A Few Words from the Devil's Advocate." *English Journal* 91.3 (January 2002): 59–63.

Mannes, Marya. "How Do You Know It's Good?" *The Essay*. Ed. Michael F. Shugrue. New York: Macmillan, 1981.

National Council of Teachers of English and International Reading Association. *Standards for the English Language Arts*. Urbana, IL: National Council of Teachers of English; Newark, DE: International Reading Association, 1996.

Scholes, Robert. *The Rise and Fall of English: Reconstructing English as a Discipline*. New Haven, CT: Yale UP, 1998.

Sontag, Susan. *Against Interpretation, and Other Essays*. New York: Farrar, Straus & Giroux, 1966.

Stein, Sol. *Stein on Writing: A Master Editor of Some of the Most Successful Writers in Our Century Shares His Craft Techniques and Strategies*. New York: St. Martin's, 1995.

Thody, Philip. *Lyrical and Critical Essays by Albert Camus*. Trans. Ellen Conroy Kennedy. New York: Alfred A. Knopf, 1968.

CHAPTER FIVE

# *Rhetoric, Literature, and the Ruined University*

EVE WIEDERHOLD
*University of North Carolina at Greensboro*

When contemplating the institutional and theoretical relations between composition and literary studies, perhaps the question should be this: Why should professors who teach literature care about the institutional subordination of composition programs?

Compositionists have told and retold the sad story about composition's institutional history with varying degrees of nuance. Accordingly, the theoretical differences that privilege the teaching of literature over composition emerged in the late nineteenth century after the German model of education and its focus on disciplinarity was imported to the United States and took shape as the research university. Programs in the general study of liberal arts, which heretofore had included four years of study in rhetoric, no longer fit the dominant epistemological paradigm. They were replaced with studies in literature, configured as the accumulation of a specialized knowledge about authors, historical periods, and literary genres. As literature programs expanded in the early twentieth century, the scope of rhetorical study diminished, and thorough attention to the acquisition of communal ways of knowing gave way to the one-year, functionary composition course. Since the early 1970s, compositionists have challenged restricted representations of work in the field, a project that continues to the present day.[1]

There are, of course, other versions of this history, but the Ur-tale of the ascendancy of poetics at the expense of rhetoric has inspired many compositionists to restore rhetoric's centrality to the field in order to eliminate, once and for all, that damning reduction of composition to grammar, to spell out in amazingly innovative ways the cultural significance of writing programs and their relevance to democratic inquiry, and to demonstrate that composition study is an intellectual endeavor that qualifies as a research discipline. In addition to critiquing the logic that situates poetics as a domain of study that surpasses work conducted on behalf of rhetoric and composition, countless analyses have articulated the material consequences of that logic for those who teach first-year writing courses and receive inadequate pay, benefits, and job security.

Given how structural inequities within the academy have motivated so much of the work in the field of rhetoric-composition, one might expect our departmental colleagues to be galvanized as well, especially those who are interested in redefining disciplinary domains that, in today's contexts, seem "insular, elitist, exclusionary, reactionary" (Ian 279). Indeed, congruence can be found among scholars in rhetoric-composition and in literary-cultural studies in their respective critiques of the epistemological frameworks that have objectified knowledge and created the conditions for producing competition over whose knowledge base has more value. Scholars in both disciplines have explored how framing the study of English in terms of an acquisition of knowledge has validated the hierarchies embedded within modernist conceptions of rationality, citizenship, and what it means to be educated. Literary theorists have questioned whether to organize studies in English in terms of historical categories that reinforce entrenched Eurocentric norms when naming which authors deserve study; compositionists have challenged culturally biased conceptions of literacy by pointing out that language use arises within competing intellectual and social environments. Indeed, scholars in both fields have examined how the dominant cultural machinery is sustained when interpretive practices claim to be disinterested and apolitical.

But in spite of curricular and theoretical overlap, a disconnect remains, evidenced in the continued lack of attention by literary-cultural studies theorists to the scholarship offered by their associates in rhetoric-composition, whose work often gets regarded as less theoretically sophisticated, and by the kind of instruction that takes place in writing classrooms taught by those trained in literary studies, where, if Sharon Crowley is to be believed, no matter what the innovations from compositionists, current-traditional models prevail.[2]

In other words, reasonable argument made to institute equity is not working. The commonplace, which suggests that to garner institutional recognition, compositionists should make a reasonable case by providing evidence of the field's intellectual content, tracing its history, and articulating its core curriculum, is produced by the very logic that has subordinated rhetoric to poetics in the first place. It incorporates a principle of positivity that has organized Western thought around the idea that the facts make the case—or the academic discipline. As such, reason seems to contain its own persuasive power, a premise suggesting that if, after all the demonstrations, composition programs fail to be held in high esteem, then the problem lies with the proof offered, not with the expectation that their value be described in a reasonable way. Indeed, in spite of all the analyses over the past three decades that underscore how the language of reason is a social construct and not a neutral conduit of truth, members of the academy are expected to remain entranced with the type of knowledge and speech formation that is culturally identified as intellectual and rational. Presumably, we all recognize reason when we see it.

Such a presumption will be unacceptable to those who have contemplated how our experiences are always mediated by the signifiers made available in culture to name those experiences. That languages influence our attitudes and perceptions is applicable to the ways that scholars react to, judge, attend to, and ignore each other's work. Given Foucault's analysis of how the terms that precede us structure our interests by creating the conditions by which we come to knowledge, how has prioritizing the language of reason affected what grabs the attention and compels the interests of colleagues within English programs?

These observations are pertinent to the prospect of fostering collaboration between faculty in literature and composition because they ask that any discussion aim to do more to promote change than identify new program goals, departmental policies, and classroom practices. The parameters of discussion should be revised to also address why some proposals galvanize while others fail, and how dominant ideologies affect what gets recognized as a collective issue. Such a revision would expand the domain of reform to examine how the historically constructed oppositional relationship between poetic and rhetoric has influenced our interpretive habits—how it has made given concepts (or identities and histories) recognizable, meaningful, and significant (or not) to those of us who perform different kinds of work within the academy. I believe that a lack of attention to the ways in which we have been conditioned by academic discourse to adopt respective attitudes about the variety of work in the field constitutes a major barrier to the impetus for change. Until scholars think more carefully about how modernity's unquestioned powers linger in the ways that we talk to each other and reference that talk when evaluating whose work has merit, the speech acts of the marginalized (including those offered by workers in rhetoric-composition) will remain virtually invisible to those who hold disciplinary authority. And the exclusionary practices that have characterized past study within English departments will be reproduced.

## Acknowledging Rhetors

One argument about the historical formation of English studies that did garner cross-disciplinary attention was made in Bill Readings's posthumously published *The University in Ruins*, which analyzed how study in literature programs can no longer be legitimated by humanist narratives that speak of literature's ability to transmit culture and civilize readers. Rather, contemporary humanistic study is being shaped by the needs of corporate culture, an influence that is most noticeable in programs that promote the pursuit of excellence, an empty signifier that can be invoked to justify any number of administrative goals and pedagogical practices.

Readings's indictment of the corporate academy issued a rallying call to those academics who have promoted cultural studies and critical literacy in scholarship and teaching and, in the process, have envisioned their work as intervening in dominant culture's bland ability to reproduce itself. But rather than affirm the cultural studies approach as a valid alternative to the regularizing pull of capitalism, Readings offers a bleak assessment of the kind of instruction that it has made possible. Ostensibly, the turn to cultural studies seems to provide an antidote to both the pursuit of excellence and modernist orthodoxies that conferred cultural prestige on "high art." But in Readings's estimation, the cumulative effect of recent explorations into the connections between social constructs and our worldly perceptions has been depressing: cultural studies offers a limited goal of critiquing signifying practices in dominant cultures and does not intervene to change the power dynamics embedded in the status quo. While the study of something as broad as *culture* promises a dispersion of topic and methodology, a focus on critique does not necessarily counteract (and indeed can perpetuate) the logic of those modernist narratives that have depicted knowledge as an object to be collected and transmitted in environments set aside for "learning." Critique seems to throw a wrench in the bureaucratic machinery that aims to increase knowledge production, but according to Readings, the potential dispersion of interest and practice continues to be recuperated into a system that values the accumulation of disciplinary knowledge as a way of assigning the comparable worth of people, departments, and institutions.

To dispel the culture of critique, Readings advocates a return to rhetoric, arguing that the teacher be envisioned "as *rhetor* rather than *magister*, one who speaks in a rhetorical context rather than one whose discourse is self-authorizing" (158; original emphasis). Readings hopes to shift expectations about how teachers and students communicate by reformulating the conventional construction of knowledge as an object to be exchanged between experts and novices, emphasizing instead the sociopolitical purposes and contexts that circulate and disrupt coherent paradigms that would explain how instruction takes place. His Lyotardian-inspired framework is at odds with modernist epistemologies that value knowledge production over a respect for the contingencies and situatedness of heterogeneous discourses expressed in local areas like the classroom. Pedagogy, he writes, "is a relation, a network of obligation" that must be disassociated from the "lure of autonomy, of independence from all obligation" (158). Readings's interest in rhetoric is less concerned with examining how rhetoric lost its central position in academic study, and more concerned with identifying a theoretical framework that might alter how scholars envision their professional identities. The "advantage" of a rhetorical approach, he explains, "would be to recognize that the legitimation of the teacher's discourse is not immanent to that discourse but is always dependent, at least in part, on the rhetorical context of its reception. The *rhetor* is a speaker who takes account of the audience, while the *magister* is indifferent to the specificity of his or her addressees" (158; original emphasis). A rhetorical approach, he argues, does not attempt to deliver "the true, real meaning" of interpretive practices but instead provides a forum in which to think through how to participate in culture (103).

At this point, the compositionist who has been nodding in agreement might be tempted to slap her forehead and utter two words: James Berlin. Berlin's work in the 1980s and 1990s helped shape an entire branch of study that connected rhetoric-composition programs to cultural studies by integrating poststructuralist theory with rhetoric's concern with audience responses and historically contingent methods of inquiry. Long before *The University in Ruins* was published, Berlin analyzed how the material conditions that led to the formation of English departments were designed to serve the economic and social needs of those in power, and his work explored how power is reproduced through institutional policies that, for example, place more value on the "consumption" of texts written by literary authorities than on students' own productions (185). Much of Berlin's work expanded on Foucault's to consider how discursive practices create conditions for knowing that can conceal a will toward dominance. He explored how dominant discourses interpellate us in ways that shape conceptions of not only what exists, but also what is possible (78), arguing that when we deploy discursive conventions without question, we effectively do not think about how our perceptions are influenced by culturally encoded signs (57–58). After interrogating the political and intellectual concerns central to the poetics/rhetoric opposition, Berlin advocated a rhetorical pedagogy that envisioned change engendered by redefining literacy as social action; he believed that students need to be equipped with rhetorical strategies that will allow them to critically reflect upon and participate in public discourse arenas.

That Berlin's corpus was not mentioned by Readings affirms an argument Readings makes himself: that entrenched conceptual schemes precede and influence how we read subsequent expressions in ways that can prevent us from understanding what another is saying, especially if they use terms we do not recognize. Power relations determine who is obligated to undertake the work of translation when language is not shared, and the onus to find a way to "make sense" typically falls upon the group that has less cultural authority. In this case, one might wonder if the legacy of the poetics/rhetoric opposition contributed to rendering composition theory irrelevant (or perhaps not known) to Readings.[3] The trajectory of Readings's argument led him to offer an extended analysis of how the professorate's investment in cultural power intersects with the historical formation of English departments. Berlin, instead, directed his scrutiny of this same history toward an examination of how it has affected the teaching of student writing. Their different emphases bear traces of the interests of their respective disciplinarity identities, but this marking is not itself neutral. Dana Harrington has examined how the literary scholar who emerged in the nineteenth-century academy came to his identity *by* differentiating his field from rhetoric, which meant rejecting an interest in student prose and devoting attention instead to the disinterested study of aesthetic texts believed to be produced by mysterious mental processes of poetic genius (255). The attention given to student writing was regarded as pragmatic rather than intellectual and eventually "relegated" to composition, a strategy of exclusion that enabled literary scholarship to claim membership in the university devoted to research. It is interesting to note that not only did Readings not consult the work of Berlin (or others in the composition field); instead, he summoned the specter of celebrated Miltonist Stanley Fish as rhetoric's representative (159).

An investment in the historical privileging of the literary is also evident in the way Readings frames his argument. Even though he does not seek a return to an era in which English professors imagined themselves as noble crusaders for the hearts and minds of students, his text conveys a nostalgia for the clarity of authority and control embedded within those narratives lost to time. Consequently, his pejorative assessment of the university reads like an admonition to those who might still be seduced by the story of the "heroic journey" one undertakes when studying literature. Perhaps, as Readings suggests, humanities professors are in a state of mourning about the disappearance of the "professor-as-hero" narrative that seemed to provide both a personal identity and a professional rubric for organizing attitudes about the value of our labor. But if one never took that narrative seriously and never desired such control, then it is possible that the current state of affairs need not be read as one involving "ruin." Indeed, the idea of "ruin" may seem untranslatable to those of us who would never have credibly embodied the image of the cultivated professor in that long ago era, and who instead have worked to devise ways of pushing past such categories by, for example, contemplating how disruptions to representational traditions might affect how teachers respond to students' texts.

If the goal of critique is to disrupt dominant conceptual schemes that name and order interpretive acts performed in the university, scholars and teachers might explore the cultural assumptions perpetuated by the various narratives that categorize work within English studies. Theorists in literary-cultural studies and rhetoric-composition seem to be speaking different languages and, as a result, performing different acts within the university—the former occupied with "high theory," the latter with "everyday practice," especially pedagogy. From these perceived categorical differences, the normative conceptual hierarchies emerge: rhetoric-composition continues to be identified as a utilitarian, service-oriented discipline that promotes a "purely functional literacy" (Bartholomae 19) that serves the interests of the state. This reputation precedes the work produced by compositionists and contributes to marginalizing that work (especially at culturally esteemed "research" institutions). Even more importantly, the disciplinary focus on the mundane and "everyday" seems by definition irrelevant to metadiscursive critique. Composition scholars interested in critiquing university practices must respond to this prior context, so that every attempt to voice their concerns must also work to prove the intellectual legitimacy of their arguments. The inverse—that "high theory" practitioners be required to work to understand what compositionists are saying—is not a cultural requirement, as Readings's silence indicates.

Consequently, the *fact* of dialogue will not necessarily displace the structure of values so deeply embedded in the ways we evaluate who is credible, pertinent, and worth our time. But focusing on why some issues appear to be irrelevant can serve as a way to read power, that is, as a way to read how categories are placed within overarching interpretive grids to conserve old methods for determining who is worth listening to. As we engage in dialogues, we might also question the legitimacy of the identity categories that are most familiar to us as a way of noticing how ideologies are inscribed within departmental institutions and practices. Indeed, the immediate recognition of a given categorical marker should give us pause since it will mark not only understanding but also the very act of interpellation itself.

## Adjusting Attitudes

But in our attempts to revise tradition, we need not limit ourselves to adding to the pool of analyses that rationally explain how cultural terms structure our experiences. Lynn Worsham argues that we can modify our tendency to rely upon entrenched interpretive frameworks by examining our emotional commitments to particular ways of life, many of which "support the legitimacy of dominant interests" ("Coming" 106). She explains that "the primary work of ideology is more fundamental than the imposition of a dominant framework on meanings" (106). Ideology exerts an influence by training us not only to acknowledge and understand the cultural terminology circulating in dominant culture, but also to acquire an emotional-physical sense of the appropriateness of a given logic or disciplinary regime. Worsham analyses how our emotions are "schooled" through a kind of pedagogic violence that inculcates individuals to adopt seemingly nameable—and therefore predictable—affective relations to the world, habituating us not only to experience categories of emotion already identified but also to naturalize those experiences.[4] One lesson we learn is to find satisfaction in the status quo. "[I]deology works most effectively through emotion to interpellate us as particular kinds of subjects who are not ideally disposed—that is to say who ideally do not have the affective disposition—to question or to sustain resistance to the structures of subordination through which we are constituted as subjects" (106).

Resistance is further discouraged because we do not have languages available to talk about how affective ideological binds between individuals and social milieus are "complex and often contradictory," at times unarticulable, remaining "just beyond the horizon of semantic availability" (106). Consequently, even if individually professors are willing to question how their professional identities are emotionally constituted, academic culture does not provide languages to sponsor such scrutiny. Indeed, as Suzanne Clark has observed, language practices within the academy are organized to effect the exclusion of speech formations identified as emotional and to obscure how the performance of this specific exclusion defines and reproduces the intellectual class (97).

A focus on the "pedagogy of emotion" can challenge the binary oppositions that sustain hierarchies between terms such as reason/emotion and poetics/rhetoric, and it can contest the represented history of disciplinarity as a rational structure that materialized after objective judgments were made about the intrinsic value of program policies. Were we to acknowledge the extent to which our judgments about the legitimacy of academic practices and policies are emotionally charged and ideologically produced, we might alter the frameworks that govern what becomes sayable in departmental dialogues and, in the process, alter perceptions and emotional experiences of our individual and collaborative work. How, for example, might a discussion about changing the department's curriculum proceed if participants disclosed which narratives about the purposes of learning secured their faith, which disappointed, and which they want to continue to believe in as they consider program revision? Typically, we do not talk about how our emotional attachments to various cultural narratives inform our perspectives about departmental goals and policies.[5] And, in departmental contexts, we rarely think about how difficult it is to find a language to communicate those complicated emotional investments, described by Worsham as "the tight braid of affect and judgment that is socially and historically constructed and bodily lived" (105). That fostering such public discussion seems unlikely—even sentimental—only demonstrates how tightly the ideology that subordinates emotion to reason has gripped our enculturated perspectives. These observations are significant not only because they point to the imposition of dominant frameworks but also because they bear upon the question of how to initiate reform. Given that academic arguments continue to be conducted as if we're most persuaded by logic, rhetoric's subordination is perpetuated in practice, and the demand that everyone speak the dominant language is reaffirmed.

Worsham's analysis is applicable to theorists contemplating the legacy of the poetics/rhetoric opposition on attitudes about reforming disciplinary structures within departments. The structure of disciplinarity is so entrenched within the academy, it seems to have intrinsic value, but the rubric poses problems for those of us working under the banner of rhetoric-composition. Scholars in the field have neither staked out a static object of study nor developed a "unified set of commitments" (R. Miller 175), evident from the variety of issues compositionists address that range from critical analyses of culture inspired by Berlin to concerns with pedagogies and classroom interactions to quasi-scientific examinations of students's composing processes. Even if everyone did agree that composition's primary concern involves student writing, whether this focus should name a disciplinary specialty or be positioned as point of intersection between rhetoric-composition and literary-cultural studies is itself a topic of debate.

Susan Miller, for example, has offered some of the most trenchant analyses of how composition studies has been discursively positioned to serve the needs of other more "important" fields of inquiry in the university. The cultural categories that construct student writing as inherently problematic and in need of a "fix" simultaneously establish a seemingly logical purpose for composition programs: to provide a "rescue" (*Textual* 38). This logic perpetuates visions of the "dour" compositionist whose main objective is to deliver "praise or blame" ("Writing" 43) and affirms the view that a more complicated interest in aesthetics resides in the study of literature. Her proposed alternative, however, does not challenge the logic of disciplinarity that contributes to such categorizing, but suggests instead that composition be renamed "writing studies." Miller maintains that the new name will "place a nonevaluative spin on the more traditional label" (41) and signify that the intellectual interests of the compositionist are not limited to managing student writing; they encompass the study of textual communication as "an enduring socialized site" (43) with historical and contemporary relevance. This expansion of composition's domain can be referenced to identify a disciplinary specialty. "Our own archive readily shows how the twentieth-century formation of composition first depended on our knowing more about composing than others do. We find identity there, in taking up what, who, to what ends, and especially *how* people have written and do write" (52; original emphasis).

But other compositionists would not work toward equity by carving out a competitive identity for composition. Susan Brown Carlton, a student of Berlin's, has noted that she and Berlin initially disagreed about whether composition scholars should stake out an allegiance to rhetoric by continuing to configure it as poetics' opposite and thereby raise the stature of composition studies "to equal poetic-centered literature" (2). Carlton maintains that such an approach does not produce the requisite structural change to alter exclusionary power dynamics, arguing that "disciplinarity establishes limits on our capacity to transform educational practices" because it continues to ensure that only experts qualify as having knowledge and the ability to produce what is worth knowing (3). She instead proposes "self-reflexive analyses" that produce "a nonoppositional relation for poetic and rhetoric, one that is neither standard nor revisionary, but subversive," which she defines as "cross(ing) the divide" that has separated "reading and writing, scholarship and pedagogy, theory and practice" (6). Carlton adds that teachers and scholars cannot merely add to an arsenal of already established disciplinary practices. Instead, "categories must be reconstituted" (6).

The bind: if we don't name how our programs provide access to a specialized body of knowledge, our programs will probably not get recognition. But as Carlton and Readings each argue, the demand *to* identify and categorize interferes with reform because it resituates knowledge production within the existing organizational structures in ways that can obscure how and whether "knowledge" is produced. In any attempt at reform, we confront the familiar problem of having to use conventional terms to facilitate recognition of what we are proposing, even if we are attempting to describe practices and goals that do not fit recognizable rubrics.

The emotional impact of having to live with this bind does not get much public attention, but its force is inscribed in the discourses of our everyday practices. From proposing grants to composing year-end statements of our accomplishments, we are required to make claims about how our expertise contributes to a system that constructs knowledge as cultural capital. Besides quantifying the number of publications we've accumulated, many of us are required to provide concrete evidence of the "excellence" of our teaching by reporting on how students evaluate our work, as if the teacher-student relation can be summed up numerically or with signifiers such as "outstanding" and "average." And we must articulate our commitment to working within such a system when outlining plans for the future, making promises to continue to accomplish all that is expected of us (promising, by extension, not to fail or be subversive).

Once we do make such claims, they will be situated within competing narratives that already exist to describe the purposes of study in our respective fields, which for composition encompasses a variety of imagined activities that range from raising the consciousness of students to helping them acquire agency to encouraging them to participate in social inquiry to the most contentious, imparting skills that will get them a job. Our attitudes and emotional investments in the various narratives that identify the purposes of study in the humanities will shape our reactions to each other's justifications. And they will be further shaped by the legacy of the history that has situated literary study as superior because of disinterest in the pragmatic training intrinsic to rhetoric. I suspect that many difficulties in communication between literature and composition faculty erupt because of differing cognitive and emotional reactions to narratives of purpose. Although we can continue to try to reason with each other, and eloquently argue (as does Paul Kameen) that serving the needs of business and developing students' critical capacities to question discourses of authority are not mutually exclusive, those who retain a fondness for the image of the professor-as-hero and who see their work as offering an escape from corporate bureaucracy will not likely be persuaded. The history that has identified composition as utilitarian may prevent those enamored with "the tradition" from hearing that many of us who work on composition's behalf are equally concerned with the possibility that programs in English are "framed through the requirements of the corporate culture" (Kameen 37), even as we reject the dichotomy that would separate "the real world" from "the ivory tower."

In our attempts to reconstitute categories, those who seek change will encounter problems when trying to translate their work to those who have embraced conventional conceptions of what constitutes successful scholarship and pedagogy. As we chronicle these paradoxes, we can also attend to the languages we use to negotiate them to consider how terms that facilitate dialogue are anchored in part by the reproduction of linguistic practices that then reinforce expectations about whose language will function in what way in a given context. When expectations and interpretations of what language is supposed to *do* are uncritically reproduced, ideology has taken control and exerted its influence in invisible ways. To loosen the grip, educators need to break their routines and "interrupt" (as Readings suggests) everyday language practices that influence how we assign credibility to speakers. The question of the future of disciplinarity cannot be decided solely on objective analyses of the merits of maintaining or dismantling disciplinary structures. Our varying commitments to reform will be affected by our varying emotional investments in institutional norms.

# Conclusion

As we rethink work in the humanities, we (like any other collective) confront the possibility of experiencing a kind of terror induced by the breakdown of familiar organizational structures

(Carlton 2). That possibility tends to remain in the realm of the unsaid, part of the unacknowledged context surrounding any local discussion of reform that nonetheless affects what visions of the future people are willing to accept. Readings's call to rethink categories and acknowledge the politics of coercion embedded within Western epistemologies poses a huge challenge. It says to professors: Give up your position of power, your points of reference, your horizon of expectations, and that historical mission that has guided work within the classroom but is now being put in the service of a corporate machine. Give up the tiny bit of cultural capital and authority that you have and replace it with . . . an unknown. If the possibility of terror brought on by that challenge cannot be addressed directly, we can at least gesture at it by shifting questions about the relationship between perceived histories in English studies and imagined futures.

A rhetorical examination of why some proposals earn our commitments would recognize multiple claims, complex relations between them, and contradictory ways of testing claims. It would address what rhetoric has always addressed: What is effective, to whom, and under what circumstances? Rather than identify how collaborations between literature and composition faculty can "advance knowledge" and enable scholars to continue to compete for scarcer and scarcer resources, those of us practicing in different disciplines might initiate a different type of discussion by "going public" about how relationships between ideology and emotion affect perceptions and experiences of academic work. Although we must acknowledge the discursive contexts that precede our inquires, we need not simply acquiesce to them; we can counter the "curricular and theoretical drift" that functions to reproduce entrenched attitudes and practices by exploring our varying allegiances to competing narratives that describe the scope and purpose of study in English. The simultaneity of cognitive and emotional acts embedded within this approach can be both critical and generative, by offering other frameworks for imagining and telling stories about the kind of work we do. We also might think about renaming the domain in which we labor. Readings suggests using the term "post-historical university" to remind us that the academy is not a static object, but a changing idea. He invokes this label to "insist upon the sense that the institution has outlived itself" (6). I would suggest a revision and propose the noun "postuniversity" to signify not a sense of loss over an irretrievable past, but ambivalence about past and future categories that have been and will be used to name and justify what goes on in institutions that, for many, should be set aside for learning.

## Notes

1. For elaborations on this history, see T. P. Miller; Brereton; Crowley; Berlin.
2. For other statements about the exclusions of composition study from literary theory, see R. E. Miller; Jarratt.
3. The lack of dialogue between the two theorists speaks to a potential loss made more poignant by the tragic coincidence of their untimely deaths. At the least, the loss of the possibility of their exchange might provide an impetus for a renewed productive collaboration that would consider how dialogues in the past have been shaped by the perception that composition and literature scholars do not speak the same language.
4. See Worsham's "Going Postal" for a full discussion of this argument.
5. There is, however, a growing interest in the study of emotion and academic culture. See, for example, Laura Micciche's important discussion of the disappointment experienced by Writing Program Administrators.

## Works Cited

Bartholomae, David. "What Is Composition and (If You Know What That Is) Why Do We Teach It?" *Composition in the Twenty-first Century: Crisis and Change.* Ed. Lynn Z. Bloom, Donald A. Daiker, and Edward M. White. Carbondale: Southern Illinois UP, 1996. 11–28.

Berlin, James A. *Rhetorics, Poetics, and Cultures: Refiguring College English Studies.* Urbana, IL: National Council of Teachers of English, 1996.

Brereton, John. *The Origins of Composition Studies in the American College, 1875–1925: A Documentary History.* Pittsburgh: U of Pittsburgh P, 1995.

Carlton, Susan Brown. "Social Epistemic Rhetoric: Traditions, Revisions, Transformations." http://www.english.ilstu.edu/mediations/carlton.html (accessed 7 October 2005).

Clark, Suzanne. "Rhetoric, Social Construction, and Gender: Is It Bad to Be Sentimental?" *Writing Theory and Critical Theory*. Ed. John Clifford and John Schilb. New York: Modern Language Association, 1994. 96–108.

Crowley, Sharon. *Composition in the University: Historical and Polemical Essays*. Pittsburgh: U of Pittsburgh P, 1998.

Harrington, Dana. "Composition, Literature, and the Emergence of Modern Reading Practices." *Rhetoric Review* 15.2 (1997): 249–63.

Ian, Marcia. Letter to editor. *PMLA* 112 (1997): 279–80.

Jarratt, Susan. "Rhetoric in Crisis? The View from Here." *Enculturation* 5.1 (2003). http://enculturation.gmu.edu/5_1/jarratt.html (accessed 7 October 2005).

Kameen, Paul. "Service and Subversion: The Composition of Our Work." *Critical Quarterly* 39.1 (1997): 36–41.

Micciche, Laura R. "More Than a Feeling: Disappointment and WPA Work." *College English* 64.4 (2002): 432–58.

Miller, Richard E. "Composing English Studies: Towards a Social History of the Discipline." *College Composition and Communication* 45.2 (1994): 164–79.

Miller, Susan. *Textual Carnivals: The Politics of Composition*. Carbondale: Southern Illinois UP, 1991.

———. "Writing Studies as a Mode of Inquiry." Olson 41–54.

Miller, Thomas P. *The Formation of College English: Rhetoric and Belles Lettres in the British Cultural Provinces*. Pittsburgh: U of Pittsburgh P, 1997.

Olson, Gary, ed. *Rhetoric and Composition as Intellectual Work*. Carbondale: Southern Illinois UP, 2002.

Readings, Bill. *The University in Ruins*. Cambridge, MA: Harvard UP, 1996.

Worsham, Lynn. "Coming to Terms: Theory, Writing, Politics." Olson 101–13.

———. "Going Postal: Pedagogic Violence and the Schooling of Emotion." *JAC* 18.2 (1998): 213–45.

# II

# Departmental Cultures

CHAPTER SIX

# In This Corner . . .

BARRY M. MAID
*Arizona State University*

*Question:* Why are academic politics so vicious?
*Answer:* Because the stakes are so low.

There's a part of me that thinks we need to keep that old joke in mind anytime we start talking about the problems, the rift, the disagreement, the animosity, the class warfare, the bad marriage, or the whatever between literature and composition. Ordinarily I prefer to leave class and politics out of my arguments. Yet when looking at the relationship between composition and literature, I find this to be impossible. I suspect that the relationship between the two has nothing to do with "normal" ideas of academic disciplinarity and everything to do with issues of privilege, power, and economics.

I must admit that I look at the closing sentence in that last paragraph and am a little amazed that I wrote it in 2003. It's the kind of sentence I might have written as an undergraduate in the late 1960s, but now, more than thirty-five years later, I usually see the academic world in a more measured and, I hope, more reasonable way. Still, I stand by my sentence regarding the tension in college English departments. I do so based on my own experience of spending almost my entire adult life having some relationship to college English departments, either as a student, a faculty member, an administrator, or a member of a department or program in which I taught writing (something usually associated with English departments) but that was not housed in an English department. In addition, since I have been associated with writing programs or departments since the early 1990s, I have had countless conversations over the past decade with colleagues about the situation in their own unit, whether it be an English department or an independent writing department or program.

Having spent many years as an academic, I know that disciplinary differences and disagreements don't exist just in English studies. (Indeed, the mere fact we now feel we must address the field as *English studies* and not simply as *English* should be a clue that something is amiss. I have given my own opinion of the concept of *English studies* elsewhere [see Maid].) In many ways, the difficulties faced in English departments are mirrored most closely in foreign language departments where there are schisms between those who wish to teach and study the literature written in the language and those who wish to teach and study how to teach the language to American students. College mathematics departments often see a split between the theoretical mathematicians and the faculty who teach the variety of first-year math courses. Likewise, traditional disciplines such as political science that have spawned applied disciplines like public administration and criminal justice often see difficulties when everyone is together in one not-so-happy family.

So, what makes the strife within English departments so vitriolic, so petty, so much a study for scholarly discussion? (Remember the opening joke.) I would suggest that unlike so many differences to which academics like to point, this one really is about class differences and the privileges accorded to some and denied others determined solely on their teaching schedule. Like most situations of power and privilege, it is one where both sides accept the assumption that one side has a right to be superior to the other. In this case, everyone believes that literary studies, especially theory, is somehow more important than writing. The result is that, within English departments, those who teach literature have more status than those who teach writing. None of this is new. People have commented on this for decades. However, what is important to note is that those who teach writing, though perhaps feeling oppressed, in many instances accept the notion that what they do is of lesser import than their literary colleagues. In addition, we can see more class distinction when we look at how first-year composition (FYC) helps keep English faculty teaching literature. Since English departments need cheap labor such as TAs to staff many sections of FYC, they can justify otherwise unjustifiable graduate programs. The graduate students can teach FYC while filling the graduate classes of the tenure-line faculty.

I understand that many will respond that these are old arguments. They will counter that composition now has status within departments and the academy because it now has its own collection of stars. To those who might think the argument I am about to make, that literature faculty still view themselves in aristocratic terms, is dated, I cite just one example, though many exist, and it is from a book just published. Talking about a search for non-tenure-track lecturers, Margaret Marshall says:

> Because introductory literature courses are classified at the sophomore level, lecturers must have a doctorate in literature to qualify for this assignment; a master's degree in "English or a related field" is acceptable for teaching composition even though composition instructors are also responsible for advanced courses at the junior level and literature lecturers never teach outside the sophomore level. (102)

There is one interesting exception to this tension. No one within the academy has to make excuses for rhetoric (though once we leave the shelter of our academic walls, rhetoric is often viewed with suspicion). The history of rhetoric, its relationship to composition, the first-year writing course, and all of their relationships to college English departments have now been chronicled many times by much better historians than I (see Adams, Berlin, Brereton, Connors, Crowley, Faigley, Miller, North, Russell).

Although it is important to know our own history, the questions likely to be asked by those outside college English departments are "What's the big deal? Why has this academic battle continued for so long, in so many places?" I suggest the reason is money, specifically the money associated with the required FYC course. In fact, I would venture to suggest that if FYC were not the universally required course, English might well have kicked writing out much as it kicked speech out almost a century ago. Without providing the necessary base to maintain their position of privilege, English departments would have no reason to dirty their hands with it. I would even suggest if the abolitionists, those who would eliminate the first-year requirement, would have their way, writing courses would be so marginalized in English departments that those departments would likely find a way to jettison them. This is, however, extremely unlikely to happen. The history of the last century seems to indicate that pressures within the university and from the general public about issues of literacy, even if they are based on faulty assumptions, will continue to keep the required FYC in place.

The idea that there exists an aristocratic hierarchy in college English departments is not new. Looking at how writing instruction in American universities emerged in the early twentieth century, James Berlin, in *Rhetoric and Reality*, makes the following observation:

> Three major approaches to the teaching of writing appeared between 1900 and 1920. The oldest was what is now known as current-traditional rhetoric. It was most conspicuously in force at Harvard and Columbia, but it also found a home in a number of the state universities—Illinois, Wisconsin, and Texas, for example. This rhetoric, positivistic and practical in spirit, was designed to provide the new middle-class professionals with the tools to avoid embarrassing themselves in print. In short, this was the rhetoric of the meritocracy. Its principle rival in the East was the rhetoric of liberal culture, advanced at such schools as Yale, Princeton, and Williams. This rhetoric was elitist and aristocratic, contending that the aims of writing instruction in the English department ought to be encouraging those few students who possessed genius. For the rest, courses in literature should provide lessons in taste, emphasizing appreciation, contemplation, and self-expression. Proponents of this rhetoric denied that writing courses had an important place in the college, arguing that geniuses were few and that writing instruction for the rest ought to be handled in high school. The result was not, however, the abandonment of writing instruction, but the use of a belletristic approach—courses in writing about literature. Finally, the third major approach to writing instruction emphasized writing as training for participation in the democratic process—a rhetoric of public discourse. This view, a part of the progressive education movement, was uniquely American. (35)

What is, perhaps, the most fascinating observation to take away from Berlin's observations of the development of writing instruction is that the model that emerged as dominant in American English departments is the one model that he calls "elitist and aristocratic." By creating a course in writing about literature and taking a belletristic approach in teaching that course, the first-year required course becomes not a writing course but an excuse for English faculty to teach literature in disguise. I suspect there would be little to write about if the only constituencies that were concerned about the first-year course would be the faculty who taught it. However, the first-year writing course is not just of concern to the English department. Unlike other general education classes, what is taught in FYC is clearly a concern of the entire university faculty as well as many external constituencies such as business, industry, oversight boards, and legislatures.

While those of us in the field might be concerned that external constituencies look to FYC as being something essentially remedial or something that should be taught by drill and tested by multiple choice, the reality seems to me to be that although we may argue with some of the methodologies of those who practiced the rhetorics that Berlin identified as the current-traditional and the progressive, the goals of those rhetorics—to provide professionals with appropriate literacy skills or to provide citizens able to take part in the processes of a democratic society—are clearly in line with both external constituencies and most of those who now professionally identify themselves with writing instruction. Yet, English departments, and many who find themselves teaching writing by default—because there are no jobs to be had to teach literature—still maintain the belletristic approach. Even today, it's impossible to publish a rhetoric or handbook as a textbook for FYC without at least a section on writing about literature.

## The Isolation of English

There is much in the history of the university that encourages separation and isolation from the rest of the world. It is present in our medieval roots. Yet, we are no longer living in the fourteenth century. Still, the emphasis on belles lettres and the rejection and devaluation of anything that might connect to the outside world, and especially to sources of money, has caused English departments to become even more isolated from the outside world but also isolated within the university. In some ways, English departments may only be surviving as a result of their own size. Interestingly, this rejection of the value of writing, both composition and applied writing, has cost English departments opportunities for funding. As Steve North notes:

> One obvious irony, then, was that while in the academy—in the English departments that were to stand as primary authorities on what English was—literature, and not composition or language, was then and remains the central concern, it could not attract the sought-after Federal support. A sort of corollary irony, perhaps not so obvious but important here, was that composition, the "service" course, so long considered academic dirty work, *could* attract such money. Here were circumstances that stood to make composition teaching respectable and fundable—make it, almost by proclamation, Composition with the capital C. (13)

I would suggest that the ironies that North notices are a function of aristocratic privilege. Aristocratic literature faculty are more than willing to have composition programs bring money into the department through the traditional funding method of student credit hour production. However, if compositionists were to bring money into the department through sponsored research, the money would go to the compositionists and not the literary faculty. In addition, bringing in sponsored funding automatically brings prestige in the university—a prestige that the literary faculty would not be able to match. Doing so would naturally undercut the hierarchies that exist in English departments because the underclass would be funded directly and not have to beg for the fruits of their labor from the literary lords of the manor.

## The Curse of Humanism

The tradition is for people who study English to consider themselves as part of the humanities. Perhaps this makes sense for literary scholars. I often wonder if part of the problem writing faculty face comes from when they consider themselves to be humanists. There seems to be an attraction to the humanities, and what I would suggest is the confusion on the part of many faculty between the humanities and having what I might term *humanistic values*. Several years ago at the special interest group for Independent Writing Units at the Conference on College Composition and Communication annual convention, I suggested that writing is not one of the humanities but rather an applied discipline. Even I was amazed at how vehemently my comments were attacked. Although it may be a function of my own stubbornness, I don't feel anyone really countered my statement with a reasonable counter-argument but rather argued with emotion driven by personal values. It is quite difficult for me to see that a discipline that teaches students to engage in academic writing and workplace writing should be considered part of the humanities. To my thinking, this is clearly the definition of an applied discipline. I can see an argument that creative writing would be considered part of humanistic study. I could also entertain that the belletristic essay would be classified under a humanities rubric. Still, I doubt that FYC is a universal part of general education so that the faculty can teach belletristic essays.

Though the opposition to my observation was passionate, I am not alone in connecting humanist perspectives and problems in FYC. In her *Composition in the University*, Sharon Crowley notes:

> The humanist claim upon composition is typically enacted through the practice of requiring students to read literary texts in the first-year composition course. Literally hundreds of English teachers have asserted that reading literature improves students' writing ability. A few have tried to articulate precisely how the connection between reading and improvement in writing works; generally they argue that students' grasp of style is improved by their unconscious absorption of its finer points as these are demonstrated in the work of great authors. (13)

After questioning the lack of writing pedagogy by English teachers, Crowley continues:

> Now even if one grants the point that writers can learn something about the way language works through reading, by a sort of osmosis, one need not accept the further claim that literary texts are the best readings to use for this purpose. Historically, though, English teachers have resisted suggestions that nonliterary texts be read in the first-year course. Generally, they justify the necessity of literary reading with humanistic arguments; students need to learn values, they need to be acquainted with the best that has been thought and said, and so on. (13)

I suggest that Crowley is too kind to English teachers. At best, I suspect that English teachers are driven to teach values. But whose values? The values of the cultural left or the cultural right? At the other end, I suspect English teachers simply want to teach what they like instead of what everyone, except their English department colleagues, expects them to teach. On one hand, they perceive that their values are the ones that all students must learn and appreciate. On the other, they assume that their personal tastes must be imposed on a general studies curriculum.

## My Own Personal Take

So, since the dominant mode of response in arguing for the English curriculum appears to be driven by personal needs, I, too, will give in to what appears to be the disciplinary norm and give my perspective from my own history. Like many of my contemporaries, I now discover that the history of the teaching of writing in the late twentieth century is my history. Unlike the current class of graduate students who study for a PhD in rhetoric-composition or technical communication or computer-mediated communication, I pursued a PhD in English to study literature. I saw no option, and no one really told me there was one. Although I believe it was possible to prepare a PhD area in composition at the University of Massachusetts in the 1970s, I don't seem to recall anyone actually doing so—though many of us have ended up in composition or technical communication, and many have administered and still do administer writing programs.

In the fall of 1973, I walked into a classroom for the first time as a teacher. I was a teaching assistant in the Rhetoric Program at UMass. I still have vivid memories of that day more than thirty years ago. It's one of the only memories I have where I can actually remember what I wore. (It was something that could have been worn only in the early 1970s.) I remember the books I was using, and, in fact, one of them is still on my office shelf. The course was "themed." It was called something like Writing for the Natural and Physical Sciences. As a PhD student in English, I was a little concerned about teaching a course for science students. However, it didn't take many classes for me to realize I knew much more science than any of my students.

What I didn't know was how to teach writing. I wasn't even sure I knew what rhetoric was even though I was teaching in something called the Rhetoric Program. My situation was typical of most of the new TAs at UMass. Knowing this, the Rhetoric Program had several forms of training for us. First of all, the new TAs were required to take a class in teaching writing. It was taught by Charles Kay Smith. I will admit that I learned a lot in that class. I also learned much from some other TAs who had been teaching in the program for some time. Patti Cowell, now of Colorado State, was a tremendous help.

Much of the reason I was both innocent and ignorant about rhetoric and writing is that I saw myself as an English student. To my mind, then, and to most students of English, what mattered was literary studies. I already had two degrees in English. Yet, the only writing courses I had taken were the required two semesters of what was called Freshman English at the University of Wisconsin. I had been forced to take the second semester only because my TA felt that everyone needed two semesters. As a result, he gave no A's. Getting an A in the first semester would have meant I would have not taken the second semester of the course. In retrospect, I suspect he was right. I did need at least two semesters of college writing. Unfortunately, the courses I took at Wisconsin in 1966–1967 did me little good at all.

Part of the reason I tell my own story is because it's so typical of faculty of my generation. We ended up teaching writing because we discovered we liked it after we started doing it, or because we saw it as an opportunity to have a pathway into an academic career that literary studies could not offer us, or a combination of the two. In my own case, though I began teaching in the UMass Rhetoric Program with absolutely no real idea of what I was doing, I quickly discovered that teaching writing was not only challenging but also intellectually interesting work. Thanks to the leadership in the Rhetoric Program of Jane Blankenship, Sara Stelzner, and Annette Rottenberg, interestingly out of the Speech Communication Department, not English, and the support I had from those English faculty who worked most closely with the Rhetoric Program, most notably Kay Smith, John Nelson, and Charlie Moran, I was able to develop some degree of expertise in teaching writing.

The result of my experience in the Rhetoric Program was that though I finished my PhD with a literary dissertation, I still ended up with a fulltime job. Even though it was a non-tenure-track job with the Special Services Project at the State University of New York–Plattsburgh, it was still a job. It also helped to give me new insights into college English departments and writing programs. Since I was not in the English Department but in a unit that reported to Student Affairs, I began to gain a perspective from the outside. Sometimes having an outside perspective can be a most educational thing. I came away from that experience convinced of two things: all academic programs need to be housed in Academic Affairs—not Student Affairs, and all basic writing instruction, including tutorial services, needs to be completely integrated with the rest of the writing program. I've often commented, most often about writing centers, that they be located in Academic Affairs (Simpson and Maid). The issue that I haven't addressed often is my contention that writing programs should be whole and not fragmented. Though the seeds of that idea were planted in Plattsburgh, I had my opinion confirmed in the early 1990s when I was sitting in a meeting with a panel of external reviewers who were charged by the Arkansas Department of Higher Education with looking at developmental education. Our basic writing course was one of the programs they were reviewing. At that meeting, one of the reviewers said they were pleased with our program and expected that it worked so well because our entire writing curriculum—from basic writing to our MA program—flowed together and had a coherence that other programs seemed to lack. In retrospect, the observation of programmatic coherence is an important one. I suspect that part of the reason for the lack of disciplinary respect that writing programs commonly feel is because they are often and easily fragmented.

## An Aside from the Personal

Think for a moment if the American university had developed along lines not quite like the present disciplinary structure. What if, for example, in the early part of the twentieth century there had been an emphasis on what might be called the "studies approach"? What if all literary specialists were not housed in English departments but in departments of American studies or medieval studies or similarly organized units? Clearly the long battle between composition and literature would have never existed. For decades, composition would have been housed in something like rhetorical studies departments. There would be no huge English departments. The discussion among literary scholars might even be wondering whether a discipline of literary studies existed. We might even carry this fantasy scenario a bit further by imagining if literary specialists were trying to find some commonality in what they do, in order to attain disciplinary status, they might focus on the fact that they teach students how to read texts.

As implausible as this may now seem, it's really similar to what has happened to writing studies over the past century. Divorced from its roots in rhetoric, alienated (partly because of the humanities bias against utility) in many places from its applied side in technical and professional writing, and focused only on delivering a first-year service course, is it no wonder that composition has struggled to proclaim itself first of all a discipline worthy of being taken seriously in the academy?

## The Personal Again

As I reflect back on my experience at SUNY–Plattsburgh, one more significant factor contributed to my development in thinking about writing studies during that time. I became part of the original group that formed the SUNY Council on Writing. As program chair for the first conference that was held in Albany in May 1980, I invited Lee Odell to give the keynote address. His title was "Composition: A Discipline." Back in 1980 Odell presented a convincing argument that composition was, indeed, a viable academic discipline. However, more than two decades later things haven't changed that much. We still operate under the assumption that only a trained specialist can teach literature, but anyone with a short training workshop can teach composition. Academic disciplines don't send new teachers into classrooms without even one course in disciplinary training.

I'll suffer you with just one more reference to my personal history. The very first CCCC convention that I attended was the 1985 conference in Minneapolis. There I heard Maxine Hairston give her "Chair's Address," later published in *CCC* as "Breaking Our Bonds and Reaffirming Our Connections." There's a part of me that wishes that Hairston had so inspired me that I actively changed the course of my career as a result. The reality is that I was troubled by what I heard. Having been trained in English departments, having been estranged from an English department while working in Special Services in Plattsburgh, I was, at that point, too thrilled being an assistant professor of English to want to rock the boat. I was too young, too naive in my own profession, and too profoundly untenured to understand the accuracy of her perceptions and the depth of her wisdom. My own personal reality, and this remains so for many writing faculty today, was that my tenure was to be determined by the literary aristocrats.

## Is There a Solution?

The easy answer is "absolutely not." First of all, most writing faculty believe they belong in English departments. Until this changes, and there is nothing happening to make it change, I expect we'll be seeing the same arguments and histories fifty years from now. Since most PhDs in writing areas are offered through English departments, most faculty will continue to see their roots as being in English. In fact, many still, at some level, accept the old argument of literary privilege. In addition, though the relationship between literature and writing faculty in many departments is tenuous at best, many writing faculty, caught up in the culture of English departments that is "they against the world and the rest of the university," support the notion of The Department. Finally, there are several English departments, and I can easily point to two, where it appears to an outsider that the structure really works well. I would also suggest that the reason those units work well is more a function of personality and intelligent hiring—not any notion of disciplinary integrity. Indeed, if there were a real cohesive thing such as English studies, I would suggest that agreeable, not acrimonious, departments would be the norm.

Although I suspect writing programs to continue to be housed in English departments, what are the other options? The obvious answer, and one that I have commented on regularly, is for independent departments of writing. We saw what appeared to be a movement in that direction from the early to the late 1990s. In 1993 we saw separate units emerge at the University of Texas at Austin, San Diego State University, and the University of Arkansas at Little Rock. Those units were formed with different levels of planning. By the end of the 1990s, units, such as the one at Grand Valley State University, were formed with significantly more planning. While it appeared that a real trend was beginning, we seem to see no new units being formed. I would suggest that the end to what seemed to be a trend corresponds to the current economic downturn. The reality is that new units cost money. Presidents and provosts are less likely to explore new units when they are looking at cutting costs. Frankly, I think it highly unlikely for us to see new units emerge unless the economy gets better. The only legitimate argument I expect for creating a new unit would be one that would bring money into the university instead of costing more.

Is there any hope for writing studies when they seem to be firmly entrenched within English departments? If there is, I would think the faculty of those departments need to focus on handling two crucial issues: curriculum, and promotion and tenure. If we look at the problems writing studies have endured within English departments, most of the issues revolve around literature faculty dictating writing curriculum and evaluating writing faculty based on literature faculty standards. The real issue, then, appears to be how do we give writing faculty autonomy over their own curriculum and their own professional lives?

Once, years ago, as chair of English, more just to see my provost's response than to be taken seriously, I suggested that English become a college, and I could be dean of English. I argued we had more faculty and produced more student credit hours than the College of Business. In retrospect, my teasing remarks may have had more credence than even I realized. Colleges are made up of units that are similar but different. The key is that the individual units, the departments, are the prime determiners of issues of curriculum and of promotion and tenure. While it is highly unlikely, especially under the current economic situation, to talk about creating a new college, it might be possible to create a new kind of sub-unit, perhaps a school, that would separate writing and literature faculty from having significant influence over their decisions in curriculum and in promotion and tenure. It would be exceptionally difficult for literature faculty to retain aristocratic notions of privilege when they have no control over any meaningful part of the lives of writing faculty. And if literature faculty chose to maintain those aristocratic values, it would have no impact on others.

If a large English department were to be reorganized, what would it look like? I expect there are multiple models. We might look at the new School of Life Sciences in the College of Liberal Arts and Sciences at Arizona State University. In that new unit, research affinities control organization. That's one possibility. Curriculum might be another. What is clear is that just having two sub-units, writing and literature, is not appropriate.

Creating new, multiple sub-units to address issues of curriculum and of promotion and tenure might not physically separate writing from literature, but it should do something even more important. To repeat what Hairston told us in 1985:

> I think the time has come to break those bonds—not necessarily physically, although in some case that may be a good idea—but emotionally and intellectually. I think that as rhetoricians and writing teachers we will come of age and become autonomous

professionals with a discipline of our own only if we can make a psychological break with the literary critics who today dominate the profession of English studies. (275)

We have still not come of age. And as Hairston suggests, the only way to do so is if we free ourselves from the psychological ties we have to literature and English as it has been defined for the past hundred years. Aristocrats may always view themselves as aristocrats who deserve privilege, but they only retain those privileges when others grant them. The ultimate irony is that writing faculty have no one to blame but themselves. They need to stop blaming their literary colleagues and simply take their discipline and their destiny into their own hands.

# Works Cited

Adams, Katherine H. *A History of Professional Writing Instruction in American Colleges: Years of Acceptance, Growth, and Doubt.* Dallas: Southern Methodist UP, 1993.

Berlin, James A. *Rhetoric and Reality: Writing Instruction in American Colleges, 1900–1985.* Carbondale: Southern Illinois UP, 1987.

Brereton, John C., ed. *The Origins of Composition Studies in the American College, 1875–1925: A Documentary History.* Pittsburgh: U of Pittsburgh P, 1995.

Connors, Robert J. *Composition-Rhetoric: Backgrounds, Theory, and Pedagogy.* Pittsburgh: U of Pittsburgh P, 1997.

Crowley, Sharon. *Composition in the University: Historical and Polemical Essays.* Pittsburgh: U of Pittsburgh P, 1998.

Faigley, Lester. *Fragments of Rationality: Postmodernity and the Subject of Composition.* Pittsburgh: U of Pittsburgh P, 1992.

Hairston, Maxine. "Breaking Our Bonds and Reaffirming Our Connections." *College Composition and Communication* 36 (1985): 272–82.

Maid, Barry M. "More Than a Room of Our Own: Building an Independent Department of Writing." *The Writing Program Administrator's Resource: A Guide to Reflective Institutional Practice.*

Ed. Stuart C. Brown, Theresa Enos, and Catherine Chaput. Mahwah, NJ: Erlbaum, 2002. 453–66.

Marshall, Margaret J. *Response to Reform: Composition and the Professionalization of Teaching.* Carbondale: Southern Illinois UP, 2004.

Miller, Thomas P. *The Formation of College English: Rhetoric and Belles Lettres in the British Cultural Provinces.* Pittsburgh: U of Pittsburgh P, 1997.

North, Stephen M. *The Making of Knowledge in Composition: Portrait of an Emerging Field.* Portsmouth, NH: Boynton/Cook Heinemann, 1987.

Russell, David R. *Writing in the Academic Disciplines, 1870–1990: A Curricular History.* Carbondale: Southern Illinois UP, 1991.

Simpson, Jeanne H., and Barry M. Maid. "Lining Up Ducks or Herding Cats? The Politics of Writing Center Accreditation." *The Politics of Writing Centers.* Ed. Jane Nelson and Kathy Evertz. Portsmouth, NH: Boynton/Cook Heinemann, 2001.

CHAPTER SEVEN

## *Along the DMZ between Composition and Literature*

JOHN HEYDA
*Miami University*

In her introduction to the mid 1990s, Modern Language Association–sponsored anthology *Into the Field: Sites of Composition Studies*, Anne Ruggles Gere proposes reading the collection for its attention to representations of composition's active relations with other disciplines, including literature. Impressed by the volume's treatment of both the limitations of such characterizations and the possibilities involved with emerging, alternative representations, Gere is concerned at the same time by how prominently bridge-building metaphors figure among these depictions, seeing them as much in need of critique. These gap-bridging metaphors envision relatively uncomplicated forays into interdisciplinarity, involving "simple appropriations," the "unproblematized adoption of methods and values," "useful alliances," "unidirectional borrowing" (1). These metaphors hold only so long, however, as composition's work remains tied to "applied and mission-oriented interdisciplinary projects" and to the strict separation of theory and application such efforts enforce. Once composition parts company with such practices and seeks, instead, a more interactional relation with other disciplines, bridge-building notions no longer suffice. In their place, Gere proposes another metaphor, that of restructuring. "In this fuller expression," as she puts it, "composition theory resists boundaries and blurs distinctions between disciplines. Instead of simply borrowing from a given field, it interacts, changing and being changed." In this way, "new perspectives on the field" are created as "they introduce new terms to the discussion of composition" (3).

In exploring alternatives to bridge building, the *Into the Field* anthology proposes composition's forging new relations with a number of philosophical disciplines, among them pragmatism, hermeneutics, and phenomenology, as well as such postmodern subjectivities as cultural studies, feminist theory, and ethnography. With the single exception of an essay on composition and poetics, *Into the Field* has little to say, however, with regard to any restructuring of composition and literature that might emerge in the kind of interdisciplinary work Gere advocates. The old bridge-building metaphors crop up, perhaps not so surprisingly, in her reference to the current state of relations between composition and literature: "The bridge between composition and literature has often spanned troubled waters as the two, like stepsiblings thrust together by a marriage over which they have no control, have warily coexisted in English departments" (2). About their sometimes stormy English department marriage, Gere notes that "composition scholars have, with some justification, felt alternatively exploited and scorned by their literary colleagues who, in turn, have resented composition's financial power and envied its intellectual liveliness" (2).

Given this state of affairs, can composition and literature move together to a new, more interactional space? Gere reports on the ongoing work of building bridges between composition and literary theory via recent borrowings from critical theory, reader response theory, and deconstruction. Still, it is hard not to see here the suggestion that although composition's interactions with other disciplines have helped make boundaries more permeable, inviting new and more complex ways of thinking about composition inside and outside the academy, collaborative work involving composition and literature has left the boundaries they share largely intact, with the old disciplinary ways of thinking untouched as well.

This is particularly true of the institutional space the "stepsiblings" occupy together in those first-year writing courses still taught under composition and literature's tattered banners. Here, Gere's envisioning of the term *field* as "a complex of forces," "a kind of charged space in which multiple 'sites' of interaction appear," contends with entrenched pedagogies that work to reassert the more traditional notions of *field* as "bounded territory" marked off against other such territories (4). Instead of a "charged space," a "zone of interaction," we find a kind of academic DMZ, a demilitarized zone wherein the aggrieved parties, having long since moved on to wage new disciplinary campaigns on more distant and presumably more promising fronts, content themselves with the maintenance of token "forces" in defense of a status quo in which neither side can claim much satisfaction. With both composition and literature far busier elsewhere, life along this disciplinary boundary line has settled into a largely uneventful routine, interrupted only occasionally by salvos fired back and forth over the no-man's-land between the two camps, as with, for instance, the Lindemann/Tate debates over literature's "place" in freshman composition. Composition studies may have emerged, as John Trimbur would have it, "in a postmodern free-for-all that has blurred the lines between fields of study, that has fragmented and undermined the disciplinary projects of normal academic work," but along the DMZ erected to keep separate the contributions of composition and literature in "lit-comp" courses, signs abound that academic business as usual remains the order of the day (118).

Having taught many versions of the composition and literature course as a first-year, second-semester required writing course, I know from long experience the difficulties involved with classroom work along this DMZ. I know, too, the complications involved with trying to argue for reform in the teaching of the course. While serving as director of composition at my university's main campus, I helped organize a major syllabus revision project aimed at finding a new, third way to teach the course, an alternative to the two well-worn approaches long dominant in our program. One approach has treated the course as a writing-intensive version of an introduction to literature class, the other a composition course with literature as its theme (the all too familiar "writing themes about literature" model). Our third way envisioned the course as focused more directly on students as readers and on reading as a cultural and critical practice, drawing in part upon classroom materials developed by Patricia Harkin, later to appear in her innovative textbook *Acts of Reading*. While this revision project proved successful insofar as the department later adopted the new course as its new standard syllabus for a time, the "victory" was decidedly limited. Few continuing faculty adopted the new course plan. Most, I suspect, saw no pressing need to revise the course in the first place.

This essay recounts my experience with this syllabus revision project, setting it in its larger institutional context and examining both the hostilities and limited reconciliations between composition and literature evident in my colleagues' reactions to the effort. I discuss, too, the rationale for revising the curriculum through a "third way" emphasis on reading as critical and cultural practice. In this regard, I must note how time-honored assignments best described as "writing about literature" had come to define course content, with students continuing the threadbare practice of "finding meaning in" or "getting meaning out of" selected literary texts. Over time, these methods have enforced a "read the text, then write about the text" sequencing of tasks that can have the effect of undoing much of our first-semester composition course's emphasis on reading and writing as intertwined practices. Such traditional approaches to teaching composition and literature courses have failed, as well, to address longstanding problems with the pedagogy for such courses, specifically the inadequate reading program represented by rudimentary, more-or-less New Critical approaches.

## Revising Standard Syllabi

At the time I was named to direct the first-year writing program on Miami's main campus, I had already taught first-year writing for a number of years on Miami's regional campus in Middletown. I had always made a point of teaching the standard syllabus, perhaps out of some misguided notion that good citizens of the department did so, but more likely due to a lack of imagination on my part. Up through the mid to late 1980s, teaching the standard syllabus had meant teaching modes-of-discourse-based writing the first semester, with analytical themes-about-literature assignments the centerpiece of second semester teaching. These two syllabi had been in place for a good while, the now commonplace view that syllabi need revising periodically having not yet established itself.

*Along the DMZ between Composition and Literature*

When the revising of standard syllabi emerged as a composition program concern in the late 1980s, I found myself involved from the start. I had devoted some time over a summer writing a modest revision of the first-semester course, redesigning sections of the now process-oriented course plan to accommodate an approach compatible with the standard syllabus's recommended text, Donald Murray's *Write to Learn*. This limited reworking helped fuel discussion of what a more thorough reexamining of the course might involve, and within a couple of years I was at work again on revising the syllabus, this time as part of a team led by Susan Jarratt, who had become the program's director. This course plan, which came to be known as the "new syllabus," introduced a new socially oriented approach to writing through a dramatically different set of assignments and related readings. Students were now to write reflective (and not just personal) narratives, arguments built from work with the Toulmin model, discourse analyses, investigations of institutional values, and readings of cultural texts. Although much was made of the syllabus's ideological orientation, its challenging expressivism through its social-constructionist approach, another long-term impact on teaching would be felt soon enough as well. In the old write-by-the-numbers course plans held in place by the modes of discourse, readings were often assigned only to provide students with formats to use as models for their own writing. With newer, write-to-learn process-minded approaches, readings could become almost superfluous, so centered were such syllabi on having students concentrate on reading and responding to one another's writing. With this new course, though, reading's place in the first-semester curriculum would take on a greater role, inviting exploration of reading-writing relationships that previous standard syllabi had largely neglected.

The new course plan did more than shake up the first-semester curriculum. It exposed the gap between the syllabi approved for the first- and second-semester courses, so much so that official composition program documents had to strain to link the two courses. The year I took over as program director, the description for the first-semester course published in the *College Composition at Miami* manual for 1993–94 spoke at some length of a course "built around five language 'tools' used by writers to both reflect and create their social contexts" (23). In the next year's manual, a more fully elaborated "course philosophy" had emerged, along with a number of "theoretical assumptions." Among the course's new assumptions were that "language constructs social difference in all spheres of discourse," that the aforementioned "tools" (now known as "discourse technologies") help us "understand how language works to structure thinking and acting in several contexts," and that "reading and writing are intertwined practices" where "the writing class benefits from multiple voices and styles of writing." A stated goal of the course was "to understand how writing reflects, produces, and even transforms social relations" (15–16).

At the time I took over as director, the manual's cryptic description of second-semester course aims could say only that "the goal is to continue the writing practices begun in English 111, but to focus . . . on imaginative texts in a number of genres," adding that "English 112 reopens the category of 'literature' to the critical processes of discussion and writing. As you talk and write about your readings in 112, you are encouraged to look skeptically at the arguments for literature as universal and timeless." Besides a "course philosophy" and "theoretical assumptions," the first-semester course had a fully developed syllabus composed of five three-week-long units, each with its own week-to-week course plans, selected readings, and detailed writing assignments. By comparison, the second-semester's course description could say only that "material in English 112 is not necessarily drawn from a single period or country. Instead, a juxtaposition of a variety of literary works raises questions of changing aesthetic values through history and of cultural differences." About the writing in the course, the description said only that "essays in 112 range from literary interpretations of readings and personal response essays to persuasive pieces concerning ethical and moral issues raised by the readings" (26).

## A New Syllabus for English 112

Such was the state of our two courses, then, at the moment I became director. Plainly, my task would be to facilitate development of a new syllabus for English 112. I thought I could follow the same extended process that had brought about a new English 111 syllabus—convene a discussion group to explore possibilities, reach consensus as to a workable curriculum, assign to group members the tasks of writing the new course rationale and unit plans, and then take the completed syllabus to the composition committee and English department for approval. I thought, too, that I had the arguments to advance the project. If the new English 111 course wanted "to understand how writing reflects, produces, and even transforms social relations," English 112 could do much the same for reading. If 111 could provide students with tools "used by writers to reflect and create their social contexts," 112 could give students comparable tools for reading. Foregrounding reading in these ways could help, too, to "reopen the category of literature to critical inquiry." Beyond all of this, we had the idea that a revitalized 112 curriculum might give graduate students teaching the course a chance to share with their first-year charges ways of reading closer to those of the graduate seminar in literature than the desiccated intro-to-lit textbooks' versions of same. The first meetings I called to talk about a new syllabus drew about twenty-five faculty and graduate students, including composition faculty whom I had hoped would be friendly to a new approach. I found, though, that resistance to reworking the course was palpable. Soon enough, resentments surfaced over the idea of extending to 112 the "ideological" impetus of the first-semester course. It was bad enough, I was to hear, that the manual for the first-semester course now claimed that "when we write, we are participating in and reconfiguring already existing systems of language rather than just creating unique expressions of our inner thoughts and feelings." I heard, too, that so anti-expressivist a pedagogy was already enough of a problem for English 111 teachers without pushing it through to a second semester. Before long, attendance at meetings had dwindled to a half dozen or so, all of them graduate students. Those staying in the group soon formed a stable work team that held together for the duration of the two-year effort. The die was cast, however. The syllabus revision was now in the hands of a regional campus faculty member in a short term as composition program director and five or six graduate students, albeit five or six of the department's best.

Beyond individual teachers' resistance to creating a new 112, institutional arrangements militated against putting our new course on a sound footing. Though the first-year writing program had responsibility for the 112 curriculum, many faculty saw the second-semester course as belonging more to the department than the program. Teaching assignments had much to do with this view. For some time, all continuing faculty were obliged to teach one writing course per year; for a substantial majority of faculty, especially those in the literature program, this meant teaching 112. With literature faculty outnumbering those in composition by quite a margin departmentwide, a curricular standoff of sorts had developed in this new era of questioning and revising syllabi. Although responsibility for the first-semester course belonged to the composition program, jurisdiction over the second-semester course was becoming a more muddled affair. The composition program could authorize revision of the 112 syllabus, approve a new plan, and take it to the department for ratification, but it had no way of requiring that instructors other than first-year teaching assistants follow a new syllabus. Over the years, in fact, the first-year program had not even disabused many faculty of the notion that 112 could still be more of an Intro to Lit course than a writing course. The two-semester teacher-training seminars for new graduate students reflected this standoff as well. Students learned, soon enough, that although they had to work closely with the units of the 111 syllabus in the first semester, they could do largely what they wanted the second semester. From their point of view, relatively free rein the second term seemed only fair after having to teach from the standard 111 playbook in the first semester. In short, pushing for a new consensus on what 112 should be about and how it should be taught had run up against the commonly held view that maintaining a no-consensus status quo was best.

Perhaps the biggest obstacle to reform had to do, however, with English 112's occupying such an undertheorized space in an increasingly theory-driven academy. Rationales for the course, at least for faculty "required" to teach it, had advanced little since the 1950s, when the university's composition program was still in its infancy. As James Berlin notes in *Rhetoric and Reality*, early postwar claims for literature in composition turned on arguments no more sophisticated than that "students have difficulty in composition because they have nothing to write about," a problem easily solved by supplying literature as the subject for writing; that literature, as the section leader's salvation, "provides the 'knowledge and stimulation' that the teacher needs to keep his career alive and vital"; and that literature helps in "preserving the integrity of the individual against the tyranny of the mob" (108–9). In the years that followed, arguments crafted to defend the course took on few refinements. In Edward Corbett's 1983 essay "Literature and Composition: Allies or Rivals in the Classroom?" we learn that requiring students "to read some literature in a writing course could be a subtle way of getting them 'hooked on books.'" We learn, too, that not only are teachers "better qualified by their training and their interest to talk about the poetics of a literary text than about the rhetoric of a piece of argumentative prose," but also that "ordinary students often enjoy reading literary texts—especially the narrative forms—more than the utilitarian forms of discourse." There is the old standby as well, namely, that "the best way to show students how to write is to expose them to the consummate artists in the handling of the language" (178–79).

If, over the years, the first-semester college course in composition had attracted a tradition of complaint (famously and thoroughly catalogued by Leonard Greenbaum in 1969), the second-semester composition and literature course could be said to have invited a quite different tradition of defense, one that made our attempts to shift the focus from literature to critical reading a most daunting task. Our faculty's resistance to the new 112's more social orientation, combined with the course's relative independence within the composition program, made this tradition of defense all the harder to crack. More importantly, the faculty's longstanding defensiveness about 112 kept the department from recognizing how little enthusiasm the rest of the university had for such a throwback course, especially given its influential position as the course most likely to meet students' first-year seminar requirement. I would hear plenty about the course's shortcomings in my capacity as director of the program, however. These complaints, which centered on English 112's limitations as a writing course, were predictable enough. They brought out, plainly enough, the potential for institutional reform were the department to overcome, somehow, its decades-long bunker mentality about the course.

## The New Course Takes Shape

The English 112 revision effort coincided with my offering a new graduate seminar, Reading Theory and Pedagogy, designed to explore theoretical and pedagogical developments in introductory reading and writing courses. The hope was that this seminar, along with the aforementioned discussion group, could help in retraining a core group of instructors in new developments in reading and writing pedagogy. The seminar's syllabus had three sections, the first of which, "Reading Habits and Practices," dealt with a range of representations of readers, and histories of (instruction in) reading. The second section, "Theories and Pedagogies," took up reading theories' impact on instruction in 112-type courses, chief among them reader-response theories from Louise Rosenblatt to David Bleich. The third section, "Applications," took as its aim the designing of course materials for a new 112. The seminar helped me emphasize how much reader-response theory could offer our project. As Daniel Sheridan had noted in one of our readings, "a theory like this . . . could be adapted readily to the classroom, for unlike some literary theory—deconstruction, for example—reader response appears to be homegrown, familiar in its vocabulary, and almost automatically student-centered." In addition, "some of its main proponents—Fish, Bleich, Holland, and Rosenblatt herself—have all written from the standpoint of classroom teachers" (805).

Another step forward came with a campus visit by Patricia Harkin, who brought us work on Wolfgang Iser and gap theory she was building into her textbook for introductory courses. Chris Anderson has captured what, for us, was so groundbreaking in Iser's theory. He writes that, according to Iser, "the reading experience . . . depends on the 'gaps' or 'blanks' in a text, the gaps arising from dialogue, for example, or from unexplained events, delayed revelations, and uninterpreted concrete images." Then, "in the space left by the reticence of the author, meaning takes place. Information withheld, interpretation withdrawn, the reader is left to make inferences and connections." Crucial for us was that "for Iser the reader must actively 'assemble' the various parts of any literary text. Language can only specify the operations the reader must perform. Gaps are the most fundamental of these linguistic instructions" (Anderson 340–41).

New syllabus planning took a quantum leap forward as we realized how much gaps can do. They can attract student readers to the act of reading itself, to make their own connections and inferences, based on gaps they identify. In the process, gaps bring out that reading can be an active rather than a passive process. Further, they offer "instructions" as to how the reader can "operate" the text, "instructions" that are eminently teachable.

Soon enough, a new syllabus was taking shape. The new course came to have five units, or "sites" as we called them, each with its own defined activities, readings, and writing tasks. "Reading and Response," the first site, drew on reader-response theory in inviting students to learn about themselves and others as readers, about how responses can be texts in their own right, and about ways in which responses can vary from reader to reader. "Difficulties Reading," the second site, drew upon Harkin's work with gaps and succeeded in opening up for students new and more active relations to texts. "Reading Representations," the third site, centered on depictions of readers and acts of reading, drawn from both literary and media culture, in order to give students the chance to reflect on the often multiple readership positions they can occupy. Featured readings included short stories showcasing readers as protagonists, with these texts raising questions about the place and status of reading in experience. The fourth site, "Borders," was built on the third, examining how readership positions can change as writing engages revision and re-presentation. The fifth site, "Reading Histories and Prospects," asked students to reflect on the course, using its terms and perspectives to (re)write a chapter in their own lives as readers.

Our hope was that these sites would catch on and that instructors would join with us in building and refining them, but little of this happened. Without their support, the buy-in needed to sustain interest among the course's core constituencies failed to materialize. The project of revising the 112 syllabus went ahead in any event, culminating in department approval of our new standard the year after I returned to my regional campus post. For the next five years or so, our revision's philosophy and leading propositions defined 112 in official composition program documents. As late as the 2000–2001 edition of the *College Composition at Miami* manual, one could read:

> The standard English 112 course looks at the social and historical factors that shape the way people read, how reading is used and valued, and the relationships between reading and writing. In 112, you will continue engaging with writing as a social process, but you will examine reading as a "process" as well. English 112 assumes that the way you read is indicative of your personal history and experience, that it—like writing—reflects the ways that you understand knowledge, history, and difference. (44)

By this time, however, a new round of department-mandated syllabus revision efforts was about to bring forward yet another reworking of 112, one that would return emphasis on the literary text to its former, preeminent position, while curtailing attention to gap theory, and all but eliminating work with representations of reading and reading histories. The course overview in a recent manual, *College Composition at Miami, 2004–05* reverts to familiar claims for 112:

> English 112 focuses on the processing of reading, interpreting, constructing and supporting arguments about a literary text and aims to deepen students' understanding of writing about literature. . . . English 112 teaches students the practices of reading and interpreting literary and cultural texts with a focus on critical reading as a precondition for participation in an intellectual community. . . . English 112 introduces students to three literary elements—narrative, dialogue, and metaphor (figurative language)—that structure a variety of genres and shape meaning. (12)

Indeed, the sites we had devised—"Reading and Response," "Difficulties Reading," "Reading Representations," "Borders," and "Reading Histories and Prospects"—had given way to "sequences" entitled "Critical Writing and Reading Strategies," "Reading and Writing Narrative," "Reading and Writing Dialogue," and "Reading and Writing Figurative Writing." As I contemplate the return of such basic literary terms to head entire course sequences, I can only lament the retreat to a rather staid formalism for our introductory course. I am left to imagine, too, what 112 could have become had instructors been trained to teach new concepts and terms, such as Patricia Harkin offers in *Acts of Reading*. Harkin introduces any number of such concepts and terms that could help students with reading a wider range of texts than just literary ones. Besides "gaps," she takes up "interpretive communities," "reading against the grain," "reading for world" (textual, authorial, and readers' worlds), the "minimal story framework," "narratee," and "intertextuality." With our 112 course's restoration of the literary, it must also be said that our syllabus revision efforts wound up, ultimately, falling well short of the restructuring Gere imagines. Our work might have shown, at times, a "fuller expression," where "composition theory resists boundaries and blurs distinctions between disciplines," so that "it interacts, changing and being changed" (3). In the end, though, our project never opened enough space to allow colleagues in literature and composition to interact as we hoped they would.

I return to a question raised in an earlier paragraph. Can composition and literature move together to a new, more interactional space? Our English 112 revision shows how the two might interact to produce the makings of a program for active and critical reading that, at the least, might yet revitalize an otherwise moribund curriculum. Composition has made headway as a discipline in the last two decades, in no small part by challenging students' negative attitudes toward writing. Thanks to the panoply of classroom practices that have emerged in recent years, students are much more positive about writing today than they were twenty years ago. Their attitudes toward reading, though, are every bit as negative as those expressed toward writing some years back. Students freely document these negative feelings in writing their own reading histories, openly express them when asked about them in class. The venerable curricular site set aside for composition and literature courses remains the one place at the postsecondary level where students' reading attitudes, habits, and practices can become the centerpiece of instruction. Were this to happen, much might be done to address the negativity and passivity so pervasive in students' attitude towards reading. Composition and literature faculty could join forces in bringing about this much needed curricular reform, but would they be willing to step away from entrenched pedagogies long enough to collaborate on such a project? The odds are against it, but there is much to be gained if they could.

## Works Cited

Anderson, Chris. "Teaching Students What Not to Say: Iser, Didion, and the Rhetoric of Gaps." *Journal of Advanced Composition* 7 (1987): 10–22. http://jac.gsu.edu/jac/7/Articles/2.htm (accessed 10 October 2005).

Berlin, James. *Rhetoric and Reality: Writing Instruction in American Colleges, 1900–1985.* Carbondale: Southern Illinois UP, 1987.

Corbett, Edward P. J. "Literature and Composition: Allies or Rivals in the Classroom?" *Composition and Literature: Bridging the Gap.* Ed. Winifred Bryan Horner. Chicago: U of Chicago P, 1983. 168–84.

Department of English, Miami University. *College Composition at Miami, 1993–94.* Vol. 46. Department of English, Miami University, Oxford, OH.

———. *College Composition at Miami, 1994–95.* Vol. 47. Department of English, Miami University, Oxford, OH.

———. *College Composition at Miami, 2000–01.* Vol. 53. Department of English, Miami University, Oxford, OH.

———. *College Composition at Miami, 2004–05.* Vol. 57. Department of English, Miami University, Oxford, OH.

Gere, Anne Ruggles. Introduction. *Into the Field: Sites of Composition Studies.* Ed. Anne Ruggles Gere. New York: Modern Language Association, 1993. 1–6.

Greenbaum, Leonard. "The Tradition of Complaint." *College English* 31 (1969): 174–87.

Harkin, Patricia. *Acts of Reading*. Upper Saddle River, NJ: Prentice Hall, 1999.

Lindemann, Erika. "Freshman Composition: No Place for Literature." *College English* 55.3 (March 1993): 311–16.

Sheridan, Daniel. "Changing Business as Usual: Reader Response in the Classroom." *College English* 53 (1991): 804–14.

Tate, Gary. "A Place for Literature in Freshman Composition." *College English* 55.3 (March 1993): 317–21.

Trimbur, John. "Composition Studies: Postmodern or Popular." *Into the Field: Sites of Composition Studies*. Ed. Anne Ruggles Gere. New York: Modern Language Association, 1993. 117–32.

CHAPTER EIGHT

# Whole English, Whole Teachers: Maintaining the Balance between Rhetorical and Literary Expertise

DENNIS CIESIELSKI
*University of Wisconsin–Platteville*

Although much has been said regarding literature teachers' experience in the composition classroom, there is little published work on the compositionist in the literature classroom. On the one hand, although some department chairs might claim that the literature teacher will gain valuable professional experience in the *practice* of teaching composition, there is little reference to the need for these too often misplaced teachers to recognize, read, and use current composition theory. On the other hand, compositionists are often barred from the literature classroom because they are "not prepared in literature" and thus do not belong in foreign academic territory. The main point here is one of academic responsibility and can be seen more clearly in terms of pedagogy and academic preparation. Although many literature specialists have neither the training nor the desire to teach "out of their field," compositionists are generally prepared in both rhetoric and composition *and* literature, especially in rhetorical and literary theory. Compositionists also have the advantage of a preparation in pedagogical theory and practice, that is, *how* to teach; *how* to address resistant learners; *how* to work the important stuff of critical thought and writing into the everyday classroom experience.

Pedagogically, the essential difference between traditional literature teachers and modern compositionists is the difference between *savoir* and *savoir faire*, *to know* and *to know how*. Whereas the literature teacher has more than likely not had a methods course in the teaching of literature, the compositionist, due to the nature of the discipline, has had much pedagogical preparation; whereas the compositionist has not had the chance to practice her rhetorical and literary theory in the literature class and thus maintain an academic balance, the literature specialist has had ample opportunity to achieve this balance, but all too often neglects the opportunity to add composition scholarship to an already strong literature base. The problem here is not one of turf, but one of disparity and binary opposition. The solution: to repair the schism between reading and writing and get on with the business of the modern English department.

Bringing together the two disparate sides of a whole discipline would serve to create a dialogically sound faculty college of *whole English* teachers. A whole English faculty would honor and respect their professional others well enough to fill in the gaps of their own professional identity with the relevant scholarship waiting to be discovered in the no-man's-land we have created between textual consumption and textual production.

## The Problem

While placing literature specialists in the composition classroom has been a traditionally unchallenged practice, placing composition teachers in the literature classroom often causes problems ranging from discipline-driven turf wars to questions of writing's place in the English curriculum overall. Because reading and writing are inextricably joined together to form the academic entity we call English, my argument is not that one intradiscipline or another has the right to teach literature *or* composition but that we must become a community of whole English teachers prepared to do the work of English as a whole discipline.

English belongs to those who use it, and it is up to us to guide our students into using it to their cultural advantage. Thus, a whole English concept should emerge in gen-ed courses more aligned with our non-English majors who might take only one or two English classes during their university career. Because our students across the curriculum need as much textual and rhetorical understanding as anyone else who hopes to hold a university degree, we need to offer these very few courses in a unified front that represents English courses as equal parts of a whole English experience offered by professor-teachers who view English as the study of signification and democratic participation in cultural affairs.

Even in non-major courses, the turf war attitude and tacit approval of the schism between writing and literature often prevail to work against the whole English teacher model. The traditional view of literature as the pivotal concern of English denigrates writing teachers and all too often bars them from exercising their own literary expertise in the literature classroom, where they are, in almost all situations, well prepared to work. This same class distinction is the reason that literature teachers, who are generally unprepared in composition theory and practice, are compelled by administrators who see literature specialists as the profession's elite to hold forth in the composition classroom ("If she can teach Joyce, she can teach anything!"). Here is where the whole English teacher model comes to bear: to be *whole*, anyone who teaches any university-level course should obviously be prepared, well read, and current in the topic at hand. However, this is not always the case. In too many of our colleges and universities, English department heads, in their bid to maintain a traditional focus on literature, have allowed the profoundly important stuff of rhetoric and composition to be handled by nonspecialists, while writing specialists, who are generally well prepared in literature, enjoy little or no diversity in their teaching experience. The outcome here is manifold; however, a primary concern must be not only our students' often misguided composition experience but also the incomplete professional maintenance of our rhetoric and composition teachers' capacity to teach on both sides of the English schism. Thus, while literature specialists too often teach composition from no real research base, compositionists who are hired only to teach gen-ed writing run the risk of seeing their own literary proficiency (the other part of their *wholeness*) atrophy in light of a departmental policy that honors literature and those who teach it as the main concerns of the department.

## The Debate

Nowhere can we find better evidence of this ideological problem than in the lit-comp debate between Gary Tate and Erica Lindemann. Beginning at the 1992 Conference on College Composition and Communication annual convention and continuing in open forum until March of 1995 in the National Council of Teachers of English journal *College English*, Lindemann and Tate discuss the place of literature in the first-year composition classroom. Though Lindemann and Tate's conversation broaches many previously unspoken (or, at least unpublished) professional concerns such as Tate's fear of the loss of textual aestheticism in the writing class (319) and Lindemann's observation that literature in the composition class veers away from composition's "real purpose" of guidance and practice "in reading and writing the discourses of the academy and the professions" ("Freshman" 312), both correspondents neglect an even greater issue: the fact that the vast majority of literature teachers who are *compelled* to teach first-year-composition are unprepared to do so. Because of this lack of preparation, the misplaced teacher will opt to teach what it is she or he knows best: literature.

Tate, a proponent of literature in the composition class, says as much in his defense of literature in his own classroom: "In part," says Tate, "literature disappeared from composition classes in this country because it was badly misused by teachers desperate to teach literature, teachers *who should not be blamed* for trying to teach the only subject they knew" (317; emphasis added). Yet, if we should not blame these inefficient teachers, who *should* we blame for putting our first-year composition students through one full semester of misguided pedagogy? Much of the blame rests in our discipline's elitist view of literature as English's primary concern. Tate's position reinforces the elitist perspective. Rather than seeing this problem from a student-centered perspective, he sees literature itself as the victim of rhetoric and those he refers to as the "rhetoric police" (318). Seeing modern composition studies as the end of imagination and style in the writing class, Tate blames the removal of literature from composition for the negative comp-as-service-course persona (319), which is, itself, the product of the same elitist views from an administrational perspective—removing lit removes the important stuff.

According to Tate and a current-traditionalist administration, as long as literature holds forth in the writing class, composition will maintain an aesthetic, consumer-based position; however, when literature is displaced with noncanon or "secular" student texts, composition will fall into a more or less utilitarian labor-based position. There seems, for Tate, to be no middle ground here. A proper education in the composition classroom is to be found within the aesthetic texts of others and the students' ability to respond to them in kind. If we move toward a multigeneric, rhetorical approach, composition risks losing its identity as an English class. However, to see this as a valid problem is to see the teaching of literature as the English department's primary concern.

Lindemann's response to literature in the composition classroom deals more in process orientations and the belief that a writing course's main objective is to learn how to identify and work within the context of an ever-changing rhetorical situation. We must teach students *about* writing as rhetoric as well as *how to* write. Freshman writing, says Lindemann, "provide[s] opportunities to master the genres, styles, audiences, and purposes of college writing" ("Freshman" 312); it allows students to "join the conversation that education enables" (Tate 319). Literature-based composition courses don't reach Lindemann's expectations because they neglect process orientations in favor of a more product-oriented mode. Because lit-based composition courses are more concerned with the consumption of texts rather than their production, "students do very little writing, and what they [do] write has very little relation to the intellectual demands" of their other course work ("Freshman" 313).

Lindemann drives home her point, observing that, "A pedagogy derived from teaching literature looks and sounds different from one that encourages students to produce texts" ("Freshman" 313). This consumption versus production model relates back to Tate's fear of composition's loss of credibility in a class-conscious English department and the university at large. Yet Lindemann's use of the term *produce* is a positive view of freshman English's main purpose, which is to teach students how to produce texts to their own advantage in and for a world that will expect textual proficiency. And, Lindemann observes, this sort of writing "neither requires nor finds particularly relevant a significant role for literature" (313).

In her final response to the lit-comp debate, Lindemann notes that "Most of the responses in *College English* take exception not to Tate's position but to mine" ("Three" 287). However, the observation that her *College English* colleagues side with lit-comp rather than a more purified, proletarian composition class will, I believe, change over time. In fact, it might have changed in her favor even before the 1992 debate began. Erwin Steinberg, in his response to the 1993 *College English* discussion, quotes from *Basic Issues in the Teaching of English*, a supplement to *English Journal* published in 1959: "The typical [English] Ph.D. is almost completely void of courses dealing primarily with language and rhetoric." The statement continues, asking the question, "Is it right to assume that a beginning teacher can teach well something he has not studied directly . . . that is at best peripheral to his current training and interests?" (269). Steinberg further notes that the same publication from which he quotes offers, thirty-five years later, that "the teaching of composition is a separate matter from the teaching of literature; the study of rhetoric, language, and how people learn to write are more important to students learning to write in composition classrooms than is the study of literature." As well, the 1994 *Basic Issues* Report maintains the same observation of the English Ph.D. that it did in 1959: "The current Ph.D. in English . . . does not prepare them to teach writing either" (270). Steinberg finalizes his research (and his point) by investigating the topics and categories addressed at the CCCC convention in recent years and discovers "that literature has not had a secure place in composition since the 1930s," that we have "entered the age of rhetoric for teachers of composition" (271). However, this particular view of literature's value in the composition classroom, though heartening, comes from specialists in the rhetoric and composition field. Those teachers who do not attend and participate in composition's national forum or partake of its ever-growing research remain separated from current theory and practice in the teaching of writing and all too often enter the composition classroom with good intentions unsupported by practical research.

One of the main reasons underprepared literature specialists are placed in the composition classroom is department chairs and administrators who do not see rhetoric and composition from a CCCC perspective. Indeed, many department heads are not aware of CCCC, WPA, or NCTE research and standards. Yet, because of organizations like CCCC and the WPA, and a public outcry regarding university graduates' poor writing skills, we can see, on several campuses across the country, a new and positive regard for writing-intensive curricula and the conflation of critical reading and writing skills as well as the sort of whole English faculty that can teach at this level. Thus, the number of literature specialists placed in composition classrooms by department chairs desperate to cover incoming first-year composition quotas notwithstanding, Steinberg's research seems to bear out Lindemann's call for more rhetoric, less literature, more production, less consumption.

Though Lindemann's final hand count on the lit-comp debate might indicate that our profession has spoken on this matter, we might see in this result not so much a consensus as a collective English faculty's very slow move toward the paradigmatic change necessary to complete the ideological structure that will eventually change how we see and thus teach English in the university. Because departmental policies are, if nothing else, political, we might be able to see the slow dialectic of pedagogical change through the lens of Raymond Williams's dialectic process model. Rather than focusing on one part of this dialectic movement, Williams advises that we "recognize not only 'stages' and 'variations' but the internal dynamic relations of any actual process" (121). The primary model by which we can observe these internal relations is Williams's view of hegemony—the dominant—as a combination of *residual* and *emergent* codes "which are significant both in themselves and in what they reveal of the characteristic of the dominant" (122). The *residual* is the historical-cultural area from which the dominant has risen. Though the dominant has taken precedence, there is yet an ancestral relationship with its place of origin. The *emergent* (often defined as the "avant-garde") is the area toward which the dominant unavoidably progresses relative to the theory and practice it both influences and inspires over time. *Hegemony* is the product, then, of a dialectic movement that spurs its own growth through cultural experience and the new and ever-changing "knowledge" this experience cannot help but generate. From Williams's model, we might see a *belletristic* perspective in the composition classroom as the residual and a new rhetorical approach as the emergent, and that the incorporation of these two dialectical ends create the ever-changing middle ground of the dominant, which, it seems, is moving in the direction of rhetoric over poetics in the modern composition classroom.

The most practical response to the Tate-Lindemann debate is Jane Peterson's call to "reframe the discussion" (314). Peterson rightly sees the question of "the classification of texts assigned [in composition]" as secondary to the "nature of reading we expect from our students and the possible roles of reading in the development of [their] writing abilities" (311). Coming from a broader base of cultural studies and individual, social, and democratic learning experiences, Peterson makes a point not for the *genre* of composition texts as much as for the *way they are used*. In this sense, "imaginative literature" might work well if presented from a more rhetorical perspective rather than from the high ground of aesthetic evaluation and response exercises. It is the *teacher* who must play a pivotal role in the context of textual application. From this observation, Peterson calls for a well-rounded view of composition as a course in rhetoric regardless of what type of reading prompts one might choose. Regardless of genre, a responsible and *qualified* composition teacher will relate to her students the fact that reading is, in itself, a rhetorical application. Thus, she offers that

> [English teachers] need to discuss the nature and place of reading in the freshman course, how readers interact with texts, print and non-print, to construct meaning: how individual, social, and cultural systems shape expectations and interpretations; and how an awareness of the constructive, interpretive nature of reading verbal and nonverbal texts might promote students' writing abilities. (312)

Peterson's reading-as-rhetorical-experience aligns with James Berlin's call for cultural studies in the English composition classroom (*Rhetorics* 97–98) as a means to guiding our first-year students into efficient social-epistemic skills relative to success both in future university writing and the world beyond the classroom. Her perspective informs, as well, Doug Brent's position that reading itself is a profound exercise in rhetorical invention. Placing rhetoric within the reading experience and vice versa, Peterson addresses a goal common to both sides of the English schism, that gen-ed language-oriented courses should prepare our students for "participation in democracy" (Lloyd-Jones qtd. in Peterson 315). Thus, the argument between what can readily be seen as "lit people" defending their turf against "comp people" who are defending their turf against underprepared "lit people" (as well as planning an "invasion" into literature's territory) becomes moot in the call for teachers who are well versed and secure enough on *both* sides of the hall to be able to conflate their areas of expertise into a new tertiary role as that of a whole English teacher, an expert who comprehends the importance of our students' understanding of rhetoric from both sides of the page, from that of interpretive consumer-of-text to that of a savvy and persuasive producer-of-text. From this point a new and more provocative question must be addressed. Who are the whole English teachers in English departments-at-large, and why?

## Dialogue and Identity: The Whole English Teacher

A whole English teacher will see the English classroom as a place where students will gain a deep understanding of a text's rhetorical *and* cultural nature and will recognize that reading and writing are the constituent parts of one intellectual body that John Schilb refers to as *civic education* (5). This idea of a civic education addresses other similar theories such as James Berlin's social-epistemic rhetoric and his call for an English-as-cultural-studies policy *(Rhetorics* 77–94) and Kenneth Burke's rhetoric of identity, which he sees as a mutual identification through dialogue (*Rhetoric* 19–23), and his coincident view of literature as "equipment for living" (*Philosophy* 293–304). Essentially, Berlin's social-epistemic rhetoric sets up a discursive environment based upon the ability to enter into a dialogue with one's own cultural experience and to effectively join the conversation that precedes her or him. Berlin sees the conflation of one's ability to *read* a situation and to *respond* efficiently and responsibly within the situation's rhetorical and social-cultural context as a sign of intellectual and social wholeness. In his essay "Composition Studies and Cultural Studies," he notes that social-epistemic rhetoric "considers signifying practices in relation to the ideological formation of the self within the context of economics, politics, and power" (109). Burke's rhetoric of identity and the concept of "literature as equipment for living" derives from the same social-epistemic fabric. Seeing literature as equal to real-life experience, as "proverbs writ large" (*Philosophy* 296), our students will be able to apply rhetorical and literary devices to the analysis of and response to their own experience. Thus Burke's *sociological criticism of literature* can just as easily become a *literary criticism of society*. His dramatistic view of literature as "equipment for living" takes on very serious implications, especially when we, as teachers, discover that all writing, even student writing, is, indeed, literature and thus deserves the same attention as the canonical literature in so many of our composition classrooms. In typical Burkeian irony, if literature is equipment for living, then the reverse is true as well: living is the equipment of literature, and our students' ability to read and respond to the text of their own experience will also allow them to participate in their own cultural development.

In a whole English environment, composition courses are designed to help our students respond (and relate) to the rhetorical situation at hand. One day the rhetorical situation might be a poem or a short story; the next day perhaps an editorial; the next day it might be the campus parking problem or a political analysis; in any case the list will *always* move beyond the isolated ability to "write about literature." Berlin's social-epistemic rhetoric and Burke's practical understanding of literature as part of personal experience might lead us to an equitable and efficient use of literature as a way to further our students' ability to join in the pre-existent dialogue on the terms of those who have preceded them with respect to voice, style, and demeanor. Rather than writing for the teacher who will simply grade for form and "correctness," whole English students write to an audience of context-specific readers whose expectations will always extend beyond formalism to the writers' ability to actually connect with them. Thus, whole English teachers evaluate the writer's rhetorical and social skills as well as the current-traditional correctness all readers naturally expect in a printed text.

A whole English model addresses, as well, Paulo Freire's liberatory pedagogy, a concept based in his term *conscientizaçao* (*Pedagogy* 19) which, loosely translated, means the conscious joining of specific facts, specialties, and identities into a braid of cultural knowing necessary to democratic participation in one's social milieu. Relative to Shilb's civic education as well as Berlin's social-epistemicism, Freire's concept addresses the necessity of a whole, well-developed dialogue between an individual and her or his cultural experience. Civic education, democratic participation, and literature as equipment for living all have one thing in common: the profound importance of everyone's ability to both read from and respond to the rhetorical situations they will encounter in their life experience, in the world outside the classroom.

The shared agenda in each of these rhetoric-based educational views is that of intellectual and professional dialogue. Naturalist Edward O. Wilson describes this dialogic wholeness as *consilience*, a term that works to "rejoin knowledge separated from itself" (40). Wilson defines *consilience* succinctly as the "jumping together of knowledge by the linking of facts and fact-based theory across disciplines to create a common groundwork of explanation" (9). Hence, consilience is "the key to unification" (8) between the natural sciences and the liberal arts (the basis of a core curriculum) and has much to say regarding one's attitude toward teaching in general. This dialogic interface, this consilience, is missing in the separatist English department where too many teachers of writing are separated from the other side of their academic and professional wholeness. Consilience in the discourse-oriented classroom is an obvious improvement over isolated, product-oriented pedagogy where students are expected to produce text relative to formal codes and teacher-as-audience expectations.

However, it seems that consilience in the university English department is yet to be discovered. Specialization, in this sense, spells alienation. Without scholarship and preparation in composition studies, the literature specialist risks professional incompetence in the composition classroom. Without a consistent opportunity to work in the literature classroom, the rhet-comp specialist becomes incomplete, one-sided, and runs the risk of becoming as myopic as those who would remove English from its own constituent parts. If approached in a spirit of dialogue and collaborative pedagogy, praxis in the literature classroom will benefit the writing specialist as much as praxis in the writing classroom will benefit the literature specialist. If Wilson's consilience can solve problems dialogically, by breaching extra-disciplinary walls in a bid to meld relative research and practical experience, then it can answer the problem of a disjunctive English department by [re]joining the teachers of reading and writing at their most strategic points. When this occurs, the specialists will remain intact and become even stronger in the interface with their very relevant other.

## Unmixing the Metaphors

Although there is a diplomatic flavor in this, recognizing and negotiating the schism between literature and composition is not the answer to our problem. Rather than *bridging the gap* between two islands, we must bring them together as one. To embrace Maxine Hairston's contentious and undiplomatic statement that "Lit people do not know writing theory" and that "Composition people are learning lit theory simply to impress their former mentors" (qtd. in Schilb 13) is to accept and tacitly reinforce the wall we have erected between us. Rather, we need to see our theoretical difference as a "mending wall" that should both situate and join at their juncture what too many people see as irreconcilable binary opposites. Hairston's knee-jerk reaction to composition's professional alienation helps little in the consubstantiation of academic and intellectual identity in the whole English model. At best, her indictment represents a negative overswing of the ideological pendulum from one extreme to the other. However, as we move out of current-traditional influences in composition and New Critical approaches to literature, we can see the pendulum's swing growing increasingly tighter to do its work more prominently in the middle ground where theoretical consubstantiation can occur.

Too many dialogic metaphors work either to mediate or to separate theoretical and ideological geographies. Thus it is important to recognize certain metaphors as more efficient than others. For example, as Ann Ruggles Gere notes, a well-intended bridge metaphor might do more harm than good (1–6). Although a "bridging-the-gap" metaphor at the outset seems to be one of juncture, of joining and solidarity, the bridge metaphor must still recognize the distance between the two entities we wish to connect. Regardless of how well we build our bridges, the islands of difference are still the same distance from one another as they always were and thus maintain their traditional identities for those who would cross the bridge *to the other side*. In the case of the whole English teaching model, the key words here are *connect* and *the other side*. The bridge metaphor, though connecting two isolated entities, does little to *join* them. Because we cannot live on the bridge itself, after visiting our neighbors we will either choose to stay or choose to "go back home." Thus, the bridge metaphor works more to maintain difference than to promote consubstantiation because we cannot be in two places at once—we are on one side of the bridge or the other. Addressing this problem, Gere suggests a metaphor of *the field* (as in a field of energy), an area of interface where multiple forces join into one essential force whose nature then becomes the product of all its parts. The field metaphor illustrates the power of Edward O. Wilson's *consilience* to generate a tertiary force to the advantage of all. Rather than simply joining opposed energies, the field metaphor creates a *new* energy in much the same way Williams's dominant hegemonic force is the product of the residual and emergent tendencies that both create and are created by the dominant force's own existence. The field metaphor is, essentially, the heart of dialectic and dialogic movement in that it will build upon itself from within, while the bridge metaphor works more to recognize and reinforce rather than modify hegemonic codes.

In cases where a positive link between two irreconcilable forces that might work well together while maintaining their distance and difference, the bridge metaphor can work as an efficient rhetorical tool; however, when the need to come together as one arises, the field metaphor seems more practical. One of the concepts offered in the whole English environment is that choice of metaphor compels us into a choice of terminologies and ways of acting relative to the ways we name our needs and desires into being. Our metaphors serve as the foundation of what Kenneth Burke refers to as our *terministic screen*, the cultural and personal lens through which we see and name the world relative to our own position within it (see *Language* 44–55). Seeing language as culturally and socially generated symbolic action, Burke says, "We must use terministic screens, since we can't say anything without the use of terms. Whatever terms we use, they necessarily constitute a corresponding screen, and any such screen necessarily directs the attention to one field rather than another" (50). As creatures of desire, and as symbol-using animals, we will choose terminologies relative to our own culturally attuned needs. If we see, for example, the need for a *connection* between two isolated terms, we must see, as well, our tacit desire to maintain a certain status quo; thus we must still choose sides. However, if we see the need for consubstantiation, a true melding of others into a third body, we can see our desire to progress both dialectically and dialogically into a new sense of self; thus, through Gere's innovative field metaphor, we can create a whole new terminology that is the product of mutual identity and democratic participation. It is from this field, this metaphor of consubstantiation, that the whole English teacher will emerge.

## Whole English: Everyone Wins

There are two primary concerns regarding the whole English teacher model. One concern is, of course, our students. Echoing Lindemann's observations, an unprepared composition teacher will fall back on teaching literature because she or he has no real preparation in rhetoric-composition. In this case, students will not receive what is actually required of a college writing course. Seeing first-year composition from the traditional perspective that English is founded upon the study of literature "validates" a lit-comp pedagogy that will, to be succinct, cheat our students out of the rhetorical acuity required of practical academic, professional, and personal writing skills. One of the first things a whole English teacher must realize is that first-year composition is first and foremost a writing class and that writing is a secular skill that extends well beyond lit-comp's limited expectations. Through this initial realization, English gen-ed teachers can [re]align their methods and goals in order to teach writing in a more interdisciplinary environment. Coincident to this realignment, our students will gain from the understanding that first-year composition is dedicated to bringing them, through their own writing, into a successful participation in their real-world experience. Rather than learning what makes a poem work, our composition students need to discover what makes their world work, the source of their own voice, and the rhetorical strategies necessary to the making of meaning within the context of their own experience.

As it stands, rhetoric-composition specialists are much closer to this sense of wholeness than their colleagues across the hall and thus ought to offer some of the basics of current composition theory and practice to noncompositionist colleagues in faculty development discussion groups, seminars, and "shoptalk" in general. Likewise, our colleagues in literature, in their own bid for *wholeness*, ought to discuss with composition specialists their experiences in the writing classroom. Together in dialogue, we need to discover which theories we share, which might be new to us, and how we might use them together to maintain a sense of solidarity in an academic department that we must sustain to the advantage of our students and the university as a whole learning environment.

## Works Cited

Berlin, James. "Composition and Cultural Studies." *Composition and Resistance*. Ed. C. Mark Hurlbert and Michael Blitz. Portsmouth, NH: Boynton/Cook, 1991. 47–57.

———. *Rhetorics, Poetics, and Cultures: Refiguring College English Studies.* Urbana, IL: National Council of Teachers of English, 1996.

Brent, Doug. *Reading as Rhetorical Invention: Knowledge, Persuasion, and the Teaching of Research-Based Writing.* Urbana, IL: National Council of Teachers of English, 1992.

Burke, Kenneth. *Language as Symbolic Action: Essays on Life, Literature, and Method.* Berkeley: U of California P, 1966.

———. *The Philosophy of Literary Form: Studies in Symbolic Action.* 3rd ed. Berkeley: U of California P, 1973.

———. *A Rhetoric of Motives.* Berkeley: U of California P, 1969.

Freire, Paulo. *Pedagogy of the Oppressed.* New York: Continuum, 1989.

Gere, Anne Ruggles. *Into the Field: Sites of Composition Studies.* New York: Modern Language Association, 1993.

Lindemann, Erica. "Freshman Composition: No Place for Literature." *College English* 55.3 (March 1993): 311–16.

———. "Three Views of English 101." *College English* 57 (March 1995): 287–302.

Peterson, Jane. "Through the Looking-Glass: A Response" *College English* 57 (March 1995): 310–18.

Schilb, John. *Between the Lines: Relating Composition Theory and Literary Theory.* Portsmouth, NH: Boynton/Cook, 1996.

Steinberg, Erwin. "Imaginative Literature in Composition Classrooms?" *College English* 57 (March 1995): 266–80.

Tate, Gary. "A Place for Literature in Freshman Composition." *College English* 55.3 (March 1993): 317–21.

Williams, Raymond. *Marxism and Literature.* Oxford: Oxford UP, 1977.

Wilson, Edward O. *Consilience: The Unity of Knowledge.* New York: Alfred Knopf, 1998.

# III

# APPLICATIONS IN THE CLASSROOM

CHAPTER NINE

# Computer-Mediated Communication and the Confluence of Composition and Literature

KATHERINE FISCHER
*Clarke College*

DONNA REISS
*Clemson University*
*Tidewater Community College*

ART YOUNG
*Clemson University*

> [W]riting hypertext helps engage students in an encounter with literature, raising the possibility of a new community of critical and creative discourse. This community, whose conventions are not yet formed, can only be defined by a confluence of literature, composition, and technology.
>
> Stuart Moulthrop and Nancy Kaplan

Richard Lanham's *The Electronic Word* reminded us that the valued genres of writing have always been in flux: "First, the essay will no longer be the basic unit of writing instruction. The world will not come to an end therefore; the essay was not always the dominant form. In classical times the central expository form was the declamation; in the Middle Ages, it was the letter; now it will be something else, partaking I would guess of both declamation and letter" (127). Indeed, the letter has been literature, both secular and sacred, and the exchange of letters that characterizes electronic communication—Weblogs, discussion boards, e-mail exchanges, newsgroups, and wikis, for example—remind us that literacy for our composition and literature students is always changing. And first-year composition and introductory literature courses should be proactively at the center of these changes, which are social, political, and economic as well as educational. We must match traditional goals to twenty-first-century communication tools, genres, and environments.

Introductory college composition and literature courses should be flexible and multigenre, old and new, functional and imaginative. After all, academic papers with theses and certain conclusions are nothing like the original form conceived of by Michel de Montaigne, founder of the essay in sixteenth-century France. In fact, Montaigne's *essai* bears more likeness to multi-authored, multivoiced, inconclusive Web texts than to academic papers. The word *essai*, after all, means "attempt," not "argument." Often tentative and hesitant in voice, Montaigne played with ideas on the page without coming to conclusions. He prized questions more than answers—and isn't that a more reflective and thought-producing model for us to offer students than a locked-in-the-safe thesis-proof conclusion?

Any move toward electronic technologies for literary study and writing classes is a way to more closely achieve the *essai* and share the process of human thought. In part influenced by the accessibility of personal computers and new media development tools, the old notion of thesis-driven, single-authored texts that adhere to the rules established de facto by Francis Bacon in contrast with the playful and in-progress *essais* of Montaigne—like much about the halls of academe—may soon be a thing of the past. The multiple modes of the texts our students attend to of their own choosing and the multiple literacies that even our textbook publishers are responding to demonstrate that our academic definitions of *composing* are changing. Although academe may well hold onto prescriptive models as long as possible, neither the workplace that students will one day enter nor the practice of language demands such archaic structures. On the other hand, "English" in a first-year composition class can be a liberal art that "blurs" distinctions among composition, literature, and technology. English studies should build integrated first-year or introductory courses, rather than separate the foundation courses into introduction to composition, introduction to literature, and introduction to communications technology.

Communication technologies, including new media development tools, can promote this coordinated approach to the first-year English class. For example, online discussions of literary and nonliterary texts along with the reading of hypertext and hypermedia literature online prepare students to think in ways that are more conducive to the world that has already shaped them as well as the world they will continue to shape.

As a bonus for teaching multiple literacies in composition and literature classes, writing about essays, newspaper articles, poems, stories, advertisements, plays, and film is more engaging for most first-year composition students than it used to be since their composing options have been expanded by new technologies, new media, and related new instructional options. Online communication allows teachers and students to break from the tradition of only writing about literature into writing their own literature. Even novice and reluctant readers of literature may well find their way as writers and composers in multiple literacies when their compositions are valued by audiences that include classmates and possibly others; when their compositions are appreciated by readers, not just assessed by teachers.

When classes take place completely online, students' extensive and intensive communication can establish a dialogue or polylogue of responses both formal and informal to establish a community of learners among students who may never meet each other or their teacher. Writing builds connections among members of online classes at the same time that writing contributes to—and demonstrates—students' progress as writers and learners. Hybrid or mixed mode classes that meet regularly but that also incorporate some of the electronic communication features of online classes bring together the best features of both face-to-face and computer-mediated writing and learning. As electronic communication tools become more widespread in higher education, more classes will be hybrid, meeting sometimes in person, sometimes through video conferencing, sometimes over the

Internet, and sometimes blending two or more of these venues. As many teachers testify, when students write for each other and not just for the teacher, their awareness of audience, their experience with literature, and their attention to their language and style often increase without explicit instruction.

At our quite different colleges, teaching quite different classes in different ways, we three have discovered activities that engage our students as writers, as readers, and as composers in multiple modes and media, like the genre-crossing authors whose works we study in our classes. With technology, student authors cross borders of campus and country, writing for local and global readers and composing language for a variety of purposes. For us and for our students, composing with new technologies encourages the "confluence of literature, composition, and technology" (Moulthrop and Kaplan 8).

Here we describe some of our experiences with existing technologies for meeting the expectations of a literature-based composition course and introductory literature classes—technologies that support interactive and conversational forums for accessing language and creating context; that provide venues for composing literary and academic hypertext; that blur genres and technologies; that generate written language, visual design, and multimedia composing; and that provide new publishing opportunities. Specific examples of strategies and genres from our classes illustrate integration of the teaching of writing and literature using technology as a tool for mediation and communication.

## I. Donna's and Kate's Early Online Writing and Literature: E-mail across Colleges and Courses

Most of Donna's classes at Tidewater Community College were online, and students never were required to meet in person with their professor or each other. In the absence of face-to-face interaction, teachers and students were challenged to build learning communities and to nurture transformative learning as defined by Rena M. Palloff and Keith Pratt: "teams with guidelines for group process"; "[r]eal-life applications of learning"; "a variety of views and constructive feedback"; and "'expansive questioning' that provides context as well as question" (129). Fortunately, computer-mediated writing assignments can encourage all these characteristics across time and place using basic applications like e-mail as well as more complex multimedia.

Kate's classes at Clarke College take place both online and in traditional classroom settings. Early in the term, students meet regularly on campus and know one another face-to-face before entering their e-groups and Web-based projects. Also, since Clarke is a small private college, many students already know one another from having shared previous classes together, from living in the same dorms, or from having attended the same high schools. Although the atmosphere is friendly and supportive, it can also be somewhat insular at times. Broadening student experience beyond the Midwest through online communities offers students advantages they may not otherwise have.

In 1997, students in Kate's creative writing class at Clarke College and Donna's second-semester composition class at Tidewater Community College had a two-week e-mail exchange revolving around Sandra Cisneros's poem "My Wicked, Wicked Ways" (see Fischer and Reiss). Students wrote original poems about their own family photographs, commented on each other's drafts, and published their poems online. That long-ago e-mail exchange was for us an early example of the ways computers and the Internet could dramatize the connection between writing and literature classes as well as build communities of writers and readers beyond individual campuses. Even today, e-mail remains an excellent medium for student interaction across institutional boundaries, especially as colleges password-protect their discussion boards.

Asked to respond to classmates' e-mail letters, one student supported a suggested interpretation of Cisneros's poem but went on to open up a new avenue of inquiry: "I agree with the fact that the mother at first would become enraged if the woman her husband knows were to show up. But then later she does try to forget and go on with her life as if this anger never existed." Within this community of learners, the assignment invited both expansion of other writers' ideas and respectful disagreement, as another student wrote: "you place yourself in the father's picture. You call this 'The Typical Husband', but do you really believe this behavior is typical?" And another student responded to this view with appreciation for a new perspective on the poem: "Upon my first two readings of this poem, I had not given much thought as to how she (the speaker) acquired these wicked ways. After reading your response, I reread the poem and realize that your interpretation could be close to the truth, especially since the child was not yet born. I like the way you gave both the mother and father the responsibility for the feelings that the child grew up with." Students were creating and negotiating meaning with each other as they conversationally explored the experience of the poem.

Students not only read and wrote about Cisneros's poem about a photograph, but they also selected from among their own photographs and composed their own original poems, posting to both classes their plans for their own poems. One student wrote, "This picture was taken in the house that I grew up in while my parents were still together. I will try to include pre and post divorce feelings about my dad and sister. I want to capture what my life was like before the divorce, after the divorce, and my present feelings in the poem—in that order." The poem began:

> Before the D, we were happy
> The three of us, my sister, Dad and I.
> You can see the new blue wallpaper,
> My mother's favorite color.
> A change, my mother is happy.
> A change foreboding the need for change.

Among the final poems in this multiclass collection was "Dorthea Takes a Lover":

> This is my great aunt,
> freckled and elegant.
> She leans in a lawn chair
> near the hydrangea,
> her blouse open at the neck,
> sun on her bare knees.
> Her lover holds the camera.
> She does not smile.
> She will not marry him.
> She will not listen to the ladies,
> clicking tongues, gathering like grackle

> to muffle her voice, fancy her a bride
> with dishsoap to her elbows.
> Her naked fingers spark speculation;
> she wears desire like lipstick, heavy and damp.
> She cries for people she doesn't know
> and holds out for the morning moon
> and even here, in sunlight, she feels
> like a page torn out of a notebook.
> This is me, skirting out of the photo,
> hair flying, dress flailing. I am little.
> I know her as spearmint gum,
> lipstick-stained tissues, cigarette exhale.
> I do not know she'll die before long.
> I do not know she'll leave
> her restlessness inside me.

Kate and Donna never made distinctions between student poets in the creative writing class and student writers in the first-year composition class. They considered all the authors of the e-mail exchange to be thoughtful readers and emerging writers of poetry, as demonstrated by their correspondence and poems in this project made possible by communications technology.

## II. Expanded Media for Composing about Literature Online: Donna's Discussion Boards, Slide Shows, and Web Publications

As options for student writing online expanded beyond e-mail to include the Internet and multimedia publishable online, Donna's totally online classes were given more choices about genre and medium for their compositions. In a Web-based writing-intensive literature-rich second-semester composition class, a Web discussion board gives students allies for coming to terms with poetry, drama, and short stories as well as informal, low-stakes opportunities to try out their ideas before they attempt formal critical analyses. Typically, student authors select poems from their textbook to write about informally at a discussion board within the Blackboard course management system. Each student replies to another student by answering a question, providing an alternative viewpoint, or expanding on the classmate's ideas. In response to a classmate's comments on Claribel Alegria's "I Am Mirror," one student wrote:

> You mentioned the importance of the person hurting themselves to feel something. I feel that this element is extremely important and ties into the mirror concept. "I hurt therefore I exist" (1200). This line, to me, is what gives the poem substance. Claribel Alegria was Latin and probably witnessed poverty in her lifetime in parts of Latin America. I feel that this poem is a reflection of the pain of a society that is grief and poverty stricken and has an overbearing military presence.

Responding to Sylvia Plath's "Mirror," another student wrote: "Your assumption, however, of the woman's dissatisfaction of her image could be further clarified with the continuation of line 14 which you quoted, 'She rewards me with tears and an agitation of hands' (789). Not only is the woman so depressed that it brings her tears of sadness as you explained, but it also brought about wrath which is exemplified with the clenching of her fists."

In this second-semester composition-literature class, students also write poetry, which they publish online for their classmates. They have the option to compose slide show presentations, Web sites, or electronic poetry as well as unadorned or illustrated word-processed documents. If they choose, they may publish their poems to a wider audience through a Web site or Weblog that belongs to them, not to the college.

In the first semester of composition with its focus on reading and writing academic essays, students also write poetry and have choices of publication medium. For first-semester students, reading poetry encourages the close attention to diction and syntax that writing workshops and revision opportunities also are meant to support. Writing poetry and reflecting on their poems enhances their awareness of the impact on meaning of a word, a phrase, perhaps even a punctuation mark. For coherence with the objectives of this class, students must compose poetic versions of one of their formal academic essays and reflect on the composing process and rhetorical features of each version. The majority of students describe this assignment as the one they enjoyed most from the class, the one that asked them to write in a different genre and to think about the words and rhythms of prose and poetry but also about the different ways they could express the same ideas. Despite initial trepidation about the assignment, most students proudly published their poems in an electronic portfolio at semester's end, thus sharing their prose and poetry with family, friends, and other audiences who found their sites online. For instance, Jacqueline wrote, "When I sat down to begin writing this assignment I was horrified." Later she described her own choices: "By mentioning specific writing styles and rules in my poem I conveyed to the reader what this course taught. Since this is an online course, I decided to describe what that meant to the student by describing the resources used in the class."

Maria wrote her poem about the experience of writing her research paper and overcoming writer's block (Figure 9.1). Taking advantage of the option to present her poem and reflective essay as a slide show or Web site, she picked a PowerPoint background and graphic that she felt complemented her thinking. In her accompanying reflective essay, Maria cited both the processes that guided her writing of the poem and reflection and the visual design principles she had learned from our textbook, John Trimbur's *The Call to Write*. The first slide of her reflection reminisces about elementary school poetry assignments and relates that memory to the challenge of the current assignment (Figure 9.2).

Another student, Adam, had experience with Web construction and was also a musician; he presented his poem on a Web site that included music he composed as an accompaniment (Figure 9.3). In the reflective essay that this project required along with an original poem, Adam wrote, "I also composed a simple three-chord sea song to further enhance this poetry project. I actually surprised myself—I did not think I would be able to write a poem." Adam's multimedia poetry project is one of several course compositions he references as links in his final course Webfolio (Figure 9.4).

## III. A Story by Kate: E-Writing in Introductory Literature Class

Wild geese have been flying over the upper Mississippi River for weeks now. They began in early August, startling me. "It's too

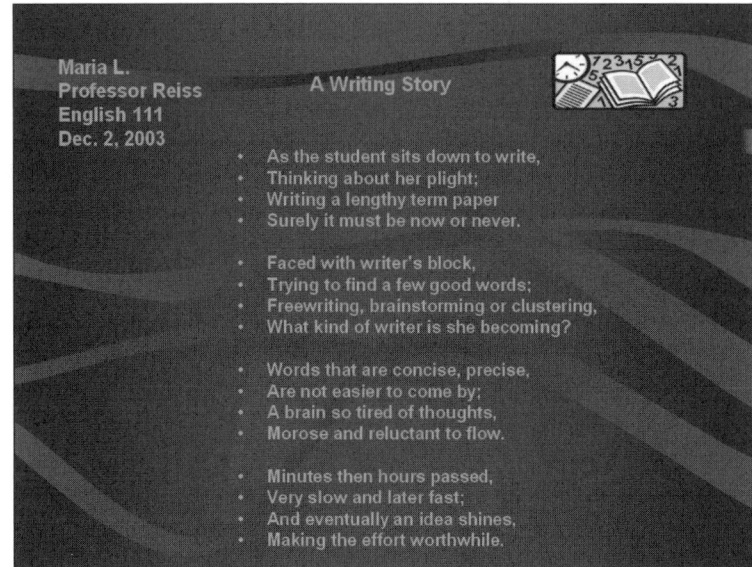

FIGURE 9.1. Maria's poem: "A Writing Story."

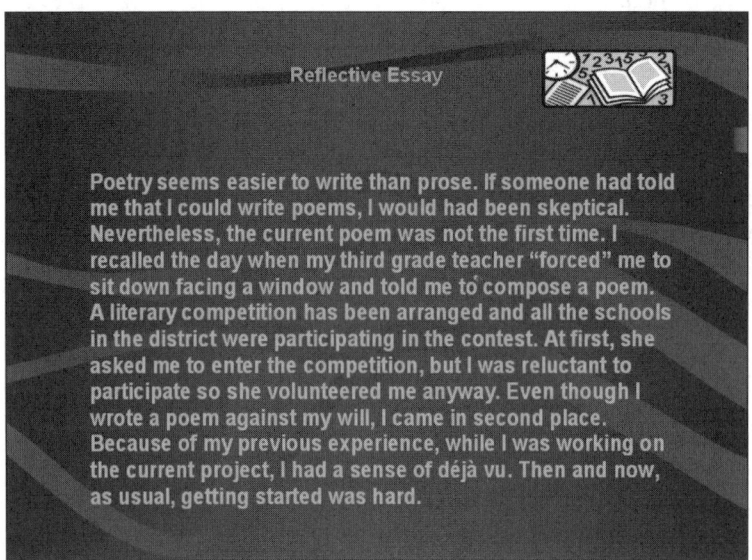

FIGURE 9.2. Maria's poetry reflection.

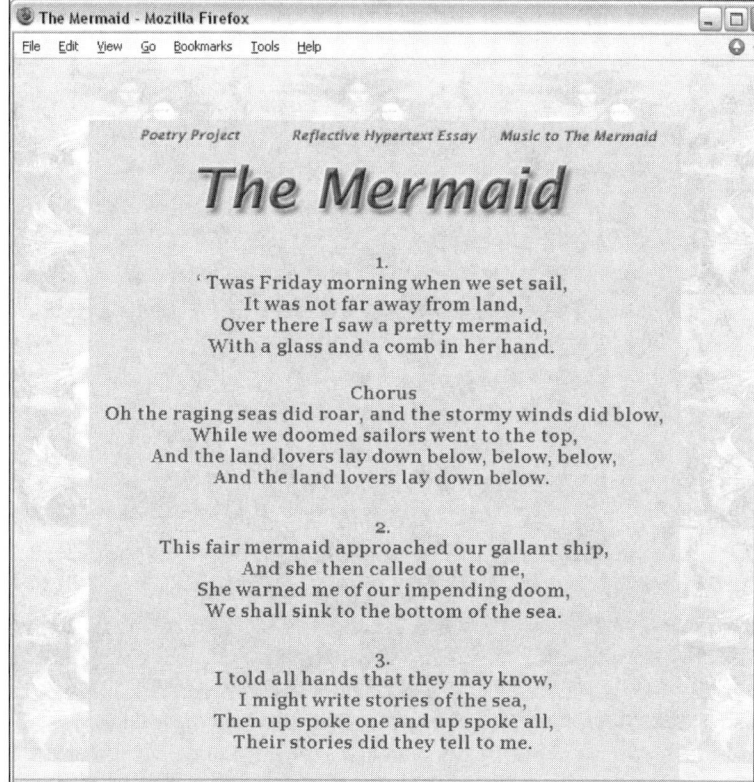

FIGURE 9.3. *Adam's poem on his Web page.*

early to go south," I thought to myself. Sipping coffee one morning on our front deck overlooking the shore, however, I realized they were flying too low and landing too quickly to be on the Big Trip. With months to go before ice sheaths the river in a frozen membrane, my feathered neighbors were only practicing, my colleague in the Biology Department assured me. Daily they work up muscle, take turns leading at the apex of their flight triangle, and train the young to fly in formation. Occasionally, I see one knock into another right in midair, only to right itself and continue flying. By October, I'm sure, they'll have it right.

The practices of writing and reading I coax in literature classes when we use e-technologies remind me of these geese learning to fly in formation. As teacher, I might take the lead, but by no

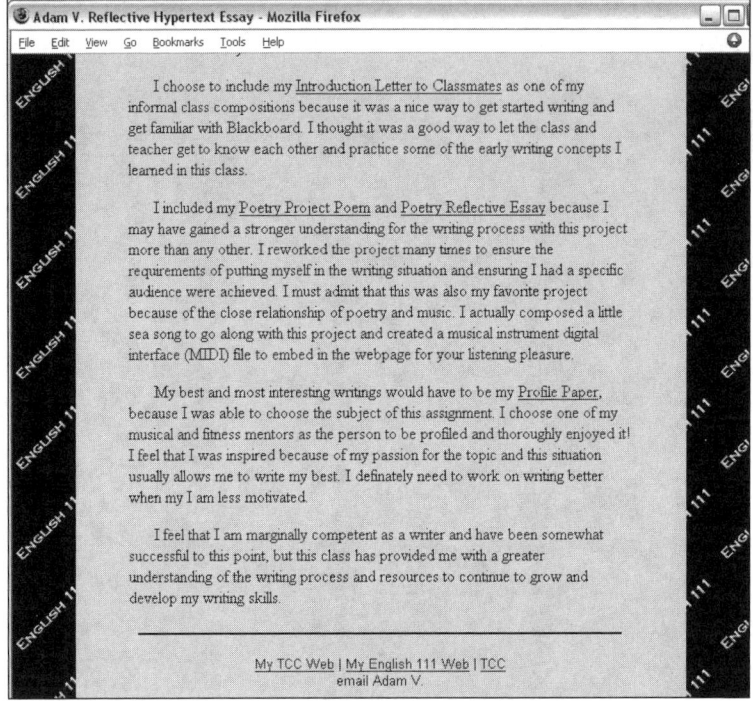

FIGURE 9.4. *Adam's reflective hypertext essay: selected hyperlinks.*

means do I keep it the entire time. It's exhausting to do so and limited—so much depends upon a single mind in such cases. Online technologies allow me to drop out of the lead of the V so that students may take over. Too, these technologies assist our gosling students in taking wing.

Approaches to Literature is an introductory course required in the General Education Program at Clarke College where I teach. Outcomes include that students be able to define and use terms and compose papers attending to the tenets of writing about literature. My English colleagues and I also hope that students who encounter interpretation of texts on a college level initially through this class will become so hooked that, regardless of academic major or career, they will be life-long readers of literature. I find that e-journals, Web site discussions, chat rooms, and WebCT lure students into literary study in ways that traditional methods do not—particularly with these students new to the field.

Although textual reference and citation, as well as reasoning and substantiation, are basic to writing about literature, they often are the most difficult skills for students to acquire. Prior to using e-technologies, I would remind students, "Remember to back up what you say," "Offer proof of your assertions from the text," and, every literature teacher's favorite, *"Use textual reference!"* During two decades of teaching, however, I found that regardless of how many workshops, exercises, and other training sessions I facilitated in the classroom, the results by the end of the semester were disappointing. Precious few students rooted their written interpretations of text in the text itself, and I felt like tossing my teaching awards out the office window.

Because I was also teaching writing and composition in a computer-assisted classroom, I decided to explore hands-on computer mediation in my literature classes as well—particularly to reinforce what had become my own personal nemesis as a teacher, student use of textual reference. Over time, I developed a three-tier approach using e-mail and chat rooms/discussion boards/collaborative writing software like Daedalus and WebCT (depending on what is available).

In the first tier, students in small groups consider a list of characters/personas/narrators from their assigned readings. Within their e-discussion group, they negotiate who will take the role of which characters. In this initial assignment, students create character sketches for their partners referring to what a character did, said, or thought in the text. Student partners respond to at least two other "characters" with questions, disagreement, or reiteration. My directions require them to quote or paraphrase from the text when doing so.

Although I'd assigned students to write character summaries before, only when they enter e-groups and have a real audience other than the teacher do they attend to using textual reference. Because peers in discussion press them for facts, they perceive more reason to deliver the goods. At this point, we're only lining up for the eventual flight formation.

In the second tier, students brainstorm face to face in the classroom, imagining modern events that might engage literary characters were they able to rise off the printed page and speak. Computers-at-the-ready offer speedy access to the *New York*

*Times*, *World Press*, and numerous other online publications providing background facts and details. With this list of contemporary issues, students return to e-discussion with group members. This time, however, students assume character roles with one another, speaking *as* their character in first person. For example, Tim O'Brien's narrator in "The Rainy River" might evaluate America's involvement in Iraq, or Elena in Judith Ortiz Cofer's "American History" might voice opinions about the English Reaffirmation Act making its way through state legislatures. When other "characters" ask questions or press for reasons, students quickly resort to additional textual reference and to more adroitly using their research findings.

As students become more familiar with grounding interpretation in texts, so, too, do they develop more self-assurance in positing such interpretations. They begin the semester offering unfounded, thin first impressions of the moral type: "What I got out of the story was how everyone can be a winner if only she works hard." A few weeks into a term using e-strategies for interpreting literature, however, they search for answers within literary passages rather than through gut reaction alone. Instead they write, "The character's desperation is revealed as she pulls out a gun and heads for the street," or "The persona is lonely because she says that she's at peace only when her lover is present (l. 12); we discover in the last stanza that he died years earlier." Too, students are attracted by what they see as "play," that is, the taking on of roles. Some comment, "We were never allowed to use first person in high school," and "I'm not allowed to be creative in writing academic papers in other classes." By now, some students are moving closer to the apex of our flight, nearly ready for leading the V.

The third tier of e-discussions invites student characters to write to other characters in their group about subsequently read pieces of literature. Within one e-group, for example, Frankie (*A Member of the Wedding*), Minnie Wright ("Trifles"), Jane ("The Yellow Wallpaper"), and Miranda ("The Grave") discuss how Virginia Woolf's feminist philosophy ("Professions of Women") could have made a difference in their own lives.

Beyond this three-tier set of exercises, students in my classes also engage in e-liaisons with students in like classes elsewhere in the country, meeting by e-mail or in chat rooms to discuss shared assigned readings. If these partnerships work well, we move on to collaborative writing assignments. Given that current college students prefer to talk by instant messenger rather than by phone, such interactions relate to their culture of communication and make the learning environment more user-friendly.

Some years, my literature students have also engaged more actively in the milieu surrounding a piece of literature thanks to e-technologies. For example, reading literature thematically arranged as Peace and War ("The Things They Carried," "Anniversary," "Death of the Ball Turret Gunner," etc.), students researched Web sites about Vietnam vets, peace activism, and post-traumatic stress disorder. E-mailing contacts listed on those sites, students corresponded via e-mail with vets, pacifists, and health practitioners in order to augment their understanding of the literature.

Although some scholars may scoff at this wild child e-play with literary art, students accomplish at least three outcomes: (1) they attend to cultural milieu and the fictional world created within the text; (2) they stretch beyond seeing a work as a single compartmentalized composition and thus are more apt to transfer learning from piece to piece; (3) they experience character and story as living art that commands their involved "ah-ha!" rather than their bored "oh-no."

Through e-interactions, students constantly challenge one another: "I don't agree" and "Where'd you get that idea?" Because discussions occur online rather than in the ether of the classroom, they are able to return to one another's challenges and consider them more carefully as well as to use them as incentive to go back to the text and hunt for credible evidence underpinning their assertions. In face-to-face classroom discussion, some students are reluctant to participate, while their more vocally gifted classmates monopolize group work. Online, however, with my stipulations that "Everyone must write at least two full screens" or "Each group member must respond to at least two other group members" (and copy entries to me), participation approaches 100 percent. Furthermore, no one talks over another or interrupts.

Once students become comfortable with attending closely to the text and assembling textual clues into credible interpretations, I instruct them in more formal writing about literature. Their attempts are far more successful than student achievement before moving into the computer classroom, and with good reason. They move solidly and confidently into taking the lead in the formation and trading it off with one another.

Students who cross the thresholds of our classrooms now are significantly different in their orientation to literacy than even their older siblings. Within my own family, for example, our oldest four children learned to read off the printed page as we spread books across our laps and pointed at brightly-colored images of dogs, trees, and seascapes. Then came Andrew in 1988. Alongside learning the alphabet, he learned point-and-click on the Macintosh Performa. His response to printed material is vastly different than that of his older siblings. While they delight in stretching out on the couch with a good book, he grows fidgety sitting for long with only a book for company. He asks, "When's the DVD or hypertext version coming out?" But give him a mouse and a CPU, and his focus sharpens as he engages with text juxtaposed by screen. He becomes talkative, animated, connected.

In *Connecting Generations: The Sourcebook for a New Workplace*, Claire Raines identifies that such millennial students prefer to work collaboratively and with technology, that they enjoy challenges but want them to be fun. There is little doubt that Andrew is far from being one of a kind when it comes to literacy. He is, instead, the profile of our current and future students, often called part of the Nintendo Generation, the Digital Generation, and the Internet Generation.

## IV. Donna's and Art's International Opportunities for Composing about Literature Online: Crossing Geographical, Institutional, and Intellectual Boundaries

In the spring of 2004, Donna and Art collaborated with Magnus Gustafsson of Chalmers Lindholmen University College in Gothenburg, Sweden, to develop an online discussion of English translations of Swedish poetry (see Gustafsson, Reiss and Young).

Students taking first-year composition at Tidewater Community College, Victorian Literature at Clemson University, and Fiction for Engineers at Chalmers Lindholmen University College discussed in long online letters using a Web discussion board the language of these poems and the ways that readers' understanding of literary works is affected by their responses to individual words and phrases as well as the rhythms in English and Swedish of Tomas Tranströmer's poems. By writing about the poems in English, students in all three classes gained insight into the way their cultural experiences and understanding of literal and figurative meanings of words affected their understanding of the poems. Students discussed the poems and translations in groups of nine or ten.

Although only one of these classes was a writing course, all three groups of students were attentive to their own writing, to the audiences reading their prose, and to the writing choices of poets and translators.

Here are excerpts from one group's discussion of Tranströmer's poem "Breathing Room: July." Wayne from Tidewater noticed immediately that each translation created a different reading experience.

> The multiple translations of this poem definitely changed the imagery that the original poem had. . . . Another example can be found in line ten of the poem. The last word of the phrase in May Swenson's translation is "lights," in Robert Fulton's translation is "straits," and in Robert Bly's translation is "bays." The three words are not synonymous and give a completely different description by that one word change in the three translations. The distinctions amongst the translations can confuse and mislead the reader into directions the poem wasn't intended to "take" the reader.

Adrian, from Chalmers and fluent in Swedish, wrote that all of the translators had changed the tone of the poem, which he perceived as calm and peaceful, with one simple word choice.

> Something that disturbs me in all of the translations is the use of the word moth as a translation to *nattfjäril*. Maybe there is no such word as "night butterfly" in English, but I think that would give a more accurate translation in aspect to the overall mood of

the poem. I don't know how you react, but I definitely don't get a pleasant image on my retina when I read the words "crawl like huge moths."

Karen from Clemson in South Carolina picked up the threads begun in Virginia and Gothenburg:

> Dear Online Classmates, I have to agree with Wayne that even slightly different word choices in translation (or in the original for that matter) can confuse and mislead the reader. . . . I especially appreciated the letter from Adrian Sparrenborn; I, too, felt the "harmony" between the man lying under the branches and the branches/tree/world. . . . I also felt the Robert Bly translation was a little jarring, but I can't explain why. I especially appreciate the reference to the "night butterfly." There is no similar word in English; unfortunately, "moth" doesn't have quite the same poetic softness and luminary quality. The night butterfly imagery, especially coupled with "hela natten / entire night," changes the whole feel of the last stanza.

This sequence of letters demonstrates that writing to each other online fostered the very actions we encourage from writing and literature students: close attention to diction and awareness of audience. References by name to other students' posts are a clear indication that these online letters are being read and taken seriously.

Continuing the online conversation, Denise from Tidewater used Robert Bly's translation, the one Karen described as "jarring," to produce what to the others was a surprising and "jarring" interpretation, since most students saw the mood of the poem as peaceful or laid-back.

> Dear Fellow Poetry Students . . . The first individual seems to be a "busy body" who even when relaxed in body, his mind "branches out in thousands of tiny branches". Seemingly, spreading himself so thin that he doesn't even realize that he has been shot right past life like a "catapult that hurls forward in slow motion."
>
> The second man is gazing out of the water in a world of his own. He is a man with the weight of the world on his shoulders. He grows older by the minute like the docks that he stands on, "They have silver-gray posts and boulders in their gut." The worry

ages him faster than necessary. The line "The dazzling light drives straight in" demonstrated that he is so engulfed in his worries that even the brightest light cannot penetrate his thought. He is lost in the ebb and tide of his life forgetting to actually live for the day.
　　The third man "spends the whole day in an open boat moving over the luminous bays" is living an image of relaxation and peace. However, in this illusion he simply falls asleep and lets life pass him by. He hides behind the walls of his home, "inside the shade of his blue lamp" and the events of his life "crawl like huge moths over the globe".

Then from Sweden, Sandra wrote:

As for "Breathing Space July" I think it was very exciting to read Denise's interpretation of it based on the translation by Robert Bly. I always found that one to be the harshest of them all and consequently the one furthest from how I perceived the original but Denise's letter made me realise why. That he uses "The man who" makes it into three stories about three different men, and with the use of several distressing words and phrases he makes them restless and unhappy.
　　"Branches out into. . . ." results in a feeling of someone splitting his attention, desperately trying to keep track of everything, whereas "rills out. . . ." creates a picture of someone floating into the tree and becoming a part of it in a sense. . . . And lets not forget the disaster with the moths—as Adrian said, it really is a shame that you don't have a word like "night butterfly". Maybe one would simply have to pick an entirely different insect that could communicate the same feeling—perhaps firefly is better. What does that convey to you?
　　My impression on reading the Swedish version is that of the forever longed for Swedish summer. That time of the year when life seems to slow down and offer a chance to live and breath. I also read into it the longing to return to nature. To lie beneath the trees, to stand by the lake, to sail all night—all these things represent freedom to me. It is funny to see how Bly seems to have interpreted it as more or less the opposite. I think it goes to show how much power the reader still has. I think Wayne is right in saying that it is best to read a poem in it's original format, at least if you want to be sure you have read what the poet intended, but unfortunately that isn't possible very often.

Adrian also reevaluates his interpretation, and thanks to Denise and Sandra, he suggests a fuller understanding of his reading experience and a better understanding of Robert Bly's translation and interpretation—albeit not an interpretation he finally endorses.

> Dear Electronic Classmates. . . . I found it very interesting to read Denise's interpretation of "Breathing Room: July", which differed quite much from my own. When I think back on my original perspective on the poem I thought more of the feeling that it conveyed to me, rather than searching for a more specific meaning in the words. Denise thinks of the first individual as a "'busy body' who doesn't even realize that he has been shot right past life". This is not how I imagined it, but this interpretation gives a completely new (and quite interesting, if I might add) interpretation of the poem, one that tells us not to waste our lives and enjoy every day we are alive. However, I'm not sure if that is the meaning the writer wanted to convey to us. Now that I have read the poem again, I think the writer wanted to say that we should take a break from our hectic lives and take the time to lie under the trees or sit by the docks and relax. The title "Andrum: Juli / Breathing Room: July" also seems to hint that one should take a breather.
>
> As a few people already have I must also agree with Wayne on the translation subject. I think that Wayne makes a very good point when he writes: "A translation can change everything about the original poem". This is something that we have all experienced from the various translations of "Andrum: Juli".

Karen then described a "cultural" reading that might have influenced the different ways readers in Sweden and readers in the southern United States were experiencing the poem.

> I wanted to comment on the Breathing Room: July comments. Thank you especially to Cheryl and Sandra for your references to slowing down and basking. I failed to see that when I initially read the interpretations. Sandra's remarks about the "forever longed for Swedish summer" helped put it in perspective. With the very mild winters and the summer heat and humidity we have here in South Carolina (and in tidewater Virginia as well), I failed to see the appeal that July would have in Sweden. For those of us that don't like the oppressive heat, "July" hardly evokes a time when we could slow down and breath easy. Only serves to illustrate that not only the author's context, but the reader's context, will affect the interpretation of a work.

These excerpts from a much longer epistolary conversation that took place over two weeks in spring 2004 demonstrate an interactive critical engagement with literature and with diverse readers of literature that cannot be reproduced in a traditional classroom. The Internet enabled our students to cross geographical and intellectual boundaries and to write insightfully, collaboratively, and effectively for engaged readers who take their words and thoughts seriously. Although students were assigned deadlines for their responses to the poems and each other, asynchronicity allowed them to read and write in their own time and in their own time zones. In this "new community of critical and creative discourse" (Moulthrop and Kaplan 8), our students have learned about writing, reading, literature, translation, interpretation, technology, and each other.

Not to be underestimated in projects like this one is the value of collaboration among colleagues working in different institutions, states, and countries. All assignment design, like the students' letters, was asynchronous, using e-mail to discuss topics and approaches that would be sensitive to their varied experience writing about literature, writing online, and writing in English. All three professors ended the assignment with enthusiasm for the ways in which students embraced this activity.

## V. Communication Technologies and the Teaching of English

As teachers of hybrid and totally online classes in both writing and literature, we recommend a variety of types of electronic communication that can support the confluence of composition and literature, two areas of instruction that focus on language and its variety for expression. Using chat and instant messaging, students can write rapidly their personal, informal responses to literary works and can participate in quick conversation with other readers. These preliminary responses are part of a process that leads to and becomes the drafting of a more formal and public commentary. Using e-mail and discussion boards, they can write more reflectively, taking time to construct and edit their words more carefully as they engage in asynchronous dialogue with others, including perhaps the authors of the very works on their contemporary literature reading lists. Instead of using writing in support of the study of literature or literature in support of learning how to write critically, online communication supports a fluid purpose that includes these approaches but focuses more on the middle ground of written conversation about literature and the production of literature as well as the consumption of literature. For specific suggestions about designing assignments, see our appendix, "Ten Tips for Generating Engaged Online Discussions about Literature."

Students write literature as well as read and study it, and they publish their informal and formal writing in platforms that demonstrate differences in genre and rhetorical context: e-mail or class discussion boards as less formal publications and Web magazines or electronic portfolios as more formal. Writing in these online environments is a particularly effective way to achieve the goal of transformative learning encouraged in *Building Learning Communities in Cyberspace* by Rena M. Palloff and Keith Pratt. Crediting Jack Mezirow for the term, Palloff and Pratt define *transformative learning* as "based on reflection and on the interpretation of the experience, ideas, and assumptions gained through prior learning" (129). Such collaborative, participatory learning that incorporates the past, present, and future experiences of the writer in response to texts canonized as literary or not classified as literary is a hallmark of compositions in online environments.

By writing, students in computer-mediated environments share more explicitly in the world of literature as authors, editors, and critics with audiences receptive to their efforts. Lines between composition, literature, and creative writing blur. After all, what *is* literature anymore, anyway? Twirling, whirling words in electronic poetry? Labyrinthine links in hypertext fiction? Who writes and who reads these new literary forms? Poets and technologists collaborate: as a result, poets learn to manipulate language in cyberspace, and techies play with visual metaphors. Recollect the shaped poems of George Herbert, the illustrated poems of William Blake, the paper Emily Dickinson folded to encase her poems, and the footnotes of T. S. Eliot as a precursor of hypertext literature and scholarship. The technologies of literature and publication, like the technologies of writing, have changed and will change. Our students need to be prepared to expect such changes and take full advantage of them and to be conversant with multiple literacies in reading, composing, and designing.

Electronic communication technologies challenge us even more than print did to ask where to draw the lines between literature and not-literature. When does an essay become creative nonfiction? How "creative" must a writer be with the facts before we have to call the work fiction rather than essay? When we consider writings by Tom Wolfe like *The Right Stuff* or Truman Capote's *In Cold Blood*, books rooted in documented fact yet obviously created when it comes to many conversations and contexts, we see a blurring. This postmodern blurring offers a response to colleagues who suggest that what students do in our literature classrooms fails to adhere to the practice of solid literary study or that the poems, plays, slide shows, animations, and drawings composed by our writing and literature students are not really interpretations, arguments, or valid critical and creative responses to experiences with literature in social context.

And not by words alone does technology help us bridge composition and literary studies—writing and reading. We admire the illuminated manuscripts of the Middle Ages but until recently have not encouraged our students to visually illuminate their academic prose. As early as 1988, in "Word and Image" John Ruszkiewicz anticipated the ease with which our students can explore the rhetoric of the visual image along with the verbal image, expressing their understanding of literary texts in multiple modes and media and thus blurring verbal and visual literacy in the effective rhetorical presentation.

> Of course, we have for a very long time lived in a world of images and a world where images combine comfortably with words. But never before have we faced the prospect of every writer having the ability to illustrate his or her thoughts almost effortlessly. What I hope we can imagine is the way that the technology can enable us to live in a more integrated world of imagination, to explore a dialectic where the literary image of metaphor is set in

vibration against what Berthoff (1981) describes as "picturable analogies." (Ruszkiewicz 7)

Although the ways to incorporate images and media into basic word-processed papers, slide shows, and Web sites have been made easier every year, the advice of Ruszkiewicz has not caught up with most first-year composition or undergraduate literature curricula and teaching. Perhaps textbook publishers are helping to lead the way with their multimedia companion Web sites and with new editions of textbooks that include a variety of visual elements such as color-coded boxes for visual coherence and photographs, drawings, and facsimiles of manuscripts. Traditional handbooks and composition textbooks now incorporate sections on visual rhetoric, treat format as presentation and design, and show students how to incorporate visuals to enhance the written word. Such recent textbooks as *Seeing and Writing* by Donald McQuade and Christina McQuade and *Picturing Texts* by Lester Faigley, Diana George, Anna Palchik, and Cynthia Selfe foreground critical response to visual images as well as composing about media and composing media.

With communication technologies, student authors can be published for audiences small (a class discussion list) or large (the World Wide Web). Many contemporary writers of fiction and poetry have Web sites; many have Weblogs or blogs. Students, too, can compose for and publish with these new technologies. Few students were able to do so when books were the primary publishing technology. Self-publication has returned to respectability with the advent of the Internet, and like Walt Whitman, Thomas Paine, Benjamin Franklin, and Elizabeth Barrett Browning, students are able to produce and disseminate their own compositions. Unlike those more famous authors of the past, who had to pay for paper, ink, printing, and distribution, often by hand delivery to willing shopkeepers or by passing out leaflets on street corners, our students can publish to the entire world with a few clicks, using the computer technologies increasingly available in their classrooms, libraries, and homes. To assume a postmodern turn, technology often allows authorship to be shared, dialogic, and multifarious.

Students are not likely to return to composing or reading literature that they perceived as dull, unilateral, and inaccessible once they cross the stage, signed diplomas in hand. Unlike more traditionally educated generations who might read something, "Because it's good for me," our students will not go so gently into that good night. The new communities we create through e-technologies make students feel more welcome in literary studies and invite them to become insiders rather than emphasizing their amateur status. If there's hope that students in our English classes will one day stroll bookstore aisles, eager for the latest offerings, and willingly write letters to the editor or volunteer to research and report on findings in the workplace, we are convinced it begins in college with learning literary interpretation and writing as fascinating, lively, interactive activities. Only then will students find, as Mary Oliver suggests, that

> the world offers itself to your imagination
> calls to you like the wild geese, harsh and exciting—
> over and over announcing your place
> in the family of things.

## Appendix: Ten Tips for Generating Engaged Online Discussions about Literature

In electronic environments, responses to literary works and to critiques of literary works are dialogic rather than solitary and foster ongoing written conversations among readings and readers. To encourage flexible assignment design for active engagement in online class discussions, these suggestions are necessarily general and should be revised to fit the delivery method (face-to-face classes with some electronic discussions, for example, or totally online classes), the type of electronic communication (e-mail list, discussion board, or Weblog, for instance), and the course content and emphasis.

1. Carefully integrate electronic discussions into course goals, not as add-on assignments. Participation should be mandatory, and on-time participation is crucial to establishing a conversational, academic exchange.

2. Give students credit but not necessarily grades for prompt, engaged participation. Without intervening in the students' dis-

cussion, you may provide feedback in an e-mail or discussion board message or in person to the entire class mentioning insightful ideas generated by the discussion and encouraging further reading, thinking, and conversation.

3. Offer precise directions with clear expectations: scope, approach, tone (courteous and respectful of various viewpoints), length (minimum and maximum—we recommend 250–350 words), diction (such as "edited conversational"), form or genre (letter or memo or report). You may want to provide a model of a good post.

4. Consider integrating Internet research, in which students include relevant Web addresses as active links in their messages to each other—for example, a Web page from the Blake Archive or a Pre-Raphaelite painting from the Victorian Web. When appropriate, encourage students to incorporate visual images and multimedia.

5. In your guidelines for the discussion, encourage explanations, examples, questions, speculations, alternative viewpoints, and connections to personal experience.

6. Develop topics and assignments that will elicit engagement with the literature as well as the answers and responses you seek. Sometimes you'll want to be quite specific about topics and approaches; sometimes you'll want a more open-ended assignment, allowing the first person who posts to determine the topic and approach.

7. Encourage or require students to quote from the literary texts and from their classmates' posts when they respond to each other within groups and when they write their tests or papers on the topics they discussed online.

8. Have students include their own and one or more classmates' posts in their final course portfolios along with reflection on what was learned from the e-discussion process.

9. Assign small groups—for example, five to seven students—who read and respond to each other. Every group's posts should be available to the whole class, but students need only read their own group's writing.

10. Develop a heuristic—for example, here's an adaptable approach that can be made more fluid or more directive.

    a. First post: Respond to the reading or assigned topic with specific reference to the reading. Include a brief summary, select a specific focus or point, develop that point with explanations and examples, and invite commentary from classmates about a particular concern, not the whole post, ending with an invitation or question.

b. Second post: Read all the posts in your group and then respond to the first post of a classmate who has not yet received a reply. Include specific reference to the main idea of the classmate's post and to the assigned reading or topic, expand on the classmate's ideas with additional information or ideas or offer an alternative viewpoint on the topic and support your position with references to the reading or posts by other group members. Perhaps raise questions and speculate further on the topic.

c. Third post: Respond to the person who answered your first post with appreciation for their response and an explanation of ways their message increased your own understanding or stimulated your thinking. Remember your audience is a specific individual plus your whole class.

d. Additional post: Summarize all the messages from your group and analyze for primary points, similarities and differences, and other observations about the group's thinking.

e. Additional post: For a subsequent post, respond to one or more classmates from a different group than the one in which you have been participating.

f. If the class meets face to face, gather the writing group to discuss the issues in person and report orally to the class as a whole.

## Works Cited

Adam's Webfolio. "For Students" and "Sample Student Webfolios" links. *Webfolio Project* by Donna Reiss. Modified 30 July 2005. http://wordsworth2.net/webfolio/ (accessed 10 October 2005).

Cisneros, Sandra. "My Wicked Wicked Ways." *My Wicked Wicked Ways*. New York: Knopf, 1992.

Faigley, Lester, Diana George, Anna Palchik, and Cynthia Selfe. *Picturing Texts*. New York: Norton, 2004.

Fischer, Katherine, and Donna Reiss. *Portraits in Poetry—Our Wicked Ways*. Tidewater Community College and Clarke College Spring 1997 Collaborative Reading and Writing Project. Modified 3 November 2004. http://wordsworth2.net/projects/wickedways (accessed 10 October 2005).

Gustafsson, Magnus, Donna Reiss, and Art Young. *Cross-Cultural Collaborations among Swedish and American Students*. Modified 11 June 2005. http://www.wordsworth2.net/projects/crosscultural collabs (accessed 10 October 2005).

Lanham, Richard A. *The Electronic Word: Democracy, Technology, and the Arts*. Chicago: U of Chicago P, 1993.

McQuade, Donald, and Christina McQuade. *Seeing and Writing*. Boston: Bedford, 2000.

Moulthrop, Stuart, and Nancy Kaplan. "Something to Imagine: Literature, Composition, and Interactive Fiction." *Computers and Composition* 9.1 (1991): 7–23. http://www.hu.mtu.edu/%7Ecandc/archives/v9/9_1_html/9_1_1_Moulthrop.html (accessed 10 October 2005).

Oliver, Mary. "Wild Geese." *New and Selected Poems: Vol. I*. New York: Beacon Press, 2004.

Palloff, Rena M., and Keith Pratt. *Building Learning Communities in Cyberspace: Effective Strategies for the Online Classroom*. San Francisco: Jossey-Bass, 1999.

Raines, Claire. *Connecting Generations: The Sourcebook for a New Workplace*. Menlo Park, CA: Crisp, 2003.

Ruszkiewicz, John. "Word and Image." *Computers and Composition* 5.3 (August 1988): 9–15. http://www.hu.mtu.edu/%7Ecandc/archives/v5/5_3_html/5_3_1_Ruszkiewicz.html (accessed 10 October 2005).

Trimbur, John. *The Call To Write*. 2nd ed. New York: Longman, 2002.

CHAPTER TEN

# Composing English 102: Reframing Students' Lives through Literature

EDITH M. BAKER
*Bradley University*

As we have seen from the diversity of positions in the chapters of this book, omnipresent problems of first-year composition are what texts to teach—even whether any texts should be studied—and how much instruction in literature and/or rhetorical strategies should be incorporated. Nevertheless, instructors who incorporate imaginative literature in college-level composition classes promote textual analysis, sensitivity to language matters, and attention to rhetorical strategies, skills needed throughout students' college careers. Students are also invited to move from insular concerns to an understanding of worlds beyond their lives and classrooms. Literature can thus play a pivotal role in the composition classroom, teaching students skills useful not only for their college careers but also for becoming astute citizens of a global world, which Dominic DelliCarpini asserts is a major purpose of composition. As I present arguments for the inclusion of literature in first-year composition (FYC), I am grounding my teaching strategies in classroom applications, tested at a rural community college in northern Arizona and a regional, private university in northwestern Illinois.

I also explain how an instructor can use literature to develop strategies to stimulate students' critical thinking abilities and to challenge the "culture of excellence," which author Bill Readings fears is invading our universities. As instructors of FYC we attempt to teach students not only how to consume texts but also how to acquire "the living unity of knowledge, the understanding of the place of knowledge in the world" (Readings 76). Such knowledge cannot be measured; it is a thinking process that is impossible to limit. Because Readings calls "Thought" "nonproductive labor" (175), he reminds us of its rarity in many institutions of higher education: as faculty we are challenged "not how to turn an institution into a haven for thought but how to think in an institution whose development tends to make Thought more and more difficult, less and less necessary" (175). Indeed, the challenge to promote Thought is before us as faculty who teach the citizens of tomorrow. Our very habits of mind, not to mention our attempts to spark students' thinking, are at stake.

We can begin with a study of imaginative literature and use it to stimulate learning. To teach students the thinking skills necessary to critique dominant power structures, as well as the disciplines within the university—not to mention an academic culture that might privilege "excellence" over genuine thinking and learning—is certainly to create a critical thinker. Such a thinker might then challenge Elizabeth Flynn's assumption in "Composing as a Woman." She begins with a premise about male and female narratives of the constructed self. When students write narratives about their lives, they often produce literature. When students can reframe the experiences of their lives, they gain perspective and distance. An instructor can always suggest strategies to turn narratives into literature, such as plot, motivation, character development, even thematic hints.

Flynn also posits the theory that "men's narratives stress individuation rather than connection," whereas "the narratives of female students are stories of interaction, of connection, or of frustrated connection"; narratives of male students are "stories of achievement, of separation, or of frustrated achievement" (Flynn 428). Our questioning student might note that not all distinctions between gendered narratives follow that precise "either/or," single narrative pattern. Some freshmen students, both male and female, may create personal narratives of both individuation and connection. To train students to recognize dominant patterns, however, will aid them in understanding other narratives they encounter. In Bill Readings's terms, students have learned "Thought" and utilized the process of thinking in understanding their past and present lives. As students turn their narratives into literature, they also are reading literature about other characters with similar experiences. The iterative process reinforces the thinking and learning.

To move students from self-centered positions and to an understanding of other narratives is certainly a goal of freshman composition. In *The University in Ruins*, Readings confirms a widely accepted tenet of acquisition of knowledge as a "*process rather than the acquisition of knowledge as a product*" (67; original emphasis). The methods by which we develop critical thinkers in FYC vary significantly. Just as current pedagogy blurs distinctions of gender constructions and no longer assumes "male and female" narratives have only one pattern, so freshman composition in the new millennium has expanded to include cultural studies, writing across the curriculum, and study of belles lettres, to name just a few approaches. Our definition of *literature* in this new millennium has at the same time expanded to include more than established, canonical cultural artifacts and belles lettres.

In 1812, the *OED* definition of *literature* was "the body of writings produced in a particular country or period or in the world in general"—especially as "applied to writing which has claim to consideration on the ground of beauty of form or emotional effect" (qtd. in Horner, 4). More recent *OED* definitions have narrowed to include "acquaintance with 'letters' of books; polite or humane learning" (qtd. in Harrington 261, footnote 2). How did the "ground of beauty of form or emotional effect" become "polite or humane learning"? Certainly a cultural overlay was developing in the nineteenth century, coincident with Matthew Arnold's conception of education as illuminating ideas for people through teaching specific books, which would dispel darkness and ignorance. Lists of books taught in some curricula today are evidence of this approach, such as Bloom's lists of important concepts and authors.

Many FYC instructors today have studied imaginative literature and are knowledgeable about concepts such as "ground of beauty" and "emotional effect." They are able to discuss such matters as unity, theme(s), catharsis, connotation, and rhetorical stances in composed works. Many of us might also concede that a great number of printed materials, from printed material on the Internet to an art gallery showing of mixed media (poetry and visual art combined) often achieve "emotional effects." Teaching students not only to decipher the effects, but also to find and perhaps challenge the claims, is certainly another purpose of a FYC class, which may incorporate multiple forms of literature on its way to teaching students to be astute thinkers.

In my experience of thirty years of teaching at five different institutions, I have noted that students arrive at a university with some verities, but most students are eager to embrace and confront the study of new ideas, disciplines, and cultures. By reading imaginative literature, students often achieve insight into the self they are making in the present and learn the rhetorical power of the construction of future selves. Ultimately, they leave behind the personal nature of constructing their own narratives (reframed in literature) and move into a rhetorical understanding of worlds beyond their ethnocentric concerns. One example of teaching students to achieve a broader perspective is the yearlong course LITCOMP, which Wayne Booth and his colleagues taught at the University of Chicago in the early 1980s. He developed the approach in a first-year course: "The Making of Constitutions" (Booth 76). Students and faculty also explored other topics, such as the French Revolution, from multiple perspectives, teaching students that many angles (and voices) about an experience exist (77–80). By reading and comparing primary documents and texts from learned authorities, students thus learned to challenge a singular interpretation of material. Students used a range of texts as the primary means of understanding multiple perspectives. Today, the approach of required "core courses" at institutions such as Harvard and the University of Chicago is based upon this philosophy of analyzing and understanding multiple perspectives about a singular topic or series of events. Faculty members from across the disciplines often teach seminar courses in their areas of expertise.

A literature-based FYC course, then, can become a site where students are exposed to worlds beyond their own. Students gain knowledge of multiple approaches to a single topic. Literature can also be a catalyst to help students understand how those encounters are framed in writing; composition thus allows students to reinvent not only themselves, but also metaphors and narratives of their lives. As students understand themselves, they may gain new perspectives. Students read literature and write narratives about themselves, which may be shaped into literature with a beginning, middle, end, character development, and plot motivation. An example explains this process. In the early 1990s, a student in my English 102 class at Yavapai College in Arizona both read and wrote her way into the future, after an analysis of "The Yellow Wallpaper" by Charlotte Perkins Gilman. A doctor's wife in my FYC class, whom I will call Marilyn, made the observation that the husband John in "The Yellow Wallpaper" treated the narrator of the short story in the same patronizing manner as her own husband treated her in the present. She was startled to realize that not much had changed in some women's roles in almost one hundred years. As she began to write about her experiences, she began to re-create her life in a narrative. She wrote a fairy tale, changing the ending and updating her story for the twenty-first century. Tilly Warnock would say that the "revising" of her life was caused by and reflected in literature (1996). Over the last fifteen years, I have observed that Marilyn has since written herself into a future as a fully functioning member of another family, not completely subjective to a patriarch. As she discovered her own voice, she coincidentally developed as a writer and embraced new roles. She understood that her bewilderment in identifying her roles could be placed in a larger context of a society that was also conflicted about roles, whether it be in Gilman's time at the start of the twentieth century or one hundred years later. She progressed from her personal narrative to an understanding of women's roles; with that new knowledge, she fashioned a different future. Marilyn, in short, became a critical thinker, willing to critique and act to change the power structures in her own life.

By beginning with construction of the self (or selves), students can expand their worlds to embrace other cultures, disciplines, and ideas, just as Marilyn did. As James Moffett states, "looking back" (beginning with first person) is for autobiography; that step leads to "looking into," which is "going from first person to third person, from writing about self to writing about others, and from first-hand information to second—and third—hand information" (180). Such assumptions may offer a rationale for the construction of research projects in FYC. Students sometimes create multiple genres in the reading and writing about lives. Literature pulls us outside ourselves to force us to look at our lives. By gaining distance, we can place our situation in historical context. Students eventually develop abilities to incorporate ideas of a non-self-referential nature, make analogies, draw parallels, create inferences—in short, develop all those critical thinking abilities that are considered the hallmark of thoughtful, nonbiased people. Marilyn had moved from revising her autobiography into asking rhetorical questions about societies and women's roles. In the process, she rewrote her own future. Writing was the means to effect this change, but reading Gilman's short story "The Yellow Wallpaper" also sparked her reflection. To develop a syllabus that provokes students to question their world, as Marilyn did, is always the challenge for a thoughtful instructor. An instructor needs to be careful to select not only texts that reflect dominant cultural values. If the course syllabus is confined to canonical literature, students may not learn to critique contemporary issues and power structures. Today, many instructors have broadened their definition of *literature* to embrace noncanonical literature texts. Literature can help students question and change their worlds; this reason is significant for inclusion of literature in first-year composition.

Terry Eagleton develops additional definitions of *literature* and thus suggests another reason for including literature in the composition classroom. In 1996, he states, "there is no 'essence' of literature whatsoever" (8). Not only should literature embrace "imaginative" literature, which is both "imaginary, meaning literally untrue," and "visionary" or "inventive" (17); it also can be a work that "uses language in peculiar ways" (2). Literature becomes "any kind of writing which for some reason . . . somebody values highly" (8). Rhetoric will be the tool to help us determine how performative aspects of text become discourse (179). No longer is literature a "specially privileged object" (179). Rhetoric "covers both the practice of effective discourse and the science of it" (180). Literature, for Eagleton, is subsumed within the rubric of rhetoric. We can thus incorporate multiple definitions of literature by utilizing a rhetorical stance in our first-year composition classrooms. For example, instructors can teach students to identify principles of unity in texts, as well as weasel words, connotative language, appeals to authority, and logical fallacies. Then, when students encounter ambiguity or lack of clarity in some literature, they have the skills and language to deconstruct the texts. To teach students to challenge claims, analyze target audiences, unravel connotative language, and search for principles of unity is to embrace teaching strategies that will develop critical citizens.

One only has to glance at the array of FYC readers and rhetorics to see the diversity of "literature" being taught in college classrooms today. Although some English faculty still cling to widely accepted texts (hence, the popularity of many editions of some readers), cultural critics have generally suggested more varied and recent texts; these critics argue that many diverse texts will help achieve similar goals of preparing students for their careers in the academy and as citizens. Literature, then, has a place in the composition classroom of helping students explore their inner worlds, while exposing them to other worlds. To continue with Moffett's reasoning, we note that when students look inward, eventually they begin to note patterns in other cultures and worlds and compare their own experiences (a circular relationship of the microcosm and the macrocosm). An iterative process occurs as students both read and write about their experiences with cultural institutions.

A flexible FYC instructor can approach the classroom with an anthropological perspective, focusing on universal cultural experiences. Some universal institutions prevail in all cultures: socialization of the young, kinship structures, death rituals, and initiation rites, for example. Many textbooks break down the "literature" selections into variations of these categories. Two examples of texts with a cultural studies approach are *One World, Many Cultures*, edited by Stuart and Terry Hirschberg, and *Connections: A Multicultural Reader for Writers*, edited by Judith Stanford. I have used both texts in composition classrooms and developed specific assignments and classroom strategies. At the beginning of a FYC course, I require students to summarize in writing selected articles, short stories, and nonfiction pieces on topics as diverse as children of women in prison and marriage rituals in Japan. The purpose of this summary assignment is to train students to be objective, to omit their opinions, and to focus upon major ideas of the author. In classroom discussion of the texts, we examine connotative language, inferences, and judgments, as well as cohesive devices in the texts. To practice the skill of concise expression, students write summaries about one tenth of the length of the chapters.

After students learn to summarize objectively (we do much peer work here), then they write a well-developed response (another typed page) of reaction; for that part of the assignment, students may start with expressive writing. Students write in any form they wish, but they must work on communicating coherently to fellow students. At this point, they do know that papers are usually shared with the class, but they also have the option of withholding their text. I teach students to dialogue with the text, which I hope sparks their critical thinking skills and sharpens their minds for dialogues with future texts, such as presidential debates. One example is Jamaica Kincaid's *A Small Place* about being a native and noting tourist behavior in Antigua; students react strongly to her piece. Students confront insider-outsider and colonial issues by answering protocols for writing responses: "What kind of tourist am I?" "What kind of tourist have I been in the past?" "How might I be different tomorrow?" All these topics are ways of challenging students as they turn the lens on the self as subject, motivated to reflection by Kincaid's harsh indictment of ugly tourism.

Perhaps a student's behavior as a tourist—or performance—might be different when he or she sits in a small village café in Aups, Provence, France. Just as Marilyn revised her life, so these students may be challenged to reflect thoughtfully upon their behavior in the future. Students make their worlds as they reflect upon past behavior and inscribe places for themselves in future worlds. Literature and writing *matter*; they help people create their identity. As students become engaged in the topic, they construct themselves and become articulate individuals. They suddenly care about spelling, for this is their life they are creating—and they want to tell the reader about it. Students now have a real audience of peers, who may have had similar experiences. Class discussions become authentic and self-generating, sparked by the written summary/reaction papers. From an instructor's point of view, these papers are texts that can be evaluated quickly. Initially, I suggest that students write only one to two pages. In my comments, I note completion of ideas, development with examples, engaging openings, dialogue, and other matters of grammar, style, and unity. The veteran instructor can apply principles from creative writing classes, mass communication and journalism courses, even literary criticism. Yet the instructor has required students to read and write about a text (applications that demonstrate analysis and objective summary) before the student is allowed to write expressively or critique the text. By the end of the course, students have internalized the grading criteria and are ready to write for the world of work, where no instructor is looking over their shoulder. Students also have learned to ask the challenging questions, without prompting from anyone, on their way to becoming critical thinkers.

An instructor must be rigorous in responding to the summary/reaction compositions; the key to allowing this exercise of composing to become an effective thinking and writing activity for FYC courses is for the instructor to evaluate these summary/reaction papers carefully, noting focus, organization, grammar, spelling, and logic. The instructor initially may need to provide specific writing prompts, such as requiring students to note disjunctions or similarities in the required reading and comparing them to their own experiences. The principle of working from a generalization to the specific instance helps sometimes in directing the students' writing. Sample writings might be Nicholas Gage's "The Teacher Who Changed My Life" (Stanford), Maya Angelou's "Graduation in Stamps," or Tepilit Ote Saitoti's "The Initiation of a Masai Warrior." Zora Neale Hurston's widely anthologized piece "How It Feels to Be Colored Me" also provokes thoughtful writing and discussion. After reading these selected essays in the textbook, for example, I might ask students to describe and confront in writing such topics as their own initiation experiences, moments when they were treated as "other," concepts of identity, or significant teachers. If an instructor has enthusiasm for the chosen texts, then most choices of topics will engage the students, from an entire semester on nature writing to political treatises.

To place the purpose of these summary/reaction papers in the context of FYC is extremely important. These papers replace regular learning logs or journal-writing activities in that their objective is fluency and review of content. In the reaction section, students develop critical thinking skills. Many students come to write fluently—and voluminously—by the end of the semester. Although students produce carefully crafted pieces (proofed and revised, even if done on a computer with spell check), they do not write extensive essays for the first six weeks of the course. The students review and revise, eliminating jargon, passive voice, incomplete arguments, and vague words and ideas. In the summary portion of these daily written compositions, I ask students to set context and find key points of the author's arguments (Who? What? Where? When? Why? How?). I instruct them to cite significant ideas or important quotations to aid the audience. Rather than the student writer demonstrating a bias, often he or she can find that the author exhibits one. I also have to work extensively on plagiarism issues, including the correct method of incorporating direct and indirect quotations. We review regularly the important concept that any ideas, even those paraphrased, need to be cited, with credit given to the original thinker. However, these issues are all topics for FYC, so confronting the issues in shorter papers helps students eliminate problems before they undertake documented essays.

The student's final inference ("So what does it all mean?"), after answering the five W's, is usually the start of the reaction section of this assignment. Four summary/reaction papers are due each week to ensure that students come to class with their reading assignments completed. I am direct about telling them the purposes of these assignments: sharpening their thinking skills, refining their writing skills, and composing regularly to eliminate their fear of writing. This habitual writing every week is like playing scales on the piano or shooting free throws; I tell them that if they do it regularly, they will improve as writers. And they do. I also teach students to eliminate many mechanical problems, before they begin to write longer expository and persuasive essays. In the entire semester, these weekly papers count no more than 20 percent of the grade. Usually, after the rigor of six weeks of this approach, we begin working on documented essays. Students develop pride in their writing and care about communicating to class members and the instructor. They have also learned to write to an audience about a text in a convincing voice, rhetorical skills that will aid them not only in this class but also in their future world of work.

This approach thus requires habitual thinking and composing about required literature texts. For the last few years, I have taught the FYC course in a computer lab; a portion of each class was devoted to writing. Although it required more planning for me to utilize the computer room in an efficient way, students certainly appreciated additional time to write. For such classes to work, instructors must execute much planning and evaluation of papers near the beginning of the semester. However, after about one-third to one-half of the course, they can give more freedom to students to prepare portfolio pieces and execute independent research. Students have eliminated most rhetorical, mechanical, and stylistic problems by this time; they have also addressed various writing issues, such as an analysis of audience, role, and format. Instructors may plan conferences and evaluate students' written progress reports, which can reveal additional writing problems.

After evaluating the summary/reaction assignments in the first six weeks, I then assign a one-thousand-word essay in FYC: a detailed description of an initiation event, using expressive description to set the context. Some students may have already written pieces of this essay in summary/reaction papers, so instructors can suggest that students utilize their portfolios for generating ideas. Students also mine other reaction essays or class discussion for topics or examples. Starting with an autobiographical focus, students explore inductively a personal experience from which they learned something (or that changed them in some way). After developing a narrative about the experience, the student explains and clarifies the significance of the past experience in his or her life today: the thesis of the essay. Often, this focus requires reframing the experience, rewriting the essay, and revising life patterns. Sometimes students find models in literature, such as the teenage narrator in Updike's "A and P" who indignantly quits a job because of his manager's treatment of two girls in bathing suits. Yet, the same narrator comments that "the world was going to be hard on me hereafter," when he reframes the experience later. Past, present, and future worlds collide in this piece of literature. Students both read and write about changed selves and begin to understand the concept of initiation. This initiation essay assignment teaches students specificity of detail, narrative structure, organizational patterns, and abstraction to higher-order thinking patterns (questions of significance), as well as analogical thinking (comparison to other situations). Over the years, students have produced outstanding essays on becoming a member of a swim team or adjusting to football practice (or other team sports) as initiation to "life," joining a motorcycle gang, being an unwed mother, and undergoing initiation into Navajo tribal ceremonies. Specific details add flavor to a student's generalizations about the *significance* of the experience. All essays have become important to students, and they craft their writing carefully. No other assignment in my thirty years of teaching has always produced meaningful essays by most of my students.

This initiation essay assignment consistently takes freshmen writers from stages of "looking back" (autobiography) to "looking into" to "looking beyond" (Moffett 180). Students reframe their past experiences and recast them as lessons learned to pass on to another generation. In the process, students read and write about literature and revise their lives, creating new literature for subsequent generations. "Yellow Woman" by Leslie Silko, for example, provides rich discussion about powerful sexual forces. "The Birthmark" by Nathaniel Hawthorne sparks discussion about obsessive love, something this media-savvy generation understands. Students both read and write about selected topics, as literature becomes both the spark and the result of connections between reading and composing. The process is circular, as the writing inspires the reading and vice versa.

Another argument for combining literature with composition classes is presented by Peter Elbow, who suggests a course of "half reading and half writing"; he uses writing as the "springboard" (21) to engage students in reading. In one assignment, Elbow asked students to write about "their most longstanding unresolved grudge" (21) before reading *The Tempest* by Shakespeare. Conventional thinking of many instructors advocates using reading as a springboard for writing topics, but to require students to write before reading has been very effective for Elbow.

An additional argument for incorporating literature in a composition course is provided by Gary Tate: he says that to teach a writing course without studying Shakespeare or other great models is analogous to trying to teach a music course without listening to Bach or Mahler (317). The history of many English departments across the country can certainly be traced to this philosophy, as many institutions have required specific literary texts over the years. Indeed, composition has grown as an unruly stepchild within most literature departments, and even today, in this period when many more faculty have been trained in rhetoric and composition, most composition courses are still taught by faculty trained in literature or by literature folks who tarry briefly along the way to teach composition. Linda Bergmann also identifies stealth literature instructors, who teach literature because that is what they know best and prefer to teach. However, a place exists in composition for literature, as long as the instructor remembers that she or he is teaching a composition class.

Another argument for a study of literature in FYC is a moral position. The writer Jackie French Koller suggests that a composition course that includes excellent models of "good" writing creates a "better individual" (qtd. in Harrington 258). This argument moves beyond models for writing styles to models for ethical behavior, certainly something difficult to prove in this era of verifiable and visible outcomes. Nevertheless, attention to models could provide information that might make a student more self-reflexive. To discuss moral issues in class also would allow students to reflect upon ethical questions, and they could create reflective pieces in their journals. Always, however, there would be the question about who is selecting the models and for what purposes, topics fraught with contention. No two faculty members in any English department would probably ever agree upon selected texts. Yet many choices could yield fruitful discussions. An example might be a moral discussion of stealing, which a reading of Victor Hugo's works could evoke. Is it fair to steal bread to feed one's family? What should be the consequences of that act? Students can think about and write their answers to questions that many people might confront.

The arguments about the moral value of literature and appreciation of the discipline are aligned with many English department missions. Reading literature in writing classes provides continuity to an English department sequence. The writer Gregory Jay, in responding to the Tate-Lindemann debate, argues that such an approach would "reintegrate the freshman program with the rest of the Department" (676). Finally, English professors know literature; they are authorities who have read texts carefully, multiple times. They are very capable of teaching students to undertake the same processes, applying critical thinking skills. The caution would be for instructors to relate the literature to composition, first and foremost, and not just execute literary analysis. A sample assignment might be for students to analyze a literary character, such as Hamlet, and write a character sketch. In writing the sketch, students would practice the organizational skills of categorizing information and supporting generalizations with specific detail. At Yavapai College in Arizona, where I taught for fifteen years, I often used the character sketch as a composition assignment. That English Department was proud of the fact that instructors had always taught "literature" in their second-semester composition course. They were referring primarily to "imaginative" literature, belles lettres. Leon Knight of North Hennepin Community College says that literature has also been taught there for over twenty-five years (Jay et al. 676). The danger of incorporating only "imaginative" literature, however, is that some instructors may focus solely on the literature and forget the "composing" part of the course. After all, literature professors know literature, especially their period or field. Remembering that the student is learning to compose the self—and is being introduced to academic writing—must be a priority when using literature in a composition course.

Instructors who argue for a broader definition of *literature* would counter that close textual analysis of literary elements in written texts detracts from writing issues. Stance, voice, point of view, context, aims, purposes—all these rhetorical matters are complex and could be diluted with excessive attention to literary analysis. Many students arrive at college with expectations about texts and a firm belief that they know everything about Mark Twain's *Huckleberry Finn*, F. Scott Fitzgerald's *The Great Gatsby*, or Joseph Conrad's *Heart of Darkness* (texts frequently studied in high school AP English classes). When students attempt to transfer these preconceived ideas to other works of imaginative literature, essays often become a pastiche of many critics' approaches, incorrectly documented or not thoroughly developed. The students' voices—not to mention their critical thinking—sometimes become lost in the process. Another problem that an instructor confronts in the classroom is that if a text does not follow student expectations of traditional conventions (and literature previously studied), then (so the students reason) it must not be good literature. How does one evaluate Leslie Silko's *Storyteller* or N. Scott Momaday's *House Made of Dawn* or *The Way to Rainy Mountain*? Or how does creative nonfiction fit into traditional categories of writing? How does a short story collage or fragmentary literature reveal unity? This contemporary writing often breaks forms and may be similar to writing that students will encounter in the future.

Yet the Native American texts mentioned in the previous paragraph can provide effective models for instruction, as honors courses at the University of Arizona demonstrate. In assigning essays that model these innovative Native American texts, instructor Anne-Marie Hall has required essays in which students create legends and stories about their families. Students composed a three-part essay, which created a myth and explained the students' connections to that myth. The final product was an essay of collage in three sections, but with unity of theme. Students and faculty in those classes also debated composition issues, such as "Are legends and myths *literature*?" Students created narratives about their own families. They mined family members' memories for lore and tried to verify its historical accuracy.

Another course sequence that illustrates the connections between literature and composition is Western Civilization 111 and 112 at Bradley University, a two-semester sequence that fulfills the FYC writing requirement. Students have written papers about family members who undertook migrations and have attempted to trace the historical context of the migrations. By interviewing family members and reading historical literature, students come to understand their place in social and historical movements. Students "compose" their lives not only by imagining the life of an ancestor but also by understanding the ancestor in the historical context. One requirement is that students must attempt to find a primary source from the period about which they are writing. This approach to composition in a yearlong course in western civilization is one more example of instructors expanding their definitions of *literature*; students are writing across the curriculum. Erika Lindemann has argued that such an approach is one possible alternative to traditional FYC courses because students "explore the sites of composing found in the academy" (316). Such an approach focuses more on "producing" texts, not "consuming" them (313).

The fact is that any instructor of composition may use almost any imaginative literature if she or he incorporates rhetorical discussions of voice, stance, purpose, audience, persuasion, and message or content, as well as literary elements. The texts may be advertisements, student papers, Shakespeare, historical papers, or even anthropology monographs. Gary Tate argues that we should "adopt a far more generous vision of our discipline," excluding "*no* texts" (321). Such an approach would "end the self-imposed censorship that for more than two decades has denied us the use of literature in our writing classes" (321).

We continue as composition and literature professors to debate and compose approaches to FYC. Just as our discipline of English is composing itself, so are the members within the rhetorical community of FYC defining their territory (literature and/or composition?) and assignments, which often include both reading and writing. Andrea Lunsford writes that "we aim . . . for the active, the continuing, the gerundive and participial—*composing*" (78). Sometimes the discussion takes a gendered turn. Lynn Z. Bloom composes herself in "Teaching College English as a Woman"; Nancy Sommers writes "I Stand Here Writing"; and Robert Connors produces "Teaching and Learning as a Man." Peter Elbow writes about "Being a Writer vs. Being an Academic"; the September 2001 issue of *College English* is a symposium on "Twentieth-Century Literature in the New Century" (Hoberek et al.). Contained within that issue are a special focus on "personal writing" and "storying our lives," topics that illustrate the ongoing debate about not only the content of FYC but also the form, for both instructors and faculty. Individuals such as Jane E. Hindman and Deborah Brandt emphasize personal writing and story in their assignments. Steinberg at the Conference on College Composition and Communication annual convention in Atlanta in 1999 discussed the genre *creative nonfiction*, which encompasses these diverse forms of writing. As long as instructors remember to emphasize the connections between composition and literature, students can create and read multiple forms of literature.

Composition specialists, rhetoricians, and literature faculty also are aware of connections between literature and composition, sometimes fraught with tensions. As the CCCC mines its "usable past [the last fifty years]," John Heyda chronicles the history of its formation in "asserting itself against literature and as composition" (667). Tate writes that only one in five programs in 1992 incorporated literature (presumably imaginative literature), according to Richard Larson's national survey of freshman writing programs (317). If we instructors can broaden our definition of *literature* to include multiple forms and a variety of texts, we can provide the arena for students to compose themselves—and to challenge the larger world, even as they prepare to enter it.

By helping students confront and engage with multiple texts and become critical readers and writers in the academic community, we can also help English departments define themselves and facilitate reconciliations between the literature and composition faculty. Students and faculty alike might produce documents such as Daphne Desser's "Reading and Writing the Family: Ethos, Identification, and Identity in My Great-Grandfather's Letters." Rather than arguing "either/or" for literature in FYC, we might realize—and teach students—the circular relationship of literature and composition. In the process of collapsing and articulating our boundaries for FYC, we also provide space for students to develop a critical consciousness, both about their own lives and the academic world in which they will perform for the next few years. We also are challenging them to learn skills for the world of work. As we create space for students to reframe their worlds, we compose ourselves—clarify the discipline and mission of English departments—and create a world of critical thinkers, who will push us forward during the twenty-first century.

# Works Cited

Angelou, Maya. "Graduation in Stamps." *Connections: A Multicultural Reader for Writers*. Ed. Judith A. Stanford. 2nd ed. Mountain View, CA: Mayfield, 1997. Originally published as Chapter 23 in Angelou, *I Know Why the Caged Bird Sings* (New York: Random House, 1969).

Baym, Nina, et al., eds. *The Norton Anthology of American Literature*. Shorter 6th ed. New York: Norton, 2003.

Bloom, Lynn Z. "Teaching College English as a Woman." *College English* 54.7 (November 1992): 818–25.

Booth, Wayne C. "'LITCOMP': Some Rhetoric Addressed to Cryptorhetoricians about a 'Rhetorical Solution to a Rhetorical Problem.'" Horner 57–80.

Brandt, Deborah, et al. "The Politics of the Personal: Storying Our Lives against the Grain." *College English* 64.1 (September 2001): 41–87.

Connors, Robert J. "Teaching and Learning as a Man." *College English* 58.2 (February 1996): 137–57.

Desser, Daphne. "Reading and Writing the Family: Ethos, Identification, and Identity in My Great-Grandfather's Letters." *Rhetoric Review* 20.3/4 (2001): 314–28.

Eagleton, Terry. *Literary Theory: An Introduction*. 2nd ed. Oxford: Basil Blackwell; Minneapolis: U of Minnesota P, 1996.

Elbow, Peter. "Being a Writer vs. Being an Academic: A Conflict in Goals." *College Composition and Communication* 46.1 (February 1995): 72–83.

———. "The War between Reading and Writing and How to End It." *Rhetoric Review* 12.1 (Fall 1993): 5–24.

Flynn, Elizabeth A. "Composing as a Woman." *College Composition and Communication* 39.4 (December 1988): 423–35.

Gage, Nicholas. "The Teacher Who Changed My Life." Stanford 185–90.

Gilman, Charlotte Perkins. "The Yellow Wallpaper." Baym et al. 1658–71.

Hall, Anne-Marie. Personal correspondence about English 109 (Honors English), University of Arizona, Tucson. March 2003.

Harrington, Dana. "Composition, Literature, and the Emergence of Modern Reading Practices." *Rhetoric Review* 15.2 (Spring 1997): 249–63.

Heyda, John. "Fighting over Freshman English: CCCC's Early Years and the Turf Wars of the 1950s." *College Composition and Communication* 50.4 (June 1998): 663–81.

Hindman, Jane E., ed. "Special Focus: Personal Writing." *College English* 64.1 (September 2001): 34–40.

Hirschberg, Stuart, and Terry Hirschberg, eds. *One World, Many Cultures*. 3rd ed. Boston: Allyn & Bacon, 2000.

Hoberek, Andrew, et al. "Twentieth-Century Literature in the New Century: A Symposium." *College English* 64.1 (September 2001): 9–33.

Horner, Winifred Bryan, ed. *Composition and Literature: Bridging the Gap*. Chicago: U of Chicago P, 1983.

Horner, Winifred Bryan. "Historical Introduction." Horner 1–13.

Hurston, Zora Neale. "How It Feels to Be Colored Me." Baym et al. 2096–2100.

Jay, Gregory, Elizabeth Latosi-Sawain, Leon Knight, and Jeanie C. Crain. "Four Comments on 'Two Views on the Use of Literature in Composition.'" *College English* 55.6 (October 1993): 673–79.

Kincaid, Jamaica. *A Small Place*. New York: Farrar, Straus and Giroux, 1988.

Lindemann, Erika. "Freshman Composition: No Place for Literature." *College English* 55.3 (March 1993): 311–16.

Lunsford, Andrea. "Composing Ourselves: Politics, Commitment, and the Teaching of Writing." *College Composition and Communication* 41.1 (February 1990): 71–82.

Moffett, James. *Active Voice: A Writing Program Across the Curriculum*. Upper Montclair, NJ: Boynton/Cook, 1981.

Readings, Bill. *The University in Ruins*. Cambridge, MA: Harvard UP, 1996.

Saitoti, Tepilit Ote. "The Initiation of a Masai Warrior." Hirschberg and Hirschberg 96–106.

Sommers, Nancy. "I Stand Here Writing." *College English* 55.4 (April 1993): 420–28.

Stanford, Judith A., ed. *Connections: A Multicultural Reader for Writers*. 3rd ed. Mountain View, CA: Mayfield, 2000.

Steinberg, Michael. "Creative Nonfiction." Conference on College Composition and Communication Annual Convention. Atlanta. 25 March 1999.

Tate, Gary. "A Place for Literature in Freshman Composition." *College English* 55.3 (March 1993): 317–21.

Warnock, Tilly. "Revising a Life." U of Arizona Spring Conference. Tucson. March 1996.

CHAPTER ELEVEN

# *The Missing Voice in the Debate: What Students Say about Literature in Composition*

MARY T. SEGALL
*Quinnipiac University*

The debate about the use of literature in the composition classroom is palpable in many English departments. In those departments that require students to pass a two-semester sequence of composition for the core curriculum, the first semester frequently contains the reading and writing of essays, while the second semester combines an introduction to literature with continued instruction in essay writing. Not surprisingly, the arguments both for and against this curricular design are ones persuasively articulated in 1995 by the contributors to "Symposium: Literature in the Composition Classroom" (Steinberg et al.). As the debate continues, I find myself revisiting the cogent arguments of Erwin Steinberg, Michael Gamer, Erika Lindemann, Gary Tate, and Jane Peterson. Each offers a different vantage, but one voice is missing. The theoretical, pedagogical, and historical views in "Symposium" seem dependent on the professional's vantage, with only an indirect perspective from the students who, of course, are the ones who have to live with our perceptions, whatever they may be. To gain the students' perspective, I administered a questionnaire to first-year students, who do indeed have much to say about the use of literature in the composition classroom.

## Description of Samples and Methodology

This study was conducted in March 1995 at Quinnipiac College (now University), a four-year liberal arts institution located in Hamden, Connecticut. At the time of this study, the incoming class numbered 1,312. A one-page questionnaire was distributed just after midterm week to all students (N = 1,105) enrolled in the second semester English 102 composition classes. Students were invited to respond voluntarily and anonymously to the questionnaire and to submit their responses in a sealed envelope. Of the 1,105 students enrolled in EN 102 at that time, 501 (or 43.5 percent) chose to respond.

## Description of the Questionnaire

Students put check marks next to the printed responses they felt best reflected their opinions, except for the last question, which invited a written response. An original copy of the questionnaire is appended (see the appendix). The questions asked the students to identify (1) in which course (EN 101 or EN 102) they grew most as a writer or improved most in their writing, (2) what factors they believed accounted for that growth, (3) which course they thought was more relevant for the kinds of writing they would do in the future, (4) in which course they did the most writing, (5) what kinds of readings they thought best to include in a composition course, and (6) their reasons for their responses to question 5. All students who responded to the questionnaire (see Table 11.1) had passed English 101, the first-semester core expository writing course, which requires six essays (with multiple drafts), several smaller writing assignments, and readings from a rhetoric reader. The students were currently enrolled in the second-semester English 102 course, which was designed to integrate an introduction to literature with continued instruction in composition, and which required four papers in reference to the literature assigned that semester.

Not all students responded to the invitation to write out their reasons for their answers to question 5, but for those who did, I have provided generic responses, since the responses differed only slightly in word choice and word order. The 130 students (24 percent) who favored nonfiction readings in a composition course gave various reasons, represented below:

Nonfiction was "more interesting" (16 students)

"We will need nonfiction for our future jobs and other course work" (15 students)

"I understand it better because the answers are right there and it is easier to find the facts" (12 students)

TABLE 11.1. Student Responses to Questionnaire: Number and Percent

| Survey Questions | Responses Checked by Students | Number | Percent |
|---|---|---|---|
| 1. In which course did you grow most as a writer or improve most in your writing? | EN 101<br>EN 102 | 267<br>281 | 49<br>51 |
| 2. What factor(s) do you believe accounts for your answer to question #1? | Quality of instructor's teaching<br>I liked the readings better<br>Factors in my personal life<br>Type of writing assignment<br>I spent more time on writing assignments<br>I sought extra help from the instructor or tutors | 295<br>165<br>70<br>299<br>179<br>96 | 53<br>30<br>13<br>54<br>32<br>17 |
| 3. Which course do you think was more relevant or helpful for the kinds of writing you will do in the future? | EN 101<br>EN 102<br>Both EN 101 and 102 equally | 127<br>127<br>289 | 23<br>23<br>53 |
| 4. In which course did you do more writing? | EN 101<br>EN 102<br>Both EN 101 and 102 equally | 263<br>89<br>192 | 48<br>16<br>35 |
| 5. What kinds of readings are best to include in a composition course? | Nonfiction (essays, articles)<br>Imaginative literature (short stories, drama, poetry)<br>Both of the above | 130<br>290<br>168 | 24<br>53<br>30 |

"Nonfiction deals with real life" (11 students)

"Nonfiction is easier to write about, to analyze, and to argue" (11 students)

"In nonfiction, there is no interpretation, and I find interpretation difficult" (8 students)

"I just like it better" (7 students)

"I do not like poetry!" (4 students)

"Nonfiction is more controversial and I can comment on the author's thoughts" (3 students)

"I can better see the different styles of writing" (2 students)

"Nonfiction broadens topic choice" (1 student)

"Nonfiction promotes more thinking" (1 student)

No reason given (39 students)

Of the 290 (53 percent) respondents who identified imaginative literature as the best reading to include in a composition course, students listed the following reasons:

"Imaginative literature is more interesting" (90 students)

"I prefer it" or "I like it better" (34 students)

"Imaginative literature is easier to read and to write about" (28 students)

"It is more creative and I can use my imagination" (24 students)

"Imaginative literature makes you think more deeply" (22 students)

"There are more ideas and more to write about" (17 students)

"It is more fun" (15 students)

"I can express my opinion more" (13 students)

"Imaginative literature helps you grow as a writer because you can learn more writing techniques and styles" (10 students)

"I have had enough nonfiction in other courses and need a diversion" (7 students)

"I love to read" (2 students)

"Fiction promotes more class discussion" (2 students)

No reason given (26 students)

Of the 168 students (30 percent) who favored including both fiction and nonfiction in a composition course, students gave the following reasons:

"You can write on anything" (29 students)

"A variety is good" (24 students)

"We should learn about or be exposed to both" (20 students)

"I enjoy both" (18 students)

"Using both gives a broad experience, expands the mind, and stimulates the imagination" (14 students)

"Both are important and beneficial" (14 students)

"You can learn from all types of reading and writing" (13 students)

"We need both for growth in writing and reading skills, especially critical thinking and analysis" (13 students)

"A mixture is good because it suits everyone's needs" (8 students)

"A mixture is good because it is good practice for future reading and writing" (6 students)

"Using both keeps the class more interesting" (5 students)

Using both genres "better reflects reality" (1 student)

"Nonfiction is good for education but I need fiction for escape" (1 student)

No reason (2 students)

Three students suggested that "it is not what we read, but how it is taught that matters." Only 11 students (2 percent of the total group) wrote comments that reflected discontent with any kind of reading. Their responses fell into two categories: "I don't care" (2 students) or "I have trouble with reading and writing about anything" (7 students).

## Discussion of Student Responses

Two of the more salient claims in the debate on literature in the composition classroom are that the use of literature results in a tendency for teachers to lecture more and to attend less to student writing, and that the majority of students find little pleasure in or use for imaginative literature in their preoccupation with achieving career goals. The results of this student questionnaire raise questions about the validity of both these claims.

As Erwin Steinberg observes from his review of conference presentations and journal articles, the profession continues to see no "symbiotic relationship between literature and composition" ("Imaginative" 271), and he suggest that historic bias in favor of expository reading and writing in composition exists because of the belief that students are better served in their other academic courses and in their jobs (268). In her 1993 *College English* article, "Freshman Composition: No Place for Literature," Erika Lindemann offers an eloquent defense for the exclusion of imaginative literature from composition classrooms, citing that 75 to 80 percent of class time is spent in "teacher talk" (312). She accounts for the loss of attention to student writing in the following way:

> A pedagogy derived from teaching literature looks and sounds different from one that encourages students to produce texts. Literature teachers are conscious of the difference. Not only do they sometimes express misgivings about the writing teacher's use of group work and peer evaluations, but they also report clear preference for teaching by lecture and discussion . . . . If students get to write a paper or two, they must assume the disembodied voice of some abstruse journal. (313–14)

Presumably, some teachers who prefer lecture mode do so because, as Jacqueline Bacon suggests, "it is often unnerving for professors to see themselves as 'facilitators' rather than 'experts'" (511). If, as Lindemann argues in "Three Views of English 101," we lack the "common ground" to arrive at a pedagogy that envisions the use of literature beyond product-centered-teacher-as-expert (300), then we are, indeed, at an impasse.

In his article "Fictionalizing the Discipline: Literature and the Boundaries of Knowledge," Michael Gamer concedes that "asking students to appreciate a literary masterpiece enshrined on a pedestal . . . will not produce the kind of process-oriented course that focuses on drafting and revising, and that sounds more like a writing workshop than a lecture course" (281). However, Gamer correctly points out that bad teaching "goes across all academic disciplines" and that the problem is not the literature itself, but rather the uninformed teachers who teach it (281). As Gary Tate writes in "Notes on the Dying of a Conversation," "the limitation of teachers, though evident, is insufficient reason to banish imaginative literature from the composition classroom" (304). The "pedagogical sins of the teachers in the past," that Tate refers to in "A Place for Literature in Freshman Composition" (317) need not, as one questionnaire respondent wrote, cause us to "neglect a whole category of writing!" In fact, Peter Elbow testifies that his work in composition has enriched his teaching of literature because "I can now teach a 'product' of literature by using active, experiential workshop activities I learned as a teacher of writing—and thereby increase the chances of students actually *experiencing* the literary work and the critical concepts we are studying" ("Culture" 535; original emphasis).

Other voices, past and present, argue for a marriage of informed pedagogy and the use of imaginative literature in teaching composition. Jane Peterson, in "Through the Looking-Glass: A Response," envisions a learning-centered classroom that does not privilege either the student or the content (317). Patricia Bizzell, in "Opinion: 'Contact Zones' and English Studies," contends that inclusion of any readings "relevant to the issue being contested" (167) would integrate composition and rhetoric, and in doing so, the "boundaries between 'content' (literature) and its traditional inferior pedagogy (composition), are usefully blurred" (168). Dan Morgan, in "Connecting Literature to Students' Lives," promotes a "student-centered approach [in which] an eclectic, flexible pedagogy that responds to students as individuals and to specific group dynamics [would] mean empowering students to draw conclusions, comment, disagree, genuinely respond to the literature studied" (495). Morgan specifically identifies as desirable those methodologies others view as occurring only in process-centered writing classes: collaboration, freewriting, small-group activities, reader-response journals, and portfolios (496). Particularly pertinent to those of us teaching developmental students, Louise Rosenblatt, in "The Transactional Theory: Against Dualisms," reminds us that the reading process, regardless of genre, is an impressive mixture of cognitive, referential, analytic, affective, and aesthetic transactions, dependent on purpose. She cautions us against reduction and "separation of the two activities [reading and writing] and against waxing prescriptive with either" (383). Also arguing against such dichotomies, Peter Elbow reinforces the connection between the affective power of language and cognition when he writes, "I'd argue that we can't harness students' strongest linguistic and even cognitive powers unless we see imaginative language as the norm—basic or primal" ("Culture" 536).

The responses on the student questionnaire show support for both arguments and reveal the complexity of the issue. For example, an almost equal distribution of students checked EN 101 (49 percent) and EN 102 (51 percent) as the course in which they grew most as writers. This distribution would seem to indicate that a composition course in which the readings are primarily imaginative literature can do, in the students' view, at least an equal job of attending to student writing as the expository writing course, EN 101. The quality of teaching was identified by 53 percent of the students as the reason for their response, underscoring Gamer's claim that bad teaching is not bound to specific disciplines (in this case EN 101 and EN 102). Since the questionnaire did not ask students to specify their criteria for quality teaching, we cannot correlate the responses with those students who prefer a very directive, presentational mode of instruction. Similarly, neither can we correlate the responses with those who prefer a more experiential or Socratic instructional approach. Distaste for prescriptive teaching clearly was the reason that caused some students to prefer EN 102. The sentiment of these students is expressed in this representative generic response: "In imaginative literature, the person can express his own feelings, emotion, and imagination. In EN 101, the student has to conform to the likings of the teacher, which can be hard to do.

It's more fun to write your opinion on something and not what your teacher wants to hear."

Although the student responses were equally divided about which course most improved their writing, 48 percent said they did *more* writing in EN 101. Students did not describe the nature of the writing, but since the EN 101 syllabus includes journal writing for most readings and encourages smaller, incremental writing assignments (such as peer reviews, dialogic journals, and multiple drafts), the nature of the syllabus may account for the survey results. Another more dispiriting explanation, however, is that Lindemann's claim is true: the use of imaginative literature in a composition class does result in less attention to student writing. However, if we take together the 16 percent who said they did more writing in EN 102 and the 35 percent who said they wrote an equal amount in both EN 101 and EN 102, the combined 51 percent offers support to the claim that students can and do write as much when imaginative literature is the content for the composition course.

The ideal, it seems to me, would be for all students to write an equal amount in both EN 101 and EN 102. Further research that more finely distinguishes the nature of writing done in each course and that allows correlation between the types of writing and students' perception of their growth would be useful. Questions about the efficacy of the kinds of writing assignments in EN 101 and EN 102 remain. Perhaps, as one student wrote, emphasis on student texts alone is too limiting. Additional research would also identify the degree to which surface features may be attended to more than global features in EN 101. We can also question whether it is realistic to expect more parity between EN 101 and EN 102 than the actual results indicate, given the 49 percent versus 51 percent distribution to the question "In which course did you grow most as a writer?"

Though questions remain about the nature of the writing done in each course, the primary focus here is the type of text students prefer—fiction or nonfiction. The second claim in this debate, that students find little pleasure in or use for imaginative literature, is supported by 24 percent of the questionnaire respondents. Students expressed opinions to the effect that "Literature is not relevant to real life unless you are an English major,"

"A physical therapist will not need to write on *Hamlet* in the future," and "I would rather become familiar with true facts as opposed to a story that was written a hundred years before I was born." Such responses lend credence to Tate's view: "It is as if all these students who come to college only in order to get a better job have convinced us that a college education is primarily job training and that the task of the freshman writing course is to help make that training more effective" ("Place" 320). Several of the students who favored nonfiction wrote comments that illustrate Lindemann's observation that students "rarely connect literature with life" ("Freshman" 313). Other students in this 24 percent who favored nonfiction did so because they found interpretation difficult, as evidenced by responses such as, "You understand things better—the answers are right there," or "They are straight to the point and don't have hidden meaning." Aside from the circular reasoning of students who wrote "I just prefer it," those who prefer nonfiction genuinely feel more comfortable focusing on pragmatic reading and writing and avoiding the risks they perceive inherent in analyzing imaginative literature.

A far larger group (53 percent of the total 501 respondents) favored imaginative literature in composition. In keeping with Tate's position that "we have denied students who are seeking to improve their writing the benefits of reading an entire body of excellent writing" ("Place" 317), these respondents voiced strong desire to be creative and to use their imagination. One could well ask why these students felt they could not be creative or imaginative in an expository writing class, which again raises questions about pedagogy and faculty development. Although a few students (3 percent of the 53 percent group) viewed exposure to literature as good medicine, commenting that students should be *subjected* to all kinds of writing, most of those in favor of including imaginative literature said they found it more interesting and easier to write about. Contrary to the assumption that students do not appreciate literature or see it as useful, a 53 percent majority of those surveyed thought it highly desirable to read literature in their composition classes, and 30 percent of the total group thought a combination of fiction and nonfiction would be ideal, including those appeasement-minded students who wrote that they think there should be a variety, so that everyone could be satisfied. Together, then, 83 percent of the respondents favored inclusion of imaginative literature in freshman composition.

A look at the reasoning behind their preferences reveals a belief that, as some students suggest, "most imaginative literature are good examples of good writing, and when you enjoy what you are reading, it makes your writing better." Jane Peterson argues that teachers can use any text to teach their own agenda (312), and similarly, those students in favor of including both fiction and nonfiction reason that *what* is read in the course is subordinate to *how* one writes about it because "both require bringing ideas together and forming them into a smooth essay." In favor of using literature, Gamer asserts that literature texts "not only allow students to interact with other ways of seeing that invite reflection and writing; they also exist as sites for the construction of plural and often conflicting 'readings.'" Gamer further concludes, "This critical distinction is in no way too complex for first year students" (282). A majority of the respondents would agree, as represented by the common response that "no one specific reading is best to include in a composition course because a quality writer can easily make connections whether dealing with reality or fantasy."

The pleasure factor derived from literature is noticeably present in the students' responses, with several holding that imaginative literature "helps a reader enjoy a topic and expand the mind in interesting and fantastical ways." The survey shows that over half of the 501 respondents do value inclusion of literature for the very reasons Morgan proffers: "Books made us think, feel, and reflect, gave us the joy of discovery and the pleasure of testing and articulating our own beliefs" (492). If Dan Morgan sees literature as effective "because literature's connecting link to 'everydayness' . . . gives immediacy and accessibility" (493), so do the majority of the students in this study. When asked which course they thought was most helpful and relevant to their future writing, 23 percent checked EN 102 and 53 percent checked both EN 101 and EN 102, indicating that 76 percent of our students value what imaginative literature has to offer.

In "Symposium: Literature in the Composition Classroom," Erwin Steinberg questions why, given the strong historical bias against it, "the argument for the use of literature in the composition classroom reappears from time to time" (271). I would suggest three reasons. First, it is impossible, as Gary Tate contends, for freshman composition to be a service course to other disciplines ("Place" 319), for the same reason that Peter Elbow concludes there is no single "academic discourse"; rather, many discourses are represented in the academy ("Reflections" 153). Second, the debate continues because each institution is site specific, as Peterson explains (313–15), and as Steinberg concedes when he says, "There is no such thing as *the* composition classroom . . . they differ widely . . . since at least the 1930s" (266). Third, and perhaps most persuasively, we continue to debate the issue because many of our students, even the most career driven, desire literature in composition. To paraphrase one respondent, literature sharpens skills in reading different levels within a story and bolsters interpretive skills that are transferable to business.

Currently, the composition faculty members in my department tend to frame the debate in constructivist language, while senior literature faculty hold to more traditional poetics and literary studies, both theoretically and pedagogically. In an attempt to reintegrate the two, some of us have designed courses, such as Introduction to Literary Studies and Studies in Stylistics, as a way to reintegrate textualism and contextualism and as an attempt to offer collaborative models for future English curricula. The questionnaire results also give us an opportunity to depolarize the debate through including the perspectives of students. Knowing that 83 percent of our students do, indeed, think literature should be included in composition and that 76 percent believe doing so will be helpful to them in the future, we can begin to rethink our assumptions based, heretofore, on our professional vantage. The student responses also suggest that just as we would be hard pressed to define a generic discourse or composition classroom, our students defy singular description. Although the clear majority of students preferred imaginative literature in composition courses, we still have the 24 percent who strongly preferred nonfiction. Perhaps the most beneficial effect of this student questionnaire, however, is an invitation to listen more closely to what our students have to say about their own academic welfare.

## Appendix: Questionnaire

Please complete the following questions. The anonymous results of this questionnaire will be used for program evaluation and for research. Thank you for your cooperation.

Directions: Please check the box next to your answer:

1. In which course did you grow most as a writer or improve most in your writing?

    [ ] EN 101
    [ ] EN 102

2. What factor do you believe accounts for your answer to question #1?
(you may check more than one box)

    [ ] Quality of instructor's teaching
    [ ] I liked the readings better
    [ ] Factors in my personal life
    [ ] Type of writing assignment
    [ ] I spent more time on writing assignments
    [ ] I sought extra help from the instructor or tutors

3. Which course do you think was more relevant or helpful for the kinds of writing you will do in the future?

    [ ] EN 101
    [ ] EN 102
    [ ] Both equally

4. In which course did you do more writing?

    [ ] EN 101
    [ ] EN 102
    [ ] Both equally

5. What kinds of readings are best to include in a composition course?

    [ ] Nonfiction (essays, articles)
    [ ] Imaginative literature (short stories, drama, poetry)
    [ ] Both

6. What is your reason for your answer to question #5?

# Works Cited

Bacon, Jacqueline. "Impasse or Tension? Pedagogy and the Canon Controversy." *College English* 55 (September 1993): 501–14.

Bizzell, Patricia. "Opinion: 'Contact Zones' and English Studies." *College English* 56 (February 1994): 163–69.

Elbow, Peter. "The Cultures of Literature and Composition: What Could Each Learn from the Other?" *College English* 64.5 (May 2002): 533–46.

———. "Reflections on Academic Discourse: How It Relates to Freshmen and Colleagues." *College English* 53 (February 1991): 135–55.

Gamer, Michael. "Fictionalizing the Disciplines: Literature and the Boundaries of Knowledge." *College English* 57.3 (March 1995): 281–86.

Lindemann, Erika. "Freshman Composition: No Place for Literature." *College English* 55.3 (March 1993): 311–16.

———. "Three Views of English 101." *College English* 57.3 (March 1995): 287–302.

Morgan, Dan. "Connecting Literature to Students' Lives." *College English* 55 (September 1993): 491–500.

Peterson, Jane. "Through the Looking-Glass: A Response." *College English* 57.3 (March 1995): 310–18.

Rosenblatt, Louise. "The Transactional Theory: Against Dualisms." *College English* 55 (April 1993): 377–86.

Steinberg, Erwin R. "Imaginative Literature in Composition Classrooms?" *College English* 57.3 (March 1995): 266–80.

Steinberg, Erwin R., Michael Gamer, Erika Lindemann, Gary Tate, and Jane Peterson. "Symposium: Literature in the Composition Classroom." *College English* 57.3 (March 1995): 265–318.

Tate, Gary. "Notes on the Dying of a Conversation." *College English* 57.3 (March 1995): 303–09.

———. "A Place for Literature in Freshman Composition." *College English* 55 (March 1993): 317–21.

# *Afterword: A Complex Affirmation of Reading and Writing*

PATRICIA HARKIN
*University of Illinois at Chicago*

The variety of the essays in this volume attests to the energy and care with which our profession continually rethinks itself. More than perhaps any other academic institution, English studies is self-reflexive: it might even be argued that its history is a series of arguments about what its *content* should be. In most of these arguments, as Edward Kearns points out, the discussions of content—and of pedagogical procedures for disseminating that content—involve value. What we teach is what we value. What we teach is what we want our students to value. And values differ. While some people want the institution to concern itself with the production and consumption of valuable texts, others value themselves for eschewing value judgments altogether—preferring what they call "disinterested disciplinary inquiry." Still others reject the notion that inquiry can be disinterested but still try to avoid discussing value on the grounds that the notion is thoughtlessly ideological or elitist. Still others urge that the construction of value itself should be the institutional topic.

Discussions of value, in turn, involve class. Class affiliations manifest themselves in choices about values. Again, more than perhaps any other academic institution, English studies has historically concerned itself with the relations between class consciousness and language use. The historically vexed relations between the teaching of writing and the teaching of literary works are symptomatic of that state of affairs.

It is important to remember that history, but just as important not to repeat every aspect of it. Eve Wiederhold makes the excellent point that educators need to think through the consequences of having to depend on known terms to communicate visions of change. Known terms can restrict thinking to the institutional structures from which they emerged. One such term is *discipline*. In reading these essays, I'm struck by the disparity in the authors' uses (implied and explicit) of the word. Dennis Ciesielski, for example, argues that "we must become a community of whole English teachers prepared to do the work of English as a whole discipline." Such teachers, he believes, would be capable of guiding students through the intricacies of both the production and the consumption of texts. Ciesielski seems to hold a traditional understanding of discipline as a body of knowledge constituted by its object of study. Zoologists study animals; professors of English study reading, writing, speaking, and listening.

But for Edward Kearns, that set of circumstances is precisely the problem: efforts to make English studies into a science, in his view, have taken us away from making art of our own and assessing the value of texts we encounter; instead, they constrain us to focus on the "measurable." He looks critically at the history of the profession he loves and finds that its efforts to make itself into a discipline—by teaching "critical thinking skills" that are "essentially analytical, descriptive, and non-normative, tending toward 'objectivity,' 'accuracy,' 'measurement,' and the like"—have distracted it from the more important concerns of "value."

Edith Baker believes that "our discipline of English is composing itself": her discipline, under construction, presumably does not have a "nature" and, in her account of it, does not sound like a science. Neither does Barry Maid's. For him, the loose amalgam of practices that we call English studies doesn't have a nature; rather, it has a history. And that history is contingent. Indeed, he offers a counter-history as a thought experiment.

> What if all literary specialists were not housed in English departments but in departments of American studies or medieval studies or similarly organized units? . . . The discussion among literary scholars might even be wondering whether a discipline of literary studies existed. We might even carry this fantasy scenario a

bit further by imagining if literary specialists were trying to find some commonality in what they do, in order to attain disciplinary status, they might focus on the fact that they teach students how to read texts.

Dominic DelliCarpini finds disciplinarity constraining: he faults writing about literature, functioning as it does within closed disciplinary boundaries, for being largely isolated from the larger public forum. DelliCarpini's cogent criticism of the belief that academic (by which I understand "disciplinary") expertise is necessary to speak on political or social issues is exacerbated by the sense that the writing classroom is aesthetic, formalist, and apolitical. He urges us to recover our own sophistic traditions rooted in a civically aware liberal arts education. John Heyda's, Edith Baker's, Mary Segall's, and Katherine Fischer, Donna Reiss, and Art Young's pedagogies involve moving away from disciplinary frameworks to accommodate new media.

For English studies, the term *discipline* has always been troublesome. It's both enabling (in the sense that its regulated procedures produce and validate knowledge) and constraining (in that it restricts inquiry to those regulated procedures). And I think that the troublesomeness is usefully explained by the circumstances I mention above. Concerns with class consciousness and mobility, discursive behavior, human values, aesthetics, and a host of other considerations cannot adequately be addressed by any one discipline. Although the term tends to pop up in discussions of practice as a name for the assumptions that inform and lend prestige to that practice, its very ubiquity reminds us that the assumptions of English studies are so continuously (and appropriately) contested that it may be more useful *not* to think of English studies, composition studies, or even literary studies as a *discipline*. For me, that word is most usefully employed in Stephen Toulmin's rather narrow sense as a regulated way of raising and answering questions in the context of a common lexicon, research agenda, and representation techniques. By this definition, zoology might qualify as a discipline. A term like *mammal* can pretty much be used by any zoologist with a reasonable expectation of communicating precisely. Think, though, of *text, meaning, metaphor, value, literacy, reading, writing, speaking, listening*—the terms with which we (in every sense) *make our livings*.

I think of this circumstance as something to be celebrated rather than corrected. If English were a discipline, we wouldn't need this book, and we do very much need this inquiry into the discourses that shape our subjectivity, knowledge, and values. It is the fact that we do not have an agreed-upon lexicon, research agenda, and set of representation techniques that makes our work so flexible, and that enables us to respond (as John Heyda, Edith Baker, Katherine Fischer, Donna Reiss, and Art Young do) to the exigencies we encounter. Whereas disciplines see only what they recognize no matter where they look, the profession of English studies (as I see it) first looks at the ways in which discourse works in the world and then adapts disciplinary procedures to describe, explain, analyze and (sometimes) change them.

I make this point about the authors' use of the term *discipline*, then, not to advance a petty quibble. Rather, I suggest that, when we think about our practice, notions of what the discipline requires are perhaps less useful than contingent local judgments about what disciplinary knowledge would most help us to promote the literate behavior the situation seems to call for. As Eve Wiederhold asserts, arguments about what we should do in the future are best not warranted in *notions of discipline* that come from the past.

This is not to say that history is bunk; certainly we need to be aware of the circumstances that have brought us to where we are. Nor is it to say that disciplinarity is useless. Disciplinary frameworks can be helpful in describing the situations we encounter and in figuring out how to implement the curricular decisions those circumstances make necessary. But those decisions, in my view, should be made on the basis of a sense (however local, contingent, and imperfect) of actual conditions inside and outside the academy rather than on a disciplinary conception of a proper way to raise and answer agreed-upon questions.

The conditions in my own little corner of the academy suggest to me that teachers should include explicit attention to reading in their writing classes. The kind of attention to reading I call for would encompass all kinds of texts—not only those we refer to as "literary." Such an affirmation is, as Linda Bergmann points out, both conceptually and historically complex. For me,

- It means actively teaching—not just assigning—reading.
- That teaching entails choosing an account or accounts of reading to teach.
- That choice entails coming to an explicit—personal, theoretical, pedagogical, and ethical—decision about meaning. Individual teachers need to decide how *meaning* (the product of reading) is to be defined *for the explicit purposes of the course.*
- That definition entails an articulation of pedagogy, ethics, and reading theory.

Before arguing these propositions, I offer an anecdote that I hope will exemplify the problem as I see it.

Last spring, as part of the final exam in a course in persuasion for junior and senior communication majors, I asked my students to read an essay (outside class) and identify its claim. I chose the text carefully: its author, Walter Benn Michaels, is the head of the English Department at the University of Illinois at Chicago (where I teach). Entitled "Diversity's False Solace," his text presents a critique of the attitudes our university takes toward what it calls "diversity." "Seemingly every piece of literature that U.I.C. distributes about itself announces that we have been 'ranked among the Top 10 universities in the country for the diversity' of 'our student body'" (12). With such self-congratulatory statistics, the university seeks to attract students and money. But the "real value of diversity," Michaels asserts, is

> as a collective bribe rich people pay themselves for ignoring economic inequality.... [We like policies like affirmative action] not so much because they solve the problem of racism but because they tell us that racism is the problem we need to solve. And the reason we like to solve the problem of racism is that solving it just requires us to give up our prejudices, whereas solving the problem of economic equality might require ... us to give up our money. (14)

Thus Michaels's claim is that to the extent that it celebrates racial and ethnic "diversity," the university tolerates and even promotes inequalities of class. That is the answer I was (as we say) "looking for."

When the papers came in, I was disconcerted, but not surprised, to find that many of my students read Michaels's essay as a celebration of UIC's diverse student body. These students wrote of the importance of diversity to a great university and the advantage our diversity gives us over less diverse schools, such as the University of Chicago a few miles—and many thousands of tuition dollars—away.

How might we explain the circumstances I've just described —and what should we do about them?

Twenty-five years ago, in the heyday of *reader response*, there would have been a plethora of answers to my questions. Then, David Bleich and Norman Holland would have analyzed the students' responses for identity themes. My students want and need to celebrate their diversity, Bleich might say, as a way of sublimating hostility or feelings of inadequacy. In fact, my students last spring did constitute a remarkably diverse group—Korean, Chinese, Japanese, Indian, Turkish, Lebanese, Polish, Russian, African American, and Chicanos far outnumbered persons of western European origin in the class. Stanley Fish would have been witty and astute about students' ability to make the meaning that their interpretive community taught them to find: accustomed to hearing celebrations of UIC's diversity, he might say, and interested in increasing the value of their degrees, they read the essay as saying what they expected or wanted it to say: a UIC degree is valuable because UIC's student body is diverse. Louise Rosenblatt might have remarked that Michaels's text, richly ironic and intricately allusive, requires aesthetic as well as efferent reading, and my students read only efferently and too quickly. Frank Smith might have pointed out that reading is a process of uncertainty reduction. Anxious about jobs as they wrote the final in their last undergraduate course, my students wanted and needed to read Michaels as reducing their anxiety about the value of their degree. Even Wolfgang Iser might patiently point out that the students, however inept their mastery of repertoire, were nonetheless building consistency. Each of these answers might be called "disciplinary": Holland and Bleich work from psychoanalysis; Rosenblatt and Smith, in different ways, invoke theories of cognition; Iser, calling reading an affair of consciousness, warrants his work in phenomenological philosophy.

But the heyday of reader response is over.[1] Now, in the era of the No Child Left Behind Act and the *National Endowment for the Arts Report*, the reading behavior of college students is more often "viewed with alarm" than addressed as a theoretical inquiry. From many different quarters, calls for increased attention to reading are becoming ever more strident. Though it pains me to say it, I think that many students read neither often nor well. And I believe that courses in English studies are appropriate venues for addressing this situation. Our task, in my view, is to describe the problems and then invoke appropriate disciplinary measures to address them.

Let me try to say, more practically, what I mean. Should I call my students' readings "errors" or is it better to describe them as an effect of class? Or maybe just carelessness? But carelessness could be an effect of class. So could overwork and inadequate preparation.

My students' readings are complex responses to complex situations; they cannot simply and entirely be put down to carelessness. This was a final exam; their grades were riding on their score; they had the essay well in advance, and they had been told what the question would be. Nor is it enough—though it is surely accurate—to say that students just don't read "carefully" (anymore), with the tacit assumption that "back in the day," students (like us) read carefully. Students know how to read carefully, and they do so when they want to. But often, overcommitted, with full-time jobs and families on top of a full academic load, they economize on time by simply *not* reading.

In this essay, I consider this situation in two ways: both as a pedagogical problem and as what I call a condition of postmodernity. It's a condition of postmodernity that meaning cannot be fixed. It is a pedagogical problem that students need to read more carefully, accurately, and thoughtfully.

I think that many compositionists, for far too long, have been inclined to only one way of thinking *at a time*. We compartmentalize, thinking as theorists when we do research and scholarship and as teachers when we teach. When we think as theorists, we assert that meaning is indeterminate. In lieu of "meaning," members of English departments often talk about "readings." Most teachers have been carefully trained to look for and to celebrate all kinds of readings—mestiza, subaltern, postcolonial, queer, Marxist, psychoanalytic, performance oriented. Members of my generation, who came of professional age in the 1970s, remember all too well a time when feminist readings (for example) were simply dismissed as "erroneous." As a corollary of our theoretical sophistication, we've developed a pedagogical piety—an impulse to celebrate disparate readings and a corresponding, even corollary disinclination to call any reading "wrong."

But late at night, when I'm reading student papers, I tend to think that my students need to read (here I use an atheoretical term) "better." In these dark nights of the pedagogical soul, I find that I do not stop to define "better." I just experience it as a problem that so many students so often produce readings that I'm inclined (again, rather atheoretically) to call "wrong." I suspect that I'm not alone. Nor are teachers the only ones who worry about students' reading. The academy's increasing corporatization encourages and even mandates this kind of thinking. Parents, employers, administrators, and legislators express concern. That concern is well founded. Even as an unapologetic tenured radical, I believe that it is within the state's legitimate interest to ask us to help our students read "more accurately." And I would say (with only a little diffidence) that "more accurately" *in this context* can mean "consistently with authorial intention."

I believe that we can address this problem only by thinking as theorists and as teachers *at the same time*. When we think only as teachers, in the obvious stark binary, we can either correct (by penalizing) the "error" or uphold the student's right to her or his own reading. Both alternatives are, I think, inadequate. Penalizing the error is both unduly repressive and theoretically unsound. Accepting anything (a practice we find at the bottom on the slippery slope of students' right to their own readings) is, in the long term, a disservice. If we think only as theorists, the impulse might be to celebrate the *differance*. But merely celebrating the *differance* makes a grand narrative of undecidability and, in so doing, ignores the fact that it is also characteristic of postmodernity to avoid grand narratives. If we make a grand narrative of undecidability, we're really no more enlightened than a politician who claims that every reading problem can be scientifically solved through phonics.

Moreover, to celebrate *differance* uncritically is to place ourselves in a pedagogical double bind: we have to teach our students to read better, but we can't privilege one reading over another. There are times when the difference between a student's reading and an author's apparent intention is more accurately understood as an effect of a reading problem that it's our job to correct than as a *plaisir du texte*. This is especially true in first-year writing classes. The trick for us is to identify those times rather than elide or ignore them.

One might decide to reward intentional misreadings but penalize unintentional ones. But, of course, this alternative begs the question by presupposing that one can figure out which is which. One could differentiate by genre—misreadings of "literature" are OK but misreadings of nonfiction are mistakes. But again that nasty question-begging, this time about literariness.

The most usual middle ground—to make the difference itself the topic of discussion—is a wonderful but rather cumbersome idea. I recommend it—but not as a universal solution. If, as I did, you ask an advanced undergraduate to argue for or against a position available in an assigned reading, I think it's fair to assume that the student will be able to do that. In a "content course," teachers don't always have the class time to devote to "finding" the author's position. To "make" that time is necessarily to take it out of the time you would otherwise spend teaching the course's writing focus.

Moreover, the fact that readers often do manage to agree on meaning is really quite remarkable, and it too deserves both theoretical and pedagogical attention. Theoretically, it is interesting. Pedagogically, it provides students with the skills they need to survive in the marketplace.

Finally, I think we must accept the responsibility of teaching reading as well as writing, cumbersome though it may be. Such a choice entails taking positions on questions that, as Linda Bergmann points out in her introduction, are both conceptual and political. That is, any teacher or scholar will need to include some thought about his or her own conceptual definitions of *writing, reading,* and (however provisional, local, and contingent) *literature,* in whatever decision she makes about whether to combine them in a writing course. In such a process, the problems are formidable.

First, conceptual: I think it crucial for each teacher to be able to say as exactly as possible what she or he means by the terms *writing, reading,* and *literature* for each course she or he teaches. The alternative, as we see politically, is to allow those terms to be defined for us by, for example, federal or state government. We know, of course, that both writing and reading are complex and multifaceted activities. We learn about them through work in a number of recognized disciplines (linguistics, psychology, philosophy) and institutional formations (literary studies, semiotics, communication studies). Researchers into both reading and writing have learned to cross boundaries freely, mixing and matching methods and assumptions in order to do a local and contingent job. For example, Iser crosses linguistics, semiotics, phenomenology, aesthetics, history, visual studies, and psychology to describe what occurs when human beings encounter literary texts. Mina Shaughnessy gathered insights from linguistics, sociology, and psychology to describe the writing behaviors of her basic writers. We cannot and should not hope for a general theory of *reading writingspeakinglistening.*

So it's important to choose an account of reading (as well as of writing) that answers the purpose of each course one teaches. Compositionists are often eager to stipulate their generalized account of writing—expressive, sociocognitive, and so forth—but they less frequently stipulate the account of reading that warrants their practice. Many accounts of reading are available. Iser or Rosenblatt might be most appropriate for the courses that John Heyda and Mary Segall describe; Bleich or Holland could serve Edith Baker's goals; Stewart Hall, Patrocinio Schweickart, and Michele Wallace would all be useful for Dominic DelliCarpini.

Once having stipulated the account of reading that warrants their practice, teachers, I think, should actively teach it. As John Heyda points out, many textbooks support such a choice, offering instruction and clarification about processes of reading just as writing textbooks instruct students in developing and shaping

*Afterword: A Complex Affirmation of Reading and Writing*

their work. Grateful as I am to Professor Heyda for choosing my *Acts of Reading*, I would point out that John Schilb and John Clifford's *Making Literature Matter* and Frank Madden's *Exploring Literature* are also excellent choices.

Next, I think it important for a teacher to come to terms with what she or he means by *literature*. Many of the authors in these pages have chosen to ask their first-year writing students to encounter and write about literary works, but few of them have identified the notion of literariness they would like those students to invoke. *Literature* is a vexed term, of course, and the question of literariness has a long and even more vexed history, one that I do not propose to rehearse here. Still, I would urge that part of the decision whether to teach literature would be a decision about how and why one defines it. A special use of language? A privileged text? A cultural expression? Fiction? Technique? My personal preference is for Louise Rosenblatt's idea that literature is a text upon which one performs an aesthetic, rather than an efferent, reading. The literary theory establishment seems to have decided to "bracket out" questions of literariness entirely. Compositionists, it seems to me, need not follow suit. If a kind of text that we call *literature* is to be studied or discussed in a course whose primary emphasis is on writing, then I think a teacher owes students an account of both the reasons for the choice and his or her working definition of *literature*. For me the question would be one of objectives. If, like John Heyda, you decide to teach skills of reading literary texts, you should, as he does, know why; if, like Mary Segall, you teach literature because your students find it interesting, you might want to give some thought to discussing with them what they find interesting about it. Will the poem you ask your students to read function as evidence for an argument, or as an aesthetic object to be contemplated? Do you (like Edward Kearns) want your students to contemplate an aesthetic object? Or would you prefer to use a poem by June Jordan as evidence for an argument about police brutality?

Next, political: The difficulty of defining *literature* notwithstanding, "ordinary people" from Oprah Winfrey to Gary Tate express concern about "its" absence from our college curricula. The National Endowment for the Arts has recently published disturbing statistics about the "decline" in the reading of "literature." In the words of Dana Gioia, chair of the NEA,

> This study suggests that there are two groups of Americans emerging in this electronic age. . . . The first group takes a very active and engaged attitude toward information and society. The other group are increasingly passive consumers of electronic entertainment. Unfortunately, one group is growing, and it's not the readers. (*Newsweek*, 19 July 2004, 58)

*Newsweek* (not particularly sensitive to the genre distinctions that concern this volume) stipulates that "'literature' means simply any books that people read without guns pointed to their heads. If people read even three pages of a Harlequin Romance, it got counted," Gioia is quoted as saying (58). Many correspondents to the *New York Times* were careful to point out, however, that the statistics neglected nonfiction and therefore failed to show that the reading of nonfiction, especially in view of the election-year spate of political books, is at least holding its own.

Even so, it does seem that college students are not being taught to read per se, even in cases where reading is assigned. When I say this I mean that students are not being taught to be self-reflexive about the ways in which they make meaning. This problem may well be the inevitable result of the multiple incommensurable discourses of postmodernity as well as the political disinclination to teach any method of reading because to do so would be to risk imposing it on a multicultural student body. So it might be said without irony that our students' difficulties with reading are at least in part a side effect of our efforts to empower them to read according to their racial, gendered, ethnic, and class affiliations.

But there is all the difference in the world between the assertion that meaning is indeterminate and the assertion that meaning does not exist. The commitment to the proposition that readers make meaning can backfire when it fosters carelessness. It is one thing to encourage a student, as Judith Fetterley does, to read against the grain of the privileged masculine point of view in "Indian Camp." It's another to allow (and, by allowing, to encourage) students to derive precisely the opposite conclusion from

*Afterword: A Complex Affirmation of Reading and Writing*

the one Walter Benn Michaels intended. The academy is large enough for both enterprises, but I think that a sense of academic integrity requires us to say which approach we're taking at any given time.

It seems clear that it is appropriate for college-level educators, regardless of departmental or disciplinary affiliation, to "teach" (and not merely assign) reading as well as writing. But, of course, there's the rub. Because they are so (conceptually) multifaceted, reading and writing draw on a number of disciplines to describe and to do their local and contingent work. Attempts to see and understand how these processes occur and to figure ways of dealing with them are often hampered by institutional roadblocks—by intradepartmental division, such as the kinds that John Heyda and Barry Maid describe, by interdisciplinary competition, by the constraints of disciplinary lexicons and methods, by administrative structures within the university, and by tacit value systems like the ones that Eve Wiederhold describes.

It seems clear that both reading and writing pedagogy have suffered politically from not having a disciplinary or institutional home. This institutional homelessness and its consequent lack of power have made reading and writing more vulnerable to social and political censure, I think, than they would otherwise have been. Let me explain. When the departmental or disciplinary focus is on "literature" (a text to be contemplated, enjoyed, honored) rather than on reading (a process of comprehending, examining, engaging in dialectic with a text), the charge that education slights the reading practices of traditionally underrepresented groups is easier to make. If reading is understood as simple decoding, then, one can have right and wrong readings. But when reading is understood as interpretation, it is harder to make the case that any reading is "wrong."

None of these problems is insoluble. The contributors to this volume ameliorate them considerably. Those who favor the use of literary texts in writing courses suggest that doing so will enhance students' interest, encourage them to address important issues, become a whole person, or simply learn more about reading. Those who do not favor the teaching of literary works in writing courses *do*, however, at least implicitly, approve of critical attention to reading. I hope and believe that this volume will be remembered and honored for its insistence that the profession of English studies address the issue of how and when to teach reading, for the problems it enumerates will certainly not go away simply as a consequence of being ignored.

## Note

1. In "The Reception of Reader-Response Theory," I explain what I think happened.

## Works Cited

Bleich, David. *Readings and Feelings: An Introduction to Subjective Criticism.* Urbana, IL: National Council of Teachers of English, 1975.

———. *Subjective Criticism.* Baltimore: Johns Hopkins UP, 1978.

Fetterley, Judith. *The Resisting Reader: A Feminist Approach to American Fiction.* Bloomington: Indiana UP, 1978.

Fish, Stanley. *Is There a Text in This Class? The Authority of Interpretive Communities.* Cambridge, MA: Harvard UP, 1980.

Harkin, Patricia. *Acts of Reading.* Upper Saddle River, NJ: Prentice Hall, 1998.

———. "The Reception of Reader-Response Theory." *College Composition and Communication* 56.3 (February 2005) 410–25.

Holland, Norman N. *Five Readers Reading.* New Haven, CT: Yale UP, 1975.

———. *Poems in Persons: An Introduction to the Psychoanalysis of Literature.* New York: Norton, 1973.

Iser, Wolfgang. *The Act of Reading: A Theory of Aesthetic Response.* Baltimore: Johns Hopkins UP, 1978.

———. *The Implied Reader: Patterns of Communication in Prose Fiction from Bunyan to Beckett.* Baltimore: Johns Hopkins UP, 1974.

Madden, Frank. *Exploring Literature: Writing and Thinking about Fiction, Poetry, Drama and the Essay.* New York: Longman, 2001.

Rosenblatt, Louise M. *Literature As Exploration.* New York: D. Appleton-Century, 1938. Rpt., New York: Modern Language Association, 1976.

———. *The Reader, the Text, the Poem: The Transactional Theory of the Literary Work.* Carbondale: Southern Illinois UP, 1978.

Schilb, John, and John Clifford. *Making Literature Matter: An Anthology for Readers and Writers.* Boston: Bedford/St. Martin's, 2000.

Schweickart, Patrocinio. "Reading Ourselves: Toward a Feminist Theory of Reading." *Gender and Reading: Essays on Readers, Texts, and Contexts.* Elizabeth A. Flynn and Patrocinio P. Schweickart, eds. Baltimore: Johns Hopkins UP, 1986. 31–62.

# Works for Further Consultation

LINDA S. BERGMANN

Adams, Katherine H. *A History of Professional Writing Instruction in American Colleges: Years of Acceptance, Growth, and Doubt.* Dallas: Southern Methodist UP, 1993.

Alberti, John. "Returning to Class: Creating Opportunities for Multicultural Reform at Majority Second-Tier Schools." *College English* 63.5 (May 2001): 561–84.

Anderson, Chris. "Teaching Students What Not to Say: Iser, Didion, and the Rhetoric of Gaps." *Journal of Advanced Composition* 7 (1987): 10–22. http://jac.gsu.edu/jac/7/Articles/2.htm (accessed 10 October 2005).

Bacon, Jacqueline. "Impasse or Tension? Pedagogy and the Canon Controversy." *College English* 55 (September 1993): 501–14.

Bartholomae, David. "What Is Composition and (If You Know What That Is) Why Do We Teach It?" Bloom, Daiker, and White 383–89.

Berlin, James. *Rhetorics, Poetics, Cultures: Refiguring College English Studies.* Urbana, IL: National Council of Teachers of English, 1996.

Bizzell, Patricia. "Opinion: 'Contact Zones' and English Studies." *College English* 56 (February 1994): 163–69.

Blair, Catherine Pastore. "Only One of the Voices: Dialogic Writing Across the Curriculum." *College English* 50 (April 1988): 383–89.

Bleich, David. *Readings and Feelings: An Introduction to Subjective Criticism.* Urbana, IL: National Council of Teachers of English, 1975.

———. *Subjective Criticism.* Baltimore: Johns Hopkins UP, 1978.

Bloom, Lynn Z. "Teaching College English as a Woman." *College English* 54.7 (November 1992): 818–25.

Bloom, Lynn Z., Donald Daiker, and Edward M. White, eds. *Composition in the Twenty-first Century*. Carbondale: Southern Illinois UP, 1996.

Booth, Wayne C. "'LITCOMP': Some Rhetoric Addressed to Cryptorhetoricians about a 'Rhetorical Solution to a Rhetorical Problem.'" Horner 57–80.

Brandt, Deborah, et al. "The Politics of the Personal: Storying Our Lives against the Grain." *College English* 64.1 (September 2001): 41–87.

Braun, M. J., and Thomas P. Miller. Review of *Composition and the University: Historical and Polemical Essays*, by Sharon Crowley. *Rhetoric Review* 17.2 (Spring 1999): 339–43.

Brereton, John C., ed. *The Origins of Composition Studies in the American College, 1875–1925: A Documentary History*. Pittsburgh: U of Pittsburgh P, 1995.

Brown, Stuart, Theresa Enos, and Catherine Chaput, eds. *The Writing Program Administrator's Resource: A Guide to Reflective Institutional Practice*. Mahwah, NJ: Erlbaum, 2002.

Bullock, Richard H., John Trimbur, and Charles Schuster, eds. *The Politics of Writing Instruction: Postsecondary*. Portsmouth, NH: Boynton/Cook, 1991.

Clark, Suzanne. "Rhetoric, Social Construction, and Gender: Is It Bad to Be Sentimental?" Clifford and Schilb 96–108.

Clifford, John, and John Schilb. "Composition Theory and Literary Theory." *Perspectives on Research and Scholarship in Composition*. Ed. Ben W. McClelland and Timothy R. Donovan. New York: Modern Language Association, 1985. 45–67.

———, eds. *Writing Theory and Critical Theory*. New York: Modern Language Association, 1994.

Connors, Robert J. *Composition-Rhetoric: Backgrounds, Theory, and Pedagogy*. Pittsburgh: U of Pittsburgh P, 1997.

Corbett, Edward P. J. "Literature and Composition: Allies or Rivals in the Classroom?" Horner 168–84.

Crow, Angela, and Peggy O'Neill. "Introduction: Cautionary Tales about Change." O'Neill, Crow, and Burton 1–18.

*Works for Further Consultation*

Crowley, Sharon. "Around 1971: Current-Traditional Rhetoric and Process Models of Composing." Bloom, Daiker, and White 64–74.

———. *Composition in the University: Historical and Polemical Essays*. Pittsburgh: U of Pittsburgh P, 1998.

Damrosch, David. *Meetings of the Mind*. Princeton, NJ: Princeton UP, 2000.

———. *We Scholars: Changing the Culture of the University*. Cambridge, MA: Harvard UP, 1995.

Desser, Daphne. "Reading and Writing the Family: Ethos, Identification, and Identity in My Great-Grandfather's Letters." *Rhetoric Review* 20.3–4 (2001): 314–28.

Eagleton, Terry. *Literary Theory: An Introduction*. 2nd ed. Oxford: Basil Blackwell; Minneapolis: U of Minnesota P, 1996.

Elbow, Peter. "The Cultures of Literature and Composition: What Could Each Learn from the Other?" *College English* 64.5 (May 2002): 533–46.

———. *Everyone Can Write: Essays toward a Hopeful Theory of Writing and Teaching Writing*. New York: Oxford UP, 2000.

———. "Reflections on Academic Discourse: How It Relates to Freshmen and Colleagues." *College English* 53 (February 1991): 135–55.

———. "The War between Reading and Writing and How to End It." *Rhetoric Review* 12.1 (Fall 1993): 5–24.

———. *What Is English?* New York: Modern Language Association, 1990.

Enos, Richard Leo. Review of *The Rise and Fall of English: Reconstructing English as a Discipline*, by Robert Scholes. *Rhetoric Review* 17.2 (Spring 1999): 337–39.

Ericsson, Patricia Freitag. Outcomes Use Table. January 2005. http://www.wsu.edu/~ericsson/OS_table.html (accessed 10 September 2005).

Faigley, Lester. *Fragments of Rationality: Postmodernity and the Subject of Composition*. Pittsburgh: U of Pittsburgh P, 1992.

Fetterley, Judith. "Dreaming the Future of English." *College English* 61.6 (July 1999): 702–11.

———. *The Resisting Reader: A Feminist Approach to American Fiction.* Bloomington: Indiana UP, 1978.

Fish, Stanley. *Is There a Text in This Class? The Authority of Interpretive Communities.* Cambridge, MA: Harvard UP, 1980.

Fleming, David. "Rhetoric as a Course of Study." *College English* 61.2 (1998): 169–91.

Flynn, Elizabeth A. "Composing as a Woman." *College Composition and Communication* 39.4 (December 1988): 423–35.

Flynn, Elizabeth A., and Patrocinio P. Schweickart, eds. *Gender and Reading: Essays on Readers, Texts, and Contexts.* Baltimore: Johns Hopkins UP, 1986.

Gage, Nicholas. "The Teacher Who Changed My Life." *Connections.* Ed. Judith A. Stanford. 3rd ed. Mountain View, CA: Mayfield, 2000. 185–90.

Gamer, Michael. "Fictionalizing the Disciplines: Literature and the Boundaries of Knowledge." *College English* 57.3 (March 1995): 281–86.

Gere, Anne Ruggles, ed. *Into the Field: Sites of Composition Studies.* New York: Modern Language Association, 1993.

Goggin, Maureen. "Literature." Heilker and Vandenburg 145–50.

Gottschalk, Katherine. "The Writing Program in the University." *ADE Bulletin* 112 (Winter 1995): 1–6.

Graff, Gerald. *Clueless in Academe: How Schooling Obscures the Life of the Mind.* New Haven, CT: Yale UP, 2003.

———. "Is There a Conversation in This Curriculum? Or, Coherence without Disciplinarity." *English as a Discipline: Or, Is There a Plot in This Play?* Ed. James C. Raymond. Tuscaloosa: UP of Alabama, 1996. 11–28.

———. *Professing Literature: An Institutional History.* Chicago: U of Chicago P, 1987.

———. "The University and the Prevention of Culture." *Criticism in the University.* Ed. Gerald Graff and Reginald Gibbons. Evanston, IL: Northwestern UP, 1985: 62–82.

Green, Daniel. "Opinion: Abandoning the Ruins." *College English* 63.3 (January 2001): 273–87.

Greenbaum, Leonard. "The Tradition of Complaint." *College English* 31 (1969): 174–87.

Hairston, Maxine. "Breaking Our Bonds and Reaffirming Our Connections." *College Composition and Communication* 36 (1985): 272–82.

Harkin, Patricia. *Acts of Reading*. Upper Saddle River, NJ: Prentice Hall, 1999.

———. "The Reception of Reader-Response Theory." *College Composition and Communication* 56.3 (February 2005): 410–525.

Harkin, Patricia, and John Schilb. *Contending with Words: Composition and Rhetoric in a Postmodern Age*. New York: Modern Language Association, 1991.

Harrington, Dana. "Composition, Literature, and the Emergence of Modern Reading Practices." *Rhetoric Review* 15.2 (Spring 1997): 249–63.

Harrington, Susanmarie, Keith Rhodes, Ruth Overman Fischer, and Rita Malenczyk, eds. *The Outcomes Book: Debate and Consensus after the WPA Outcomes Statement*. Logan: Utah State UP, 2005.

Harris, Joseph. "Meet the New Boss, Same as the Old Boss: Class Consciousness in Composition." *College Composition and Communication* 52.1 (September 2000): 43–68.

Heilker, Paul, and Peter Vandenburg, eds. *Keywords in Composition Studies*. Portsmouth, NH: Heinemann/Cook, 1996.

Heyda, John. "Fighting over Freshman English: CCCC's Early Years and the Turf Wars of the 1950s." *College Composition and Communication* 50.4 (June 1998): 663–81.

Hindman, Jane E. "Special Focus: Personal Writing." *College English* 64.1 (September 2001): 34–40.

Hoberek, Andrew, et al. "Twentieth-Century Literature in the New Century: A Symposium." *College English* 64.1 (September 2001): 9–33.

Holland, Norman N. *Five Readers Reading*. New Haven, CT: Yale UP, 1975.

———. *Poems in Persons: An Introduction to the Psychoanalysis of Literature*. New York: Norton, 1973.

## Works for Further Consultation

Horner, Winifred Bryan, ed. *Composition and Literature: Bridging the Gap*. Chicago: U of Chicago P, 1983.

Iser, Wolfgang. *The Act of Reading: A Theory of Aesthetic Response*. Baltimore: Johns Hopkins UP, 1978.

———. *The Implied Reader: Patterns of Communication in Prose Fiction from Bunyan to Beckett*. Baltimore: Johns Hopkins UP, 1974.

Jarratt, Susan. "Rhetoric in Crisis? The View from Here." *Enculturation* 5.1 (2003).

Jay, Gregory, Elizabeth Latosi-Sawain, Leon Knight, and Jeanie C. Crain. "Four Comments on 'Two Views on the Use of Literature in Composition.'" *College English* 55.6 (October 1993): 673–79.

Kameen, Paul. "Service and Subversion: The Composition of Our Work." *Critical Quarterly* 39.1 (1997): 36–41.

Lanham, Richard A. *The Electronic Word: Democracy, Technology, and the Arts*. Chicago: U of Chicago P, 1993.

Larson, Richard. "Enlarging the Context: From Teaching Just Writing, to Teaching Academic Subjects with Writing." *Composition in Context: Essays in Honor of Donald C. Stewart*. Ed. W. Ross Winterowd and Vincent Gillespie. Carbondale: Southern Illinois UP, 1994. 109–25.

LeNoir, W. David. "Grading Student Poetry: A Few Words from the Devil's Advocate. *English Journal* 91.3 (January 2002): 59–63.

Levine, George. "Putting the 'Literature' Back into Literature Departments." *ADE Bulletin* 113 (Spring 1996): 13–20.

———. "Rhetoric within and without Composition: Reimagining the Civic." Shamoon et al. 32–41.

Lindemann, Erika. "Freshman Composition: No Place for Literature." *College English* 55.3 (March 1993): 311–16.

———. "Three Views of English 101." *College English* 57.3 (March 1995): 287–302.

Lunsford, Andrea. "Composing Ourselves: Politics, Commitment, and the Teaching of Writing." *College Composition and Communication* 41.1 (February 1990): 71–82.

Maid, Barry M. "More Than a Room of Our Own: Building an Independent Department of Writing." Brown, Enos, and Chaput 453–66.

Marshall, Margaret J. *Response to Reform: Composition and the Professionalization of Teaching.* Carbondale: Southern Illinois UP, 2004.

Micciche, Laura. "More Than a Feeling: Disappointment and WPA Work." *College English.* 64.4 (2002): 432–58.

Miller, Richard E. "Composing English Studies: Towards a Social History of the Discipline." *College Composition and Communication* 45.2 (1994): 164–97.

Miller, Susan. "Writing Studies as a Mode of Inquiry." Olson 41–54.

Miller, Thomas P. *The Formation of College English: Rhetoric and Belles Lettres in the British Cultural Provinces.* Pittsburgh: U of Pittsburgh P, 1997.

———. "Rhetoric within and without Composition: Reimagining the Civic." Shamoon et al. 32–41.

———. "What's Going on with English Majors? Historical Contexts and National Trends in Undergraduate Curricula." Conference on College Composition and Communication Annual Convention. San Antonio, TX. March 2004. Updated 5 May 2004. http://www.gened.arizona.edu/tmiller/ccc.htm (accessed 13 February 2005).

Moffett, James. *Active Voice: A Writing Program Across the Curriculum.* Upper Montclair, NJ: Boynton/Cook, 1981.

Morgan, Dan. "Connecting Literature to Students' Lives." *College English* 55 (September 1993): 491–500.

Moulthrop, Stuart, and Nancy Kaplan. "Something to Imagine: Literature, Composition, and Interactive Fiction." *Computers and Composition* 9.1 (1991): 7–23. http://www.hu.mtu.edu/%7Ecandc/archives/v9/9_1_html/9_1_1_Moulthrop.html (accessed 10 Sept. 2005).

National Council of Teachers of English and International Reading Association. *Standards for the English Language Arts.* Urbana, IL: National Council of Teachers of English; Newark, DE: International Reading Association, 1996.

North, Stephen M. *The Making of Knowledge in Composition: Portrait of an Emerging Field.* Upper Montclair, NJ: Boynton/Cook, 1987.

Ohmann, Richard, with a chapter by Wallace Douglas. *English in America: A Radical View of the Profession.* New York: Oxford UP, 1976.

O'Neill, Peggy, Angela Crow, and Larry Burton, eds. *A Field of Dreams: Independent Writing Programs and the Future of Composition Studies*. Logan: Utah State UP, 2002.

Olson, Gary, ed. *Rhetoric and Composition as Intellectual Work*. Carbondale: Southern Illinois UP, 2002.

Palloff, Rena M., and Keith Pratt. *Building Learning Communities in Cyberspace: Effective Strategies for the Online Classroom*. San Francisco: Jossey-Bass, 1999.

Parker, William Riley. "Where Do English Departments Come From?" *College English* 28 (February 1967): 339–351. Rpt., *The Writing Teacher's Sourcebook*. Ed. Gary Tate and Edward P. J. Corbett. 2nd ed. New York: Oxford UP, 1988. 3–15.

Peterson, Jane. "Through the Looking-Glass: A Response." *College English* 57.3 (March 1995): 310–18.

Petraglia, Joseph, ed. *Reconceiving Writing, Rethinking Writing Instruction*. Mahwah, NJ: Erlbaum, 1995.

Pratt, Mary Louise. "Arts of the Contact Zone." *Profession* 91 (1991): 33–40.

Readings, Bill. *The University in Ruins*. Cambridge, MA: Harvard UP, 1996.

Reiss, Donna, Dickie Selfe, and Art Young, eds. *Electronic Communication Across the Curriculum*. Urbana, IL: National Council of Teachers of English, 1998.

Rhodes, Keith, Irvin Peckham, Linda S. Bergmann, and William Condon. "The Outcomes Project: The Insiders' History." Harrington et al. 8–17.

Rosenblatt, Louise M. *Literature As Exploration*. New York: D. Appleton-Century, 1938; rpt., New York: Modern Language Association, 1976.

———. *The Reader, the Text, the Poem: The Transactional Theory of the Literary Work*. Carbondale: Southern Illinois UP, 1978.

———. "The Transactional Theory: Against Dualisms." *College English* 55 (April 1993): 377–86.

Royer, Daniel J., and Roger Gilles. "The Origins of a Department of Academic, Creative, and Professional Writing." O'Neill, Crow, and Burton 21–37.

Russell, David R. "Rethinking Genre in School and Society: An Activity Theory Analysis." *Written Communication* 14 (1997): 504–54.

———. *Writing in the Academic Disciplines, 1870–1990: A Curricular History.* Carbondale: Southern Illinois UP, 1991.

Ruszkiewicz, John. "Word and Image." *Computers and Composition* 5.3 (August 1988): 9–15. http://www.hu.mtu.edu/%7Ecandc/archives/v5/5_3_html/5_3_1_Ruszkiewicz.html (accessed 10 September 2005).

Schilb, John. *Between the Lines: Relating Composition Theory and Literary Theory.* Portsmouth, NH: Boynton/Cook, 1996.

———. "Scholarship in Composition and Literature: Some Comparisons." *Academic Advancement in Composition Studies.* Ed. Richard Gebhardt and Barbara Geselle. Newbury Park, CA: Sage, 1996. 21–31.

———. "The WPA and the Politics of Litcomp." Brown, Enos, and Chaput 165–79.

Schneider, Alison. "Bad Blood in the English Department: The Rift between Composition and Literature." *Chronicle of Higher Education,* 13 February 1998: A14.

Scholes, Robert. *The Rise and Fall of English: Reconstructing English as a Discipline.* New Haven, CT: Yale UP, 1998.

Schutz, Aaron, and Anne Ruggles Gere. "Service Learning and English Studies: Rethinking the Public Sphere." *College English* 60.2 (February 1998): 129–49.

Schweickart, Patrocinio P. "Reading Ourselves: Toward a Feminist Theory of Reading." Flynn and Schweickart 31–62.

Shamoon, Linda K., et al. *Coming of Age: The Advanced Writing Curriculum.* Portsmouth, NH: Boynton/Cook, 2000.

Sheridan, Daniel. "Changing Business as Usual: Reader Response in the Classroom." *College English* 53 (1991): 804–14.

Slagle, Diane Buckles, and Shirley K. Rose. "Domesticating English Studies." *Journal of Teaching Writing* 13.1–2 (1994): 147–68.

Smith, Louise Z. "Why English Departments Should 'House' Writing Across the Curriculum." *College English* 50 (April 1988): 390–95.

Sommers, Nancy. "I Stand Here Writing." *College English* 55.4 (April 1993): 420–28.

Sosnoski, James. *Token Professionals and Master Critics: A Critique of Orthodoxy in Literary Studies*. Albany: State U of New York P, 1994.

Steinberg, Erwin R. "Imaginative Literature in Composition Classrooms?" *College English* 57.3 (March 1995): 266–80.

Stygall, Gail. "At the Century's End: The Job Market in Rhetoric and Composition." *Rhetoric Review* 18.2 (Spring 2000): 375–89.

Tate, Gary. "Notes on the Dying of a Conversation." *College English* 57.3 (March 1995): 303–09.

———. "A Place for Literature in Freshman Composition." *College English* 55.3 (March 1993): 317–21.

Trimbur, John. "Composition Studies: Postmodern or Popular." Gere 117–32.

Varnum, Robin. "Composition Studies." Heilker and Vandenburg 44–48.

White, Edward M. *Developing Successful College Writing Programs*. San Francisco: Jossey-Bass, 1989.

Williams, Ashley. "Integrative Writing and Ways of Knowing Across Four Courses." Fifth National Writing Across the Curriculum Conference. Bloomington, IN. 1 June 2001.

Winterowd, W. Ross. *The English Department: A Personal and Institutional History*. Carbondale: Southern Illinois UP, 1998.

Worsham, Lynn. "Coming to Terms: Theory, Writing, Politics. Olson 101–13.

———. "Going Postal: Pedagogic Violence and the Schooling of Emotion." *Journal of Advanced Communication* 18 (1998): 213–45.

*WPA Outcomes Statement for First-Year Composition*. April 2000. http://www.wpacouncil.org/positions/outcomes.html (accessed 21 July 2001).

Young, Art, and Toby Fulwiler, eds. *When Writing Teachers Teach Literature: Bringing Writing to Reading*. Portsmouth, NH: Boynton/Cook, Heinemann, 1995.

# INDEX

Academic Affairs v. Student Affairs, 102
Academic responsibility, 124
Accountability issues, 5
*Active Voice: A Writing Program Across the Curriculum* (Moffett), 227
*Act of Reading: A Theory of Aesthetic Response, The* (Iser), 226
*Acts of Reading* (Harkin), 111–12, 121, 215, 225
Adams, Katherine H., 221
Adjunct writing teachers. *See* Faculty, temporary
Advertisements, job, 33n. 6
Aesthetics, 9, 63, 84
  vocabulary, 65–66
"Against Interpretation" (Sontag), 57
Alberti, John, 221
Alegria, Claribel, 150
*American Demographics*, 18
Anderson, Chris, 118, 221
Angelou, Maya, 179
*Apology* (Sidney), 26–27
*Architectonike*, 32
Aristotle, 17
Arkansas Department of Higher Education, 102
Arnold, Matthew, 173
Assignments
  character sketches, 184
  character summaries, 155–57
  response, 178
  summary, 177–78

Atwood, Margaret, 67
Audience, 134, 177, 178, 181
  aids, 180
Authority, appeals to, 177
Autobiography, 175, 182

Bacon, Francis, 144
Bacon, Jacqueline, 196, 221
Baker, Edith M., x, xii, 6, 10, 171, 206, 207, 214, 233
Bakhtin, Mikhail, 23, 27
Barthes, Roland, 26
Bartholomae, David, 221
Bennett, William, 25
Bergmann, Linda S., x, 1, 183, 209, 213, 228, 233–34
Berlin, James, 2, 6, 20, 45, 48, 78, 79, 96, 117, 132, 133, 221
*Between the Lines: Relating Composition Theory and Literary Theory* (Schilb), 229
Bizzell, Patricia, 197, 221
Blair, Catherine Pastore, 221
Blake, William, 164
Blankenship, Jane, 102
Bleich, David, 118, 210, 211, 214, 221
Bloom, Harold, 25
Bloom, Lynn Z., 186, 222
Bly, Robert, 160
Booth, Wayne, ix–x, 33n. 8, 174, 222
Bradley University, 185

## Index

Brandt, Deborah, 186, 222
Brandt, H. C. G., 70
Braun, M. J., 222
Brent, Doug, 132
Brereton, John C., 222
Brown, Stuart, 222
*Building Learning Communities in Cyberspace: Effective Strategies for the Online Classroom* (Palloff and Pratt), 164, 228
Bullock, Richard H., 222
Burke, Kenneth, 132, 133, 137

*Call to Write, The* (Trimbur), 151
Canon, 56–57
Capote, Truman, 165
Carlton, Susan Brown, 84
Center for Information and Research on Civic Learning and Engagement (CIRCLE), 18
Chalmers Lindholmen University College, 158–63
Chaput, Catherine, 222
Character sketches, 184
Character summaries, 155–57
Cicero, 17, 23, 33n. 5
Ciesielski, Dennis, 10, 124, 206, 235
Cisneros, Sandra, 146
Civic education, 17–33, 132, 177
  civic conversation, 18
  deliberative action, 18, 30
  democratic inquiry, 74
  demographics, 18–19
  political v. literary language, xii
  role of literature, 24–32
Clark, Suzanne, 82, 222
Clarke College, 146, 154
Class bias, 8, 93–108, 126, 205, 210
Classroom applications
  computer technology, xi, 143–70

  dialogue, 145
  polylogue, 145
  using literature to reframe lives, 171–90
  . *See also* Assignments
Clifford, John, 215, 222
*Clueless in Academe: How Schooling Obscures the Life of the Mind* (Graff), 224
Cofer, Judith Ortiz, 156
Collaboration, 158
*College Composition at Miami*, 113–14, 120
*College English*, 2, 127, 129, 186, 196
*Coming of Age: The Advanced Writing Curriculum* (Shamoon), 229
Composition
  circular relation with literature, 187
  consumption v. production models, 128–29, 186
  cultural studies, 110, 132
  dialogue, 132–35
  ethnography, 110
  feminist theory, 110
  first-year, 94–96
  hermeneutics, 110
  history in English departments, 96–97
  identity, 132–35
  models, 183
  personal writing, 186–87 (*See also* Reframing)
  phenomenology, 110
  pragmatism, 110
  process v. product, 5, 128, 198
  reframing lives through literature, 171–90
  research, ix
  role of computer, 143–70
  role of literature, 24–32, 111, 143–70, 171–90
  student preferences, 191–204

# Index

writing before reading, 182
. *See also* Composition teaching; Literature in composition classes; Rhetoric
*Composition and Literature: Bridging the Gap* (Horner), 2
*Composition and/or Literature: The End(s) of Education* (Bergmann and Baker)
  practical vision, 4
  purpose of study, 3–4
*Composition in the University* (Crowley), 99, 100
*Composition-Rhetoric Backgrounds, Theory, and Pedagogy* (Connors), 222
Composition scholars, 80–81
Composition teaching
  as applied discipline, 99, 128
  belletristic approach, 96, 97, 131
  collaboration with literary studies, 3, 111
  emotional issues, 99
  integration of programs, 102–3
  meritocracy, 96
  prescriptive teaching, 198
  pressures from literary studies, 1
  process approach, 5, 128, 198
  rhetoric of public discourse, 96
  staffing constraints, 29
  student preferences, 191–204
  training for, 100, 101
  whole teachers, 124–39
  writing teachers v. literary scholars, 54–72, 111
Computer-mediated composition, xi, 143–70, 181
Condon, William, 228
Conference on College Composition and Communication, 2, 55, 104, 127, 129–30

independent writing units, 99
*Connecting Generations: The Sourcebook for a New Workplace*, 158
Connors, Robert J., 186, 222
Connotative language, 177, 178
*Conscientizaçao*, 134
*Consilience*, 134–35, 136
Corbett, Edward P. J., xi, 117, 222
Core courses, 174
Cornell University, writing program, 47
Corporate academy, 76
Council of Writing Program Administrators (WPA), 130
  e-mail list, 4
  Outcomes Statement, 1, 8
Cowell, Patti, 101
Crain, Jeanie C., 226
Creative nonfiction, 185
Crews, Frederick, xi
Criminal justice, 94
Critical literacy, 76
  . *See also* Critical thinking skills; Literacy
Critical thinking skills, 59, 171, 175, 179
Critics and criticism, 58
  definition of, 57
  normative v. descriptive, 68–69
  writing teacher as critic, 58
Crow, Angela, 38, 49, 222
Crowley, Sharon, 2, 6, 8, 9, 23, 75, 99, 100, 223
Cult of the author, 26
Cult of the Muses, 33n. 5
Cultural anthropology, 28
Cultural materialism, 28
Cultural narratives, 82
Cultural studies, 8, 76, 77, 110, 132, 177
Culture of excellence, 171
Curriculum
  core courses, 174
  LITCOMP, 174

*. See also* Syllabus

Daiker, Donald, 222
Damrosch, David, 48, 223
Deans, 50
DelliCarpini, Dominic, xii, 3, 9, 10, 17, 171, 207, 214, 235
Departmental politics. *See* English departments
Desser, Daphne, 187, 223
*Developing Successful College Writing Programs* (White), 230
Dewey, John, 30–31
Dialogue
  classroom applications, 145
  composition, 132–35
  scholarly dialogue, 41–42, 44–51, 48
  text, 178
Dickinson, Emily, 164
Discipline
  definition of, 206, 207
  integrity, 105
  *. See also* Field
Discourse, 176
  academic, 202
  *. See also* Rhetoric; Text
Discussion boards, 149–51, 163
Diversity, 209–10
DMZ metaphor, 111–22
Doherty, Timothy, 3, 10, 36, 235
Domestic metaphors, 51n. 2
DotNets, 19

Eagleton, Terry, 176, 223
Elbow, Peter, 66, 182, 186, 198, 202, 223
*Electronic Word: Democracy, Technology, and the Arts, The* (Lanham), 143, 226
Eliot, T. S., 164

E-mail, 146–49, 163
  *. See also* E-writing
Emergent codes, 130–31
Emotion
  academic culture, 88n. 5
  categories, 81–82
  emotional investments, 83, 99
  legitimate v. bogus, 67
  pedagogy, 82
  uniting emotion and intellect in literature, 66–67, 174
English Coalition Conference, 54
*English Department: A Personal and Institutional History* (Winterowd), 230
English departments
  aristicratic privilege, 98, 107
  bridge building v. restructuring metaphors, 109–23, 135
  class issues, 93–108, 126, 205
  composition as peripheral, ix, 109–22
  creative writing, 56
  funding, 98
  history of composition, 96–97
  isolation of, 97–98
  politics, 2, 93–108
  turf wars, 126
  whole English model, 135–37
  writing program splitting from, 36–51
  writing teachers v. literary scholars, 54–72
*English Journal,* 129
English studies
  self-reflexive nature, 205
  term, 94
Enos, Richard, 7, 223
Enos, Theresa, 222
Epistemology, 74
Ericsson, Patricia, 8, 223
*Essai,* 144
Ethnography, 110
E-writing, 151–58
  international, 158–63

*Index*

tips, 167–69
*Exploring Literature* (Madden), 215
Expressivism, 9

Faculty, temporary, x, 6, 29, 95, 100, 101
   non-tenure-track lecturers, 95
Faigley, Lester, 166, 223
Feminist theory, 28, 110
Fetterly, Judith, 216, 223
Field, 136
   definitions, 110–11
*Field of Dreams: Independent Writing Programs and the Future of Composition Studies, A* (Crow and O'Neill), 38, 43
Fischer, Katherine, xi, 6, 10, 143, 207, 235
Fish, Stanley, 79, 210, 224
*Five Readers Reading* (Holland), 225
Fleming, David, 224
Flynn, Elizabeth A., 172, 224
Foreign language departments, 94
*Formation of College English: Rhetoric and Belles Lettres in the British Cultural Provinces, The* (Miller), 227
Foucault, Michel, 28
*Fragments of Rationality: Postmodernity and the Subject of Composition* (Faigley), 223
Freire, Paulo, 134

Gage, Nicholas, 179, 224
Gamer, Michael, 191, 197, 198, 224
Gap theory, 120
Geertz, Clifford, 28
Genre theory, 8

George, Diana, 166
Gere, Anne Ruggles, 109, 110, 136, 224, 229
Gilles, Roger, 47, 228
Gilman, Charlotte Perkins, 175, 176
Gioia, Dana, 69, 216
Goggin, Maureen, 224
Gottschalk, Katherine, 47, 224
Graduate programs, 95
Graduate students, 95
   as teachers of composition, x, 95, 100, 101
   *. See also* Faculty, temporary
Graff, Gerald, 8, 55, 224
Grand Valley State University, 47
Green, Daniel, 7, 224
Greenbaum, Leonard, 117, 225
Gustafsson, Magnus, 158–63

Habermas, Jurgen, 27
Hairston, Maxine, 104, 106–7, 135, 225
Hall, Anne-Marie, 185
Hall, Stewart, 214
Harkin, Patricia, 111–12, 118, 121, 205, 215, 225, 235–36
Harrington, Dana, 79, 225
Harrington, Susanmarie, 225
Harris, Joseph, 225
Hegemony, 131
Heilker, Paul, 225
Herbert, George, 164
Hermeneutics, 110
Heyda, John, 3, 5, 10, 109, 207, 214, 215, 217, 225, 236
Hindman, Jane E., 186, 225
Hirschberg, Stuart, 177
Hirschberg, Terry, 177
*History of Professional Writing Instruction in American Colleges: Years of Acceptance, Growth, A* (Adams), 221

Hoberek, Andrew, 225
Holland, Norman N., 210, 211, 214, 225
Homer, 21
Horner, Winifred Bryan, ix, 2, 226, 236
Hugo, Victor, 183
Humanism, 98–100
  moral issues and values, 99–100
Human judgment, 60
Hurston, Zora Neale, 179
Hypertext, 143
  . *See also* Computer-mediated composition

"I Am Mirror" (Alegria), 150
Identity issues, 132–35, 178, 179, 210
  . *See also* Reframing
Ideology of dominant culture, 81
*In Cold Blood* (Capote), 165
Inference, 178
*Institutes of Oratory* (Quintilian), 24–25
Institutional contexts
  accountability issues, 5
  change, 44–45
  civic education, 17–33
  organizational structures, 45
  scientific approach, 57–58
  stakeholders, 46, 48
  subordination of composition programs, 73–88
  writing program/English department split, 36–51
International Reading Association, 54, 59
*Into the Field: Sites of Composition Studies* (Gere), 109, 110, 224
Iser, Wolfgang, 118, 210, 211, 214, 226
Isocrates, 17, 25

*Is There a Text in This Class? The Authority of Interpretive Communities* (Fish), 224

James, William, 30
Jarratt, Susan, 113, 226
Jay, Gregory, 184, 226
Jordan, June, 215

Kairos, 28
Kameen, Paul, 86, 226
Kaplan, Nancy, 143, 227
Kearns, Edward A., 9, 54, 71n. 1, 205, 206, 215, 236
Kennedy, X. J., 69
Kinkaid, James, 59
Knight, Leon, 184, 226
Koller, Jackie French, 183

Language arts, 66–67
  . *See also* Literary studies
Lanham, Richard A., 143, 226
Larson, Richard, 187, 226
Latosi-Sawain, Elizabeth, 226
Leadership, 50
Learning communities, 8
LeNoir, W. David, 64, 226
Levine, George, 47, 226
Lindemann, Erica, 2, 111, 127, 128, 186, 191, 196, 200, 226
LITCOMP, 174
Literacy, 44–45, 50, 96
  definitions, 45
  as social action, 78
  . *See also* Critical literacy
Literary scholars, x, 184
  whole teachers, 124–39
  writing teachers v. literary scholars, 54–72, 111, 184

Literary studies, 59
  as basis for civic education, 24–32
  canonical literature, 133
  class issues, 94
  composition's circular relation with literature, 187
  composition teachers teaching literature, 124–39
  defenses of traditional literature, 25
  definition of literature, 62–63, 173, 176, 184, 187, 214–16
  Dewey's views on literature, 31
  emotional issues, 66–67, 174 (*See also* Emotion)
  isolationists, 47
  literary criticism of society, 133
  literature and online writing, 146–63
  literature as rhetoric, 23
  political v. literary language, xii
  postmodern theories, 33n. 7
  privileging of texts, 9
  reframing lives with literature, 171–90
  relation to composition teaching, 1–2, 143–70
  sociological criticism of literature, 133
*Literary Theory: An Introduction* (Eagleton), 223
*Literature* (Kennedy), 69
*Literature as Exploration* (Rosenblatt), 228
Literature in composition classes, 1–2, 143–70
  civic education, 24–32
  composition's circular relation with literature, 187
  definition of literature, 62–63, 173, 176, 184, 187, 214–16
  literature and online writing, 146–63
  literature as rhetoric, 23
  reframing lives with literature, 171–90
  sociological criticism of literature, 133
  student preferences, 191–204
  uniting emotion and intellect, 66–67
  . *See also* Composition; Composition teaching; Literary studies
Logical fallacies, 177
Lottich, Kenneth V., 24
Lunsford, Andrea, 186, 226

Madden, Frank, 215
Maid, Barry, 1, 3, 10, 93, 206, 217, 226, 236–37
Maimon, Elaine, xi
*Making Literature Matter* (Schilb and Clifford), 215
*Making of Knowledge in Composition: Portrait of an Emerging Field, The* (North), 227
Marshall, Margaret J., 95, 227
Marxism, 28
Mathematics departments, 94
McQuade, Christina, 166
McQuade, Donald, 166
Media, 67
*Meetings of the Mind* (Damrosch), 223
Mezirow, Jack, 164
Micciche, Laura, 88n. 5, 227
Michaels, Walter Benn, 209–10, 217
Miller, Richard E., 227
Miller, Susan, 48, 83, 227

Miller, Thomas, 2, 6, 8, 45, 48, 222, 227
Milton, John, 33n. 4
"Mirror" (Plath), 150
Modern Language Association (MLA), 55
Moffett, James, 175, 227
Momaday, N. Scott, 185
Montaigne, Michel de, 144
Moral issues and values, 99–100, 183, 205
  class issues, 205
Moran, Charles, 102
Morgan, Dan, 197, 201, 227
Moulthrop, Stuart, 143, 227
*Multicultural Reader for Writers, A* (Stanford), 177
Multicultural studies, 8
Murray, Donald, 113
"My Wicked, Wicked Ways" (Cisneros), 147

Narrative
  cultural narratives, 82
  dominant patterns, 172
  gender issues, 172
  grand narratives, 213
  self-centered positions, 173
  . *See also* Text
National Council of Teachers of English (NCTE), 54, 55, 59, 127, 130
National Endowment for the Arts, 215–16
*National Endowment for the Arts Report*, 211
Nelson, John, 102
New Critics, 24
New Historicism, 26, 27–28
*Newsweek*, 216
No Child Left Behind Act, 211
Norris, Frank, 56, 68
North, Stephen M., 98, 227

North Hennepin Community College, 184

O'Brien, Tim, 156
Odell, Lee, 104
Ohmann, Richard, 227
Oliver, Mary, 167
Olson, Gary, 228
O'Neill, Peggy, 38, 49, 222, 228
*One World, Many Cultures* (Hirschberg), 177
Online writing. *See* E-writing
*Origins of Composition Studies in the American College, 1875-1925: A Documentary History, The* (Brereton), 222

Palchik, Anna, 166
Palloff, Rena M., 146, 164, 228
Parker, William Riley, 228
Peckham, Irvin, 228
Pedagogy, 77–78, 80, 124
  of emotion, 82
  fixing meaning, 211–13
  v. high theory, 80–81
  new media use, 207
  . *See also* Assignments; Classroom applications
Peirce, Charles, 30
Perry, Bliss, 57
Peterson, Jane, 131, 191, 197, 201, 202, 228
Petraglia, Joseph, 228
Phenomenology, 110
*Picturing Texts* (Faigley et al.), 166
Plagiarism issues, 180
Plath, Sylvia, 150
Plato, 17, 20, 21
Poetics v. rhetoric, 23, 74, 131, 184

*. See also* Literature in composition classes
Poetry, 146, 150
   Swedish poetry, 158–63
Political science departments, 94
Politics. *See* English departments
*Politics of Writing Instruction: Postsecondary, The* (Bullock), 222
Portfolio assessment, 64
Postmodernity, 211–13
Power relations, 79, 80–81
*. See also* Class bias
Pragmatism, 30–31, 110
Pratt, Keith, 146, 164, 228
Pratt, Mary Louise, 228
*Professing Literature* (Graff), 55
Professor-as-hero, 80
*Progymnasmata,* 24
Public administration, 94

Questionnaire, student
   description, 192–95
   discussion, 196–202
   questions, 203
Quinnipiac College, 192
Quintilian, 17, 22–23, 24–25
*Quintilian as Educator* (Wheelock), 24–25

Raines, Claire, 158
Reader-response theory, 118–19, 210
Readings, Bill, 7, 9, 75–81, 171–72, 173, 228
*Readings and Feelings: An Introduction to Subjective Criticism* (Bleich), 221
Reading theory, 113–22, 131
   aesthetic v. efferent readings, 215
   authorial intention, 212
   feminist reading, 212
   fixing meaning, 211–13

*Reconceiving Writing, Rethinking Writing Instruction* (Petraglia), 228
Reframing, 171–90
   composing lives, 185
   construction of self, 175, 178
   historical context, 185
   looking back v. looking beyond, 182
   multiple approaches to single topic, 174
   revising lives, 175
Reiss, Donna, xi, 6, 10, 143, 158, 207, 228, 237
*Republic* (Plato), 20
Residual codes, 130–31
Resistance, 81–82
Response papers, 178
*Response to Reform: Composition and the Professionalization of Teaching* (Marshall), 227
Rhetoric
   art v. utility, 23
   civic education, xii, 20–23 (*See also* Civic education)
   history in English departments, 96–97
   literature as form of, 23, 184
   v. poetics, 74, 131, 184
   political v. literary language, xii
   relations to composition, 95
   rhetoric of identity, 132–35
   social-epistemic, 28, 132–35
   training for, 100, 101
   *. See also* Composition
*Rhetoric and Composition as Intellectual Work* (Olson), 228
*Rhetoric and Reality* (Berlin), 96, 117
*Rhetorics, Poetics, Cultures: Refiguring College English Studies* (Berlin), 132, 221

*Rhetor* v. *magister*, 76–81
Rhodes, Keith, 228
*Right Stuff, The* (Wolfe), 165
*Rise and Fall of English: Reconstructing English as a Discipline, The* (Scholes), 229
Rose, Shirley, 11n. 2, 229
Rosenblatt, Louise, 118, 198, 210, 211, 215, 228
Rottenberg, Annette, 102
Royer, Daniel, 47, 228
Russell, Cheryl, 18
Russell, David R., 229
Ruszkiewicz, John, 165, 229

Saitoti, Tepilit Ote, 179
*Savoir* v. *savoir faire*, 124
Schilb, John, 29, 132, 215, 222, 225, 229
Schneider, Alison, 229
Scholarly dialogue, 41–42, 44–50, 48
 ends of, 50–51
Scholes, Robert, 7, 45, 48, 229
Schutz, Aaron, 229
Schweickart, Patrocinio, 214, 229
Scientific approach to teaching English, 57–58
*Seeing and Writing* (McQuade), 166
Segall, Mary T., xii, 10, 191, 207, 214, 215, 237
Selfe, Cynthia, 166
Self-publication, 166
Self-reflexive analyses, 84, 205, 216
Sentiment
 legitimate v. bogus, 67
 . *See also* Emotion
Service learning, 8, 18, 32n. 1, 98, 128
Shamoon, Linda K., 229

Shaughnessy, Mina, 214
Shelley, Percy, 21
Sheridan, Daniel, 118, 229
Sidney, Philip, 21, 26–27
Silko, Leslie, 185
Slagle, Diane Buckles, 229
Slide shows, 149–51
Smith, Charles Kay, 101
Smith, Frank, 210, 211
Smith, Kay, 102
Smith, Louise Z., 51n. 2, 229
Social change, 78–79
Socrates, 21, 31
Sommers, Nancy, 186, 229
Sontag, Susan, 57
Sosnoski, James, 7, 230
Stakeholders, 46, 48, 50
Standardization, 60, 63
*Standards for the English Language Arts*, 54, 59
Stanford, Judith A., 177
State University of New York Council on Writing, 104
State University of New York–Plattsburgh, 103
Special Services Project, 102
Stein, Sol, 64
Steinberg, Erwin, 129, 187, 191, 196, 201, 202, 230
*Stein on Writing* (Stein), 64
Stelzner, Sara, 102
Student preferences, 191–204
Stygall, Gail, 230
Summaries, 177–78
Swedish poetry, 158–63
Syllabus, 176
 analysis of, 65
 revision project, 112–22
 . *See also* Curriculum

Task forces, 40–41
 discussions on organizations, 41
 discussions on theory, 41

*Index*

Tate, Gary, 2, 111, 127, 183, 186, 191, 197, 200, 202, 215, 230
Teaching. *See* Composition teaching; Literary scholars
Teaching assistants (TAs), x, 95, 100, 101
. *See also* Faculty, temporary
Teaching schedules, 94
Tenure issues, 104
Terministic screen, 137
Text
  aesthetic v. efferent readings, 215
  cohesive devices, 178
  dialogues, 178
  interpretation, 57–59, 184
  language, 177
  models, 183
  performative aspects, 176
  production v. consumption, 128–29, 186
  selection, 171, 173, 186
  unity, 177
Textual reference, 155–58
Thinking process, 172
. *See also* Critical thinking skills
Thought, 172
Tidewater Community College, 146–49, 159
*Token Professionals and Master Critics: A Critique of Orthodoxy in Literary Studies* (Sosnoski), 230
Toulmin, Stephen, 207
Transformative learning, 164
Tranströmer, Tomas, 159
Trimbur, John, 111, 151, 230

*University in Ruins, The* (Readings), 7, 9, 75–81, 173, 228
University of Chicago Press, ix–x
University of Illinois at Chicago, 210
University of Massachusetts rhetoric program, 100–101
University of Miami, 113–22

Varnum, Robin, 230
Virgil, 33n. 4
Voice, 66
Voluntarism, 18

Wallace, Michele, 214
Weasel words, 177
Web publications, 149–51
Western Kentucky University, 64
Wheelock, Frederick, 24–25
White, Edward, 49, 230
Whole English, 124–39
  debate, 127–32
Whole teachers, 124–39
Wiederhold, Eve, xii, 9, 73, 206, 208, 217, 237
Wilds, Elmer H., 24
Williams, Ashley, 230
Williams, Raymond, 130
Wilson, Edward O., 134, 135
Winfrey, Oprah, 215
Winterowd, W. Ross, 9, 48, 230
Wolfe, Tom, 165
Workplace issues, 9
Worsham, Lynn, 81, 83, 230
WPA. *See* Council of Writing Program Administrators (WPA)
*Write to Learn* (Murray), 113
Write-to-learn process, 113
Writing across the curriculum (WAC), xi, 1, 11n. 3, 38, 47, 186
Writing assessment, 60–61
. *See also* Text
Writing departments, 94, 105
  curriculum, 105–6

*Index*

integration of programs, 102–3
promotion, 105–6
split from English department, 36–53
tenure, 105–6
*Writing Program Administrator's Resource: A Guide to Reflective Institutional Practice, The* (Brown), 222

Writing teachers. *See* Composition teaching

Yancey, Kathleen Blake, 11n. 1
Yavapai College, 175, 184
"Yellow Wallpaper, The" (Gilman), 175, 176
Young, Art, xi, 6, 10, 143, 158, 207, 230, 238

# EDITORS

**Edith M. Baker** is associate professor in the Department of English at Bradley University. From 1997 to 2002, she directed the Writing Across the Curriculum Program and is presently the coordinator of composition. Previously she was a faculty member for fifteen years at Yavapai College in northern Arizona. She holds a BA from Cornell College, MA from the University of Virginia, and PhD in rhetoric, composition, and the teaching of English from the University of Arizona. Her teaching and research interests combine theory, pedagogy, ethnographic studies, American literature, and the teaching of composition. She has published review essays in *Teaching English in the Two-Year College* and articles on composition and diversity. Her most recent publication is jointly authored with Susan Berry Brill de Ramirez in *Organization and the Environment* (June 2005) and is on environmental justice in selected writings of Leslie Silko.

**Linda S. Bergmann,** associate professor of English at Purdue University and director of the Purdue Writing Lab, has started Writing Across the Curriculum programs and writing centers at the University of Missouri–Rolla, the Illinois Institute of Technology, and Hiram College. Her teaching experience includes first-year composition, undergraduate courses in literature, pedagogy, and literacy, and graduate seminars in writing program administration. She has published articles in such journals as *Language and Learning Across the Disciplines, Feminist*

*Editors*

*Teacher, A/B: Auto/Biography Studies,* and *American Studies,* and has written chapters on WAC and other aspects of teaching writing for various collections. She is currently completing a textbook on research writing.

# CONTRIBUTORS

**Dennis Ciesielski** is associate professor of English at the University of Wisconsin–Platteville, where he teaches courses in rhetoric, English language studies, composition, and literature.

**Dominic DelliCarpini** is writing program administrator of York College of Pennsylvania. He holds a BA in English from the University of Pennsylvania and an MA and PhD in English from Pennsylvania State University. His research interests, grounded in the work of John Dewey, focus on the ways that rhetoric and writing can develop more informed workers and citizens. His book on this topic, *Composing a Life's Work: Writing, Citizenship, and Your Occupation*, was published in 2005 by Longman. He is coeditor, with Jack Selzer, of *Conversations: Readings for Writing* and is an executive board member of the Council of Writing Program Administrators.

**Timothy J. Doherty** is associate professor of English and communications at Rivier College in Nashua, New Hampshire, where he also directs the writing program. His teaching and scholarly work focus on issues of conflict and community. His article "The Coalition Rhetoric of Rose Schneiderman" recently appeared in *Rhetorical Democracy: Selected Papers from the 2002 Rhetoric Society of America Conference*.

**Katherine Fischer** teaches writing and literature at Clarke College in Dubuque, Iowa. She has contributed her insights on teaching writing within the electronic environment to numerous books and journals—particularly her ideas on how students can appreciate a greater sense of the human experience through interacting creatively with both literature and computers. She is also a columnist and writer currently in the dreck stage of her manuscript, *Dreaming the Mississippi*. When not writing, you'll find her crick stomping the backwaters of the river.

**Patricia Harkin** teaches in the Departments of Communication and English at the University of Illinois at Chicago. She is the author of *Acts of Reading* and coeditor of *Contending with Words: Compo-*

*sition and Rhetoric in a Postmodern Age* and of *Configuring Virtual Worlds: Teaching with Virtual Harlem* (forthcoming). Her work appears in *College English, College Composition and Communication*, and *Rhetoric Review*.

**John Heyda** is associate professor of English at Miami University in Middletown, Ohio, where he teaches composition and film studies and serves as coordinator of English. He has published articles in *College Composition and Communication, Journal of Basic Writing, Writing Instructor*, and elsewhere. He served as director of composition at Miami University's main campus in Oxford, Ohio, from 1993 to 1995.

**Winifred Bryan Horner** is professor emerita of English at the University of Missouri and Radford Chair Emerita of Rhetoric and Composition at Texas Christian University. She has published eleven books dealing with rhetoric and composition, including a collection of diary and autobiographical excerpts, and the *Harbrace Handbook*. She has lectured both nationally and internationally—at Oxford University and the Universities of Turin, Amsterdam, Gottingen, and Edinburgh, among others. She was a visiting research fellow at the University of California, Berkeley, and a fellow of the University of Edinburgh. In 1991 a book of essays was published in her honor. She has taught composition and rhetoric for forty years and loves to teach. She has four children and has been married for over fifty years. She is currently teaching a course in memoir writing and working on a book, *Between the Lines: Memoir through Story*.

**Edward A. Kearns,** professor emeritus, taught English and humanities for 34 1/2 years at the University of Northern Colorado. During his tenure, he also served as English Department chair, director of composition, and student teacher supervisor. In the latter part of his career, Kearns was especially interested in training high school English teachers and presented programs and workshops on writing at the secondary level. Until his death in the summer of 2004, Kearns lived in Longmont, Colorado, with his wife and children, continuing his love for writing through a column on education for his local newspaper.

**Barry M. Maid** is professor and head faculty of technical communication at Arizona State University, where he led the development of a new program in Multimedia Writing and Technical Communication. Before going to ASU, he taught at the University of Arkansas at Little Rock, where he directed the Writing Center and the First

Year Composition Program, chaired the Department of English, and helped in the creation of the Department of Rhetoric and Writing. Though most of his time is now spent in program administration, he tries to keep in touch with his professional interests of computers and writing, writing program administration, and academic/industry partnerships.

**Donna Reiss** (http://wordsworth2.net/) teaches English part time at Clemson University. She retired January 1, 2005, as professor emeritus of English at Tidewater Community College. During 25 years at TCC, she directed the Writing Center and Writing-Across-the-Curriculum, Online Learning, and Distributed Teaching and Learning. Among the first faculty to teach computer-enhanced and Web-based writing, literature, and humanities classes, she also taught from 2001 to 2005 over the Internet for TCC in Virginia while living in South Carolina. She has given keynote talks, presentations, and workshops in the United States, Europe, and Australia on using electronic communication and digital portfolios for active learning in English and across the curriculum. She is coauthor of "The Poetics of Computers: Composing Relationships with Technology" in *Computers and Composition* (2003) and author of "Reflective Webfolios in a Humanities Course" in *Electronic Portfolios: Emerging Practices in Student, Faculty, and Institutional Learning* (2001). She is coeditor with Dona Hickey and a chapter author of *Learning Literature in an Era of Change: Innovations in Teaching* (2000) and coeditor with Art Young and Dickie Selfe of *Electronic Communication Across the Curriculum* (1998).

**Mary T. Segall**, assistant professor of English at Quinnipiac University, formerly directed the Freshman English Program at Quinnipiac for many years. With William R. Brown, she coauthored *Portals: Critical Reading, Writing, and Thinking* (1999), and with Robert A. Smart, she coauthored *WAC: Direct from the Disciplines* (2005), which evolved from their presentation at the 2003 annual convention of the Conference on College Composition and Communication. Her teaching and research interests include linguistics, early American literature, civic literacy, and the doppelganger.

**Eve Wiederhold** is assistant professor of English at the University of North Carolina at Greensboro. She teaches courses in rhetoric and composition, critical theory, and women and gender studies. Her publications include articles in *JAC* and *Rhetoric Review*, and she serves as executive editor of *Lore: An E-Journal for Teachers of Writing*.

*Contributors*

**Art Young** is Robert S. Campbell Chair in Technical Communication, professor of English, and professor of engineering at Clemson University. He is the founder and co-director of Clemson's Communication-Across-the-Curriculum Program. In 2002, he received the Exemplar Award from the Conference on College Composition and Communication. He is the author of *Teaching Writing Across the Curriculum* (4th ed., 2006), the third edition of which is available online from *The WAC Clearinghouse* (http://wac.colostate.edu/books/young_teaching/), and coeditor of *Bringing Writing to Reading: When Writing Teachers Teach Literature* (1996).

---

*This book was typeset in Sabon by Electronic Imaging.*
*Typefaces used on the cover were Adobe Jenson Pro*
*and Adobe Garamond Pro.*
*The book was printed on 50-lb. Williamsburg Smooth Offset paper*
*by Versa Press, Inc.*